Praise for *Don't Let Death ~~Ruin Your~~ Life*

"Jill Brooke breaks new ground in this excellent book: she provides us with a sense of direction and hope as we deal with our feelings, with our continuing bonds with the deceased, and with the changes we need to make in our lives."

—Phyllis R. Silverman, Ph.D., author of
Never Too Young to Know: Death in Children's Lives

"Jill Brooke has embraced life's most difficult problem with grace and dignity. Her guide to help go through the loss of a loved one should find a place in every American's home."

—Bill O'Reilly, host of *The O'Reilly Factor*

"The loss of a loved one, whether early or late in life, creates an ongoing grieving process that never goes away. Instead of telling us to let go of our attachments to loved ones, finally someone is showing us how to maintain our relationships by creating ways to honor our loved ones and keep them close by. Jill Brooke's book is a blessing."

—Mary Higgins Clark

"A very, very important book. One wonders why it wasn't written years ago. I would have loved to have the terrific input when I lost my dad years ago."

—Larry King

"This is truly a practical book in that death is viewed as a normal part of life and dealing with it constructively should be a more common reaction."

—*Booklist*

JILL BROOKE's articles have appeared in *The New York Times*, *USA Today*, *Redbook*, *McCall's*, and *Ladies' Home Journal*, among other publications. A former CNN correspondent, she is currently editor in chief of *Avenue* magazine, a columnist for the *New York Daily News*, and host of the radio show on parenting *What Do I Do Now?*. She lives with her family in upstate New York.

Don't Let Death Ruin Your Life

*A practical guide to reclaiming
happiness after the death of a loved one*

JILL BROOKE

Ⓟ

A PLUME BOOK

PLUME
Published by the Penguin Group
Penguin Putnam Inc., 375 Hudson Street,
New York, New York 10014, U.S.A.
Penguin Books Ltd, 80 Strand,
London WC2R ORL England
Penguin Books Australia Ltd, Ringwood,
Victoria, Australia
Penguin Books Canada Ltd, 10 Alcorn Avenue,
Toronto, Ontario, Canada M4V 3B2
Penguin Books (N.Z.) Ltd, 182–190 Wairau Road,
Auckland 10, New Zealand

Penguin Books Ltd, Registered Offices:
Harmondsworth, Middlesex, England

Published by Plume, a member of Penguin Putnam Inc.
Previously published in a Dutton edition.

First Plume Printing, February 2002
10 9 8 7 6 5 4 3 2 1

Ⓟ REGISTERED TRADEMARK—MARCA REGISTRADA

The Library of Congress has catalogued the Dutton edition as follows:

Brooke, Jill.
Don't let death ruin your life : a practical guide to reclaiming happiness after the death of a
loved one / Jill Brooke.
p. cm.
ISBN 0-525-94569-5 (hc.)
ISBN 0-452-28298-5 (pbk.)
1. Death.   2. Bereavement.   3. Consolation.   4. Thanatology.   I. Title.
HQ1073 .B75   2001
306.9—dc21   00-057299

Printed in the United States of America
Original hardcover design by Leonard Telesca

This book is dedicated to the men
who have enriched my life with all forms of love

My father, Leon
My brother, Peter
My husband, Gary
My son, Parker Leon

Acknowledgments

A friend once told me that writing the acknowledgment page is one of the favorite tasks of the author; the reason being that until then you had no idea how much work the project would require and how many people you'd have to thank. This is indeed true.

First, thanks to my bosses at CNN, who gave me this incredible professional passport that enabled me to parachute into the living rooms of the best and the brightest and glean from them their expertise and wisdom, which has subsequently been used for this book.

Aside from my CNN boss Scott Leon, I thank Bill Cosby, Alan King, Mary Tyler Moore, Rosie O'Donnell, Julio Iglesias, John Walsh, Tom Monahan, John Bell, Linda Bloodworth-Thomason, Donna Karan, Mary Higgins Clark, Carol Higgins Clark, Rupert Murdoch, Ted Turner, President Bill Clinton, Gary Winnick, Jimmy Lee, Supreme Court Justice Ruth Bader Ginsburg, Sheryl Henson, Howard Rubenstein, Donald Trump, Vince Gill, Shania Twain, Reg Green, Rep. Bart Gordon and Peter Fonda.

And then I would like to thank all the doctors, therapists, nurses, researchers, bereavement specialists, philosophers, survivors, counselors, hand-holders and real-life angels who not only enthusiastically supported this project but flooded me with research, phone numbers and perspective in the hopes that this book would shatter some of the misconceptions that contaminate the way we look at death and provide a more enlightened approach to living with loss.

I would also like to give a special thanks to the handful of people who indulged my many, many questions and gave me many hours of their time including Dr. Marvin Eisenstadt, Dr. Elisabeth Kübler-Ross, Dame Cicely Saunders, Dr. James Feldman, Dr. Gerald Koocher, Dr. Therese Rando, Dr. Joanne Jozefowski, Dr. Richard Tedeschi, Dr. Dennis Klass, Barbara Hozinsky, Dr. Phyllis Silverman, Dr. Ken Doka and Ted Menten.

Then there is the wonderful Makeda Wubneh, who Bill O'Reilly generously shared with me, to work as my research assistant. Since the topic of this book is a subject rarely discussed, finding information was often a frustrating challenge; however, she managed to unearth some real gems.

A *merci beaucoup* also to Molly Friedrich, my agent; Lori Lipsky, my editor at Dutton and her comrade in arms, Karen Murphy, who shepherded this project.

Aside from the professional help, there are those who personally made my life more pleasurable during this long process, because a project like this can be both life-affirming as well as emotionally draining. As a result, there are a few behind-the-scenes people who deserve credit for being my cheerleader during those times I really needed it.

To Leslie Lampert, for being my sanity sister, my soul sister, my best friend. I am so grateful for both your intelligence and heart. To Liza McGuirk, for your sage and sensible advice, which always calms me. To Mark Simone, for your generosity in letting me bounce ideas off you and for offering smart, savvy advice on every step of this project. To Roger Friedman, for providing me with an endless supply of amusing tidbits during our midnight chats when I stopped writing and welcomed a distraction. To Peter Brooke, for saving the first article I ever wrote and thinking it was terrific even though it wasn't.

I also would like to thank Fern Siegal, Jo Maeder, Ted Menten and Gerard Bray for reading my manuscript in its early stages and offering their opinions. Dr. Michael Plotnick will have my eternal gratitude for saving my life. I also want to thank Pei Lin Yu for her quiet support, her steady stream of caffeine and her necessary reminders that despite my ability to zone out over my work, my husband and kids still needed dinner on the table.

Another word of thanks goes to those people whose talent I am in awe of and whose work inspires me to aim higher than I would have if they weren't around as a constant reminder of what heights can be achieved. These people include Anna Quindlen, Maureen Dowd, Paul Boller, Michael Crichton, Bonnie Raitt, Sting, Gene Roddenberry, Steven Spielberg, George Lucas, Tim Robbins and Morgan Freeman.

Last but not least, I want to thank my husband, Gary, a man who makes my reality exceed my dreams on a daily basis. I love you with all my heart.

Contents

PART THREE

Finding Meaning from Loss

PART FOUR

Family Politics

PART FIVE

Making Memories Last

PART SIX
Leaving a Legacy

PART ONE

The Power of Memory

∽

"God gave us our memories so that we might have roses in December . . ."
—Sir John Barrie

1

Introduction

For many, the thrill of pending motherhood awakens with the grainy sonogram from the doctor's office, which like a paint-by-number drawing outlines the body of your child. For others, it's the excitement of the first kick, that surefire sign that someone is living inside your swollen belly. But for me, it was neither of those things. The moment I experienced the thrill was right before my baby shower.

There, on the creamy blue stationery decorated with old-fashioned bassinets, was the first time I saw my baby's name spelled out. "Please join in the celebration of the pending arrival of Parker Leon."

Such magical words. Such emotional power lying among the stream of consonants and vowels. I remember caressing the letters so very gently and mouthing the words in a hopeful whisper. Parker Leon. Parker Leon. A name is so much more than a medley of sounds. In the same way an artist uses clay to create a sculpture, parents use a name to shape a personality.

In many religions, it is customary for parents to take either the first letter or the name of a deceased relative and give it to a newborn. It is said this tradition gives the loved one who has passed away immortality.

And I hope that is true. Because Parker Leon is named after my husband's father, Perry, who died five years ago, and my father, Leon, who died more than twenty years ago. His name was Leon Brooke.

When I brought my baby back from the hospital, I hoped deep down that a remnant of my father would be reincarnated in this little boy. However, Parker, with hair the color of caramel and flesh as soft as pizza dough, didn't resemble him at all. Yet each day, I would begin a new search. Could I find something of my father in the lentil-shaped ear? Perhaps I'd see some glimmer of recognition in those Fred Flintstone feet. Or maybe, I hoped, I could see my father in Parker's dancing blue eyes, set inside a face that resembled a bright full moon. Yes, those are from him, I thought, as was his smile, so warm it could melt the icicles hanging from our living room window.

My search, I later learned, was not uncommon. My friend Alisa lost her dad when she was seven. Years later when she had her son Gregg, she noticed his pinkie finger curled in a locked position. Far from being concerned, she was pleased. Her father had had the same quirk, and this inherited trait gave her a strange form of comfort. "I have so few memories of my father, but this was vivid," she recalls. I understood what she meant.

I've waited so many years to see a sign of my father, to hear his thickly accented voice with its strong German lilt, to smell the scent of Old Spice splashed on after a shower, to see him hovering over *The Wall Street Journal* with a Tiperillo cigar dangling from his lips, laughing over a funny story about some farmer making a fortune from donkey dung.

Now my son is a living reminder of what I loved in my father. Through Parker, Leon lives on. He lives on in my son's name and in the stories I will tell him about his grandfather, stories that will make my father as real as he is in my heart, stories that, if I do my job, Parker will tell his children.

Some of Parker's mannerisms already conjure up images of my father in surprising ways. Sometimes I'll be tickling him on the floor, and he'll flash me a smile, and I will be transported back to another time and place.

These are pleasures I do not take for granted.

Anyone who has lost someone to death feels robbed and cheated. Often, the memory of a loved one becomes blurred like a Seurat painting. From a distance, it seems like a beautiful detailed landscape, but up close, there's only a collection of dots. I yearned for someone to join the dots, to fill in the spaces I didn't know, to provide a fleshed-out portrait of my father that I could see and feel and touch. Because when my father died, I was too young to really know him and not mature enough to figure out how to.

Although he had been ill for years, my parents hadn't prepared my brother and me for his death. Yet the signs were there. The plastic pill bottles sitting ominously on the dresser, the scar of his pacemaker peeking through his pajama shirt, his skin tone becoming as white as chalk. But my father would never admit any weakness. "I'm fine, sweetheart," he assured me when I confronted him. Naively, I believed him.

"Parents think their job is to protect their children and shield them from pain," explains Dr. Robin Goodman, a counselor at New York University Hospital's oncology unit. "It's almost superstitious. 'I'm not going to talk about this.' As though it will go away. Sadly, they often waste precious time that could have been spent preparing together."

Two days before Thanksgiving, my mother's screams woke me up.

Running into their room, I saw him lying down in his bed holding his stomach. I grabbed his hand and held tightly. "It will be okay, Daddy," I said, attempting to reassure him. But I was really trying to reassure myself.

Within moments his fingers started to slowly unfurl and slip away from my grasp, creating a stillness that seemed both surreal and endless. He had died of a massive aneurysm. Later I realized we had never talked about his feelings about life, or even the afterlife, nor had we discussed many things that from that moment forward would always matter.

Part of the reason is my family's history.

My mother, Celia, was five when her mother died of a heart

attack at forty-two, leaving her Russian immigrant father, who died twenty years later, alone with five children to raise. Emotions were considered frivolous, a luxury this struggling family could not afford. Like many families facing grief, the pain was repressed and never discussed. My mother emerged from this environment cool and distant, highly efficient but lacking any maternal warmth.

Almost thirty years her senior, my father, Leon, was a handsome, cultured man, who had also survived a devastating blow. During the 1930s, his family was living in Vienna as the Holocaust infected Europe. His mother, Tanya, was a true philanthropist, a woman who believed "net worth is not self-worth." She opened her kitchen on Sundays to struggling artists as well as the homeless and poor. My grandfather Alvin owned shoe factories throughout Europe. Despite their sons' pleas, my grandparents couldn't believe that harm would come their way given their position in Viennese society and their good deeds. They chose to remain in Europe while their sons fled to the United States.

It cost them their lives. My grandfather committed suicide before being taken to a concentration camp and my grandmother was killed in Treblinka.

Fifteen years later, when my father met my mother, he had become a very successful slipper salesman. She brought to the union youth and beauty. He provided security. Neither asked probing questions. That, I believe, was the attraction.

As my brother, Peter, and I were growing up, the household was curiously empty of memories. Rarely were stories told about our grandparents, or about their childhood. No old pictures peered at us from ancient silver frames.

Yet I yearned for a larger family connection. Once as a teenager, I visited my friend Fran's house and we trekked up to her attic filled with half-opened boxes and trunks of old clothing. "Can you believe my grandmother wore this?" Fran giggled as she pulled an old lace dress from a trunk. Even then, I felt a stab in my heart, because I was acutely aware that my family lacked any link to its past.

Many years after my father's death, I casually asked my mother if my grandfather had any siblings. It came as a shock that she didn't know.

"How close could you have been to Daddy if you didn't know about his childhood?" I asked.

"He didn't want me to know" was her steely reply.

As Dr. Joe Rosenthal, a New York–based therapist, observed, "People make choices in how they deal with pain. They often choose to forget as a coping mechanism. Or they choose to remember."

Unlike my mother and father, and many of their generation, I have made the choice to remember. I want to remember everything so my child will not grow up with as many questions as I did. Because having a past rich with memories blankets a child with security and a comforting sense of continuity.

The other day I thought about how pioneer women would spend the summer months cooking over a stove to preserve jams and vegetables for winter's trying times. But now I can go into my own storage closet and retrieve my preserved memories, those that I've gathered over the years, along with the ones that were given by my father directly to me. And Parker now has his own shelf, which I'm stockpiling with his personal histories, so that he, too, can visit when needed.

Because you never know when that need will come.

As the ambulance raced through the streets of New York City, its sound seemed eerily familiar. Instead of focusing on the blood that was gushing out of my body, I was entranced by the ambulance's sound. What was it?

"Miss, are you with us?" the EMS helper cried.

"Yes," I replied hazily.

His voice interrupted my thoughts and I peeked to my side, where my husband held my hand, his face tightened with fear. "Hold on," he said. "We're almost there." Another EMS helper, whose kind eyes reminded me of a Labrador's, was busy finding towels and sheets to contain the blood.

"Please, God, don't let me die," I prayed. "Please."

But the prayer wasn't for me.

Ever since my father died, I had lived every day to the fullest. In a way, those of us who have lost a parent are lucky. We realize how precious and fleeting life can be. My father's death became the prism through which I gauged everything. Boyfriend doesn't call. Not a real problem. Boss is a jerk. So what?

But this was a real problem. I was hemorrhaging and on the verge of dying. Only one in five million had this case—a cervical pregnancy—meaningless odds if you happen to be that one. An experimental treatment to slowly drain the fetus of nutrients so it wouldn't kill me had resulted in the placenta puncturing my arteries, looking for a blood supply to feed the fetus.

As I realized foggily that my life could end, my eyes filled with tears. "Oh, God, please don't make Parker go through what I did. Please don't let my son have to live a life without really knowing his mother."

At the hospital, I was rushed into the operating room, and as the anesthesiologist plunged the needle into my arm, I drifted to sleep. And then I remembered. The sound, the sound. It was the same sound as my little boy's fire truck.

"She's coming out of it," the nurse said to the doctor who then approached me. "Well, that was a close one," he said, smiling. Then his face became serious as he explained the consequences of what had transpired. I had lost over half my blood. To save me, the doctors had performed a hysterectomy. I would never be able to have another child. The recovery would be a long one.

However, I did have my other child, my only child, my son, Parker. If I had died, what would Parker have had to remember me?

Not many photographs existed of us together, because along with short-order cook and caregiver, my job was also picture taker. So Parker would have been left with drawers full of snapshots, of him giggling in delight while playing with his puppy, of him strutting like a gold-medal winner while taking his first steps. But the shots would be mostly of him alone or with his father and two older stepsisters, Vanessa and Jessica.

A handful of videos of his mother's work as a CNN correspondent would be stacked on a closet shelf, as well as cover stories from magazines and newspapers. Nothing would have context, no little notes about the struggles and joys in getting from point A to Z.

Nor would there be any videotapes telling him how much I loved him, tapes where I would have dispensed advice on everything from the importance of good table manners to my thoughts on compassion and kindness.

Missing would also be letters documenting my love for him, even on those trying days when his high-octane energy drained me to my limits.

And because he was only a year old, who would tell him enough stories so I wouldn't be a ghost, so I wouldn't be the stranger in the handful of remaining photos?

For so many years, I had kindled the memory of my father so he wouldn't be a ghost in my life. Now I realized that planting memories was one of the most important jobs for the living, my one-way ticket to immortality.

These were the thoughts that raced through my mind as I began my recovery, a recovery that required a painful mourning and inexorably forced me to examine my life more fully once again.

My sadness at times was suffocating because I had already had so many plans and dreams for my unborn child. I also was sure that my little girl, already named Annabel, would become the best of pals with her brother Parker. Parker would later be her historian, in the same way Peter is mine. Who, I wondered, would comfort him when his heart was broken and remind him that while little Willow rejected him, Lily loved him so. Who would look into his crystal ball and be able to see his life in its entirety?

Any loss rekindles the losses before, and this one took me back to another time so long ago. At sixteen, I was ill equipped to have many coping mechanisms. As an adult, you have a reservoir of resources to draw upon because you are a fully developed person. Yet when the loss occurs in childhood or adolescence, it is absorbed into the child's identity, saturating every cell.

In those days, I found meaning from my loss by defiantly making sure I would emerge from the emotional debris never having to depend on anyone again, although I was also left with the unsettling insecurity that nothing is permanent. This time, I took all my feelings of sadness and injustice, and channeled them into researching the ways human beings have coped with loss. I was determined this time to understand death and not be afraid of it.

Years ago, my father's death forced me to sort out my place in the world and turned a teenager into an adult almost overnight. This time, a death created the birth of this book.

Loss is often a muse. Loss is often a motivating force. This is the essence of this book. By finding a productive outlet for the intense emotions that the grief process triggers, many have enhanced the human experience in the arts, in business, in politics and in science. Loss also compels us to throw a lariat of love around our family and friends and appreciate more fully the precious times spent together.

Dr. Francine Cournos, a psychiatrist and teacher at Columbia University as well as the author of *City of One*, a book about her childhood as an orphan, believes that loss is a springboard for achievement. "So much attention is given to the feelings of pain associated with loss, but there are ways to use the pain in productive ways," she says. "It often provides the impetus to push one's abilities beyond safe and predictable limits. The person doesn't believe he has time to waste, because time is now a luxury. Therefore, the person becomes extremely focused."

Scratch the surface of most charities or social movements and you'll discover that they were started by someone who wanted to right a wrong. It requires someone with dogged determination and a driving, burning passion to create an organization and put it on the map. It requires people like Nancy Brinker, a single mother whose sister's death from breast cancer left her with a blinding desire to help find a cure. The Florida real estate executive John Walsh, whose son Adam was murdered, became a victim's rights advocate, which resulted in the creation of the National Center for Missing and Exploited Children. As the anthropologist Margaret Mead observed, "Never doubt that a small group of thoughtful, committed people can change the world. Indeed, it is the only thing that ever has."

Some people have channeled their feelings of emptiness into creating great works of art or music or literature. The list is impressive. Bach, Beethoven, the Beatles, Michelangelo, Leonardo da Vinci, Mark Twain, Hans Christian Andersen, Tom Stoppard, Edward Albee, Mary Higgins Clark, Eric Clapton, Ray Charles, Edith Wharton, Charlotte Brontë, Dante, Edgar Degas, Robert Frost, Voltaire, and so on.

Loss also ignites the desire to master one's environment and leave a mark on society. Dr. Pierre Rentchnick, who was a professor at Geneva University, found that boys who have lost their fathers make up the great majority of revolutionaries and political leaders. In American history, many of the towering figures who transformed and shaped democracy were children of loss. They include George Washington, Thomas Jefferson, Abraham Lincoln, Franklin D. Roosevelt as well as his wife, Eleanor—even President Bill Clinton.

Starting from earliest records, ten of the twelve Caesars also fit this pattern as did subsequent leaders such as Peter the Great, Elizabeth I, Simón Bolívar, Benito Juárez, Napoleon and Gamal Nasser.

In the past two years, I've interviewed hundreds of people about loss—survivors, bereavement specialists, researchers, doctors, nurses, therapists, social workers, historians and philosophers as well as people who overheard me speaking about the subject in restaurants or the gym and felt compelled to share their stories with me. What surprised me is how many people hungered for this information. At a restaurant, a woman at a neighboring table excused herself to ask me questions.

"I never ever discuss my brother," she confessed, her voice dropping to a whisper. "I loved him so much, but people discourage me from talking about him. You feel this pressure and it has silenced me. The silence hurts more. It's the silence that lives with you."

I then shared with her ways people can discuss loved ones without making people feel uncomfortable and the rituals we can use to keep them in our lives even though their physical presence is not with us.

Loss impacts us in so many ways. Its tentacles are far reaching, crawling into all parts of our lives. Because I don't know whether you are in the throes of early loss, when walking to the kitchen seems like a Herculean task or whether more time has elapsed and the pain is less acute, I've treated this project like a cookbook of sorts where you can sift through it to find recipes that apply to you individually.

The book will give you some direction on how to find outlets for your pain, how to find someone to talk to and how to examine various therapies available. A step-by-step guide is also provided on how to start a charity, create a family genealogy, videotape a loved one, survive holidays and anniversaries and handle family politics. It will also offer advice on making a will, planning a grand finale and creating hundreds of family rituals so that you can ensure you will always be remembered when it is your time to say good-bye.

Early in my research, I visited the wise and feisty Elisabeth Kübler-Ross. The doctor is considered the pioneer in bringing the discussion of death and loss into the mainstream with her landmark book, *On Death and Dying*. Sitting in her Arizona home, surrounded by pictures of her family and Indian artifacts, we talked about grief therapies and philosophies and how death seems so random in how it touches one family and not another.

"What do you say then to the survivors who must pick up the pieces?" I asked.

Looking at me with a knowing smile, she replied, "You can tell them that you can't change the direction of the wind. But you can control the setting of the sails."

2

Keeping the Memories Alive

Even though we can no longer touch the face of someone we love, we can still feel their presence in our lives. We can remember the scent of their perfume when it is sprayed nearby, we can relish the sound of their voice playing like a sweet melody from a recorded tape or we can caress those intimate objects that hold the power to magically link us to them, whether it's a photograph, an inscribed bracelet or an old love letter.

Death may rob us of getting a morning hug, but it cannot take away our love and memories. In fact it shouldn't, for as the poets have said for centuries, love is immortal. As you will see, that immortal love remains in many ways.

For most of the twentieth century, the prevailing view of grief therapy is that it is necessary to sever ties with the deceased. Sigmund Freud and his band of followers declared that grief is only resolved when the griever cuts old attachments and forms new ones.

Move on, they say. Let go. Get on with your life. Ridiculous, isn't it? Yet these have been the mantras of the mental health community.

"People who attempted to maintain ties with the dead were viewed as suffering from complicated mourning or being pathological," says

Dr. Craig Vickio, a clinical psychologist who teaches at Bowling Green State University. "Or they were perceived as attempting to deny their loss. Some even had their sanity questioned."

Yet some of us realize that this kind of advice is crazy. Cutting ties to our loved ones only hinders the healing process. Silence and suppression only build emotional scars and prolong the pain. They do not alleviate it. If we shut out grief, the feelings of frustration and remorse will seep out either in misdirected anger or by manifesting physical pain or emotional withdrawal. Loss is not something one should get over. Loss is something you live with. After all, what is grief but an emotion that says you have loved someone?

Therefore, you should never ignore your feelings. Be proud of your love. Your love ensures that your child, your friend, your parent or your spouse will have immortality. When you cease to talk about someone, when you stop mentioning their name, then they truly die.

Even though many of us understand this instinctively, conflicted messages hamper our healing.

Dennis Klass fought this dilemma for years. Dennis is a researcher and psychologist who teaches at Webster University in St. Louis, Missouri. He is considered a pioneer in challenging the culture's previous perspectives on grief.

"If you asked patients if they maintained relationships with their loved ones, they would confess they did," he says. "But as a therapist, you felt obligated to steer them away from this thinking. Finally, after hearing the same story time after time, it was too compelling to ignore." His subsequent research resulted in groundbreaking clinical studies that are now being used by a growing number of therapists. Another pioneer is Dr. Alan Wolfelt. He is the director of the Center for Loss and Life Transition in Fort Collins, Colorado, and calls himself part of the "responsible rebels" who advocate continued relationships with the person who died.

"Our modern understanding of grief all too often lacks any appreciation for the spiritual nature of the grief journey," he says. "In an attempt to make a science out of grief, we have compartmentalized complex emotions into neat clinical labels. The previous models are flawed because the goal was to return the person back to normal.

A death changes you forever. You are never the same. We have overlooked the journey into grief as a soul-based journey."

Because we are not taught how to mend a broken heart in school, we naturally rely on the experts to guide us, the majority of whom follow the old models of grief therapy, models that undermine what we really need.

If you ask what the dying are most fearful of, the nurses, doctors, hospice workers and therapists will tell you the same thing. Most people learn to accept the inevitable. They are not scared of dying. They are most fearful of being forgotten.

The following five steps can be taken to help keep our loved ones close by and honor their memory while integrating them into our lives which are now changed by their physical absence.

(1) First, try to remember ways in which your loved one left an imprint on you. Review the ways your loved one influences you today and how he or she impacts your daily life. Do you love cooking? Are you good in math? Do you relish mystery novels? When you speak, are there familiar phrases you use?

My friend Sally hears herself yelling at her kids, "If you mess up, you can clean up," which was how her mother scolded her in childhood. Tim's father would build train tracks that twisted like pretzels through the backyard, and now he gets great pleasure building similar mazes with his own son. Whenever I am angry, a light switch turns on in my head and I hear my father saying, "Choose your battles wisely." This sage advice guides me and influences my daily reactions. This is what psychologists call the "continuing sense of presence." By consciously recognizing that your loved one has left an imprint on you, it helps make them feel closer to you.

Bill Cosby continues to share his love of teaching with his son, Ennis. While his son was finishing his teaching degree at Columbia University, he was killed by a drive-by robber. In his early years, Ennis had struggled with school. "He worked so hard yet he wasn't getting the grades he wanted," recalls Cosby. "My wife had him tested, and sure enough, we learned that Ennis had dyslexia. Once we identified the problem, we could then work on it." The experience inspired Ennis to be a teacher, and Bill ensures that he still is.

Cosby started the "Hello Friend/Ennis William Cosby Foundation" to "celebrate the life and fulfill the goals and dreams of Ennis." As Cosby explains "Hello Friend" was a favorite phrase of his son's. The foundation is designed to develop innovative ways to help children with learning problems. For Cosby, working with the foundation connects him to Ennis. "I want to celebrate his life," he says. "This is one way to do it."

No one that we have ever loved can totally disappear from our lives. Our loved ones live on in our gestures, our mannerisms, our beliefs and our feelings. "The deceased leave their mark and imprint on our very being," says Dr. Craig Vickio. "As a result of this internalization process, the influence of our loved ones extends far beyond death."

What often happens is an editing process in which you take the best parts of the person. My father was a kindhearted man, loved by many, and I, too, put a high value on compassion and empathy. Yet he was also a man who kept secrets about his past, which robbed me of truly knowing him and my family history. As a result, I am far more forthcoming to my children and friends.

Dr. Richard Tedeschi, a researcher at the University of North Carolina and the author of "Posttraumatic Growth," considers this one of the positive outcomes from loss.

"The ongoing bonds with the deceased help survivors review past events, clarify values and attitudes in their lives," he says. "In rebuilding their belief systems, they often restructure their lives and become more focused and appreciative of their surroundings. Healthy bereaved people find new ways to relate to the person, and that's part of making something useful of this terrible experience."

Therefore, even in death, your loved one is alive in your everyday life. Too often, these realizations reside in the subconscious, but by bringing them into your conscious mind, by making yourself aware of them, your loved one can be by your side always.

(2) The second strategy is to be mindful of telling stories about the person you love. Don't feel inhibited to say, "Jack used to say," even though Jack is no longer here. Make sure you tell stories about your loved one so their influence can still be felt by others.

"The children and grandchildren who hear those stories acquire a sense of being part of a larger community of family whose traditions are both idiosyncratic and universal," says Dr. Teri Friedman, a Westchester psychologist who is also a hospice consultant on the clinical use of therapeutic reminiscence. "Both grandparent and grandchildren become part of a greater whole, and may experience a heightened sense of place in the world, a place in the family, a place in the community and a place in the cycle of life. It is a legacy that lasts many lifetimes."

Teri recently felt this impact in her own life. "My six-year-old received a nickel for a job well-done, and she was less than impressed with the amount. Consoling herself, she said, 'Well, at least I don't have to choose between a soda and a nickelodeon like your Nana and Papa had to do on their first date!' Because the stories had been passed down, the experiences of her great-grandparents born a century before, and whom she had never met, were as germane and alive to her as if they happened yesterday," says Teri. "Moreover, she was able to use this nearly century-old story to help cope with life's disappointments."

One of the reasons I love my mother-in-law's visits is that she's a great storyteller. Recently, I was tugging at my hair, trying to twist it into a French braid.

"If Grandma Bea was here, she would have helped you do your hair," Joyce said. "The things she could do with hair. Everyone in the neighborhood went to her." I never met Grandma Bea, but because of this steady stream of stories, she is now a presence in my life.

Our culture isn't always resistant to speaking of the deceased. Look at our fascination with Shakespeare, with Marilyn Monroe, with John F. Kennedy. We continue to keep these figures alive by talking about them, by putting them in movies and books and by projecting what they may have thought or done. "Not infrequently, many of us take instruction from their lives and apply it to our own," says Dr. Therese Rando, clinical director of the Institute for the Study and Treatment of Loss in Warwick, Rhode Island, and the author of *How to Go on Living When Someone You Love Dies*. "Yet, why is it considered appropriate to go to the writings of Saint Augustine to get a moral perspective on how to cope with a particular moral issue, but considered unresolved grief if you reflect how your deceased father would deal with the same issue?

"You can and should have healthy relationships with the deceased. The important issue is that there be appropriate recognition of the fact that the person is dead and that your expectations and abstract interactions with him reflect knowledge of that fact."

In the early grieving stages, some people find comfort in telling stories while others find it painful. You must be the judge of when you are ready to become your loved one's historian. Follow your heart in these matters. That's the real expert. And don't think you need to have the acting skills of Tom Cruise to deliver a good story. It is the essence of the story that is remembered, the moral lesson or the funny mishap. But one tip is worth mentioning. It helps to tell the story with good cheer so that the person hearing the story will know that it also gives you pleasure. Sometimes, people mistakenly believe that any mention of the deceased is painful.

This next story illuminates this point.

To a friend, one evening, I said, "Whenever I see James Bond movies, it reminds me of my father." The response was typical. My friend avoided eye contact, shifted uncomfortably, and conveyed the message loud and clear that the conversation was unwelcome.

Later, to another friend, I said, "Whenever I see James Bond movies, it reminds me of my father. He loved the ruggedness of Sean Connery. I wonder what he would have thought of Roger Moore or Pierce Brosnan?"

Because I framed the second statement in a way that showed that the memory gave me pleasure, we talked about my father's tastes in leading men.

Telling stories is a great gift to everyone, including your loved one. In the Jewish faith, it is said that every time you talk about someone you love, their soul is elevated closer to God.

(3) The third strategy is weaving your loved one's interests or values into the fabric of your life, a method that is also defined as identification.

"A daughter may derive joy through keeping her mother's garden or using similar flowers to start her own and thereby forge a bond, since this activity occupied a central place in her mother's life and now her own," says Dr. Craig Vickio. "Or it can be taken further. Following the death of J.R.R. Tolkien, his son Christopher pored over more than half a century's worth of his father's writings and drafted the book *The Silmarillion*." The Fiennes clan did the same thing. When their mother died, actors Ralph and Joseph Fiennes of *The English Patient* and *Shakespeare in Love* fame found an unpublished manuscript of hers and used their influence to publish it. Tracey Brown, the daughter of Ron Brown, the secretary of commerce who died in a plane crash, wrote a memoir of her father.

Sheryl Henson launched a worldwide puppet festival in memory of her father Jim Henson, the creator of such beloved characters as Big Bird and Kermit the Frog.

"I remember we went together to Dresden, East Germany, for a puppet festival. Despite the bleak surroundings, the bad hotels and the terrible food, here was this community of puppeteers who found something funny and joyful.

"My father enjoyed the company of puppeteers, and the festival was a time to share what everyone was working on. Dad had once said that he wanted to do a worldwide festival. He didn't do it in his lifetime, but we organized this international biannual festival as a tribute to his love of puppetry," she says proudly. "It keeps us connected to what he cared about."

Sometimes the connection can come from sharing the same career. "I feel a connection to my father in what I do," says designer Donna Karan. Her father, a highly respected tailor, died when she was three. "He's the best inspiration," she adds. "What I do is in my genes. I feel that. I really do."

If we care about what they cared about, we have a link to our loved ones. My father was an easygoing, loving man except when it came to the dinner table. He was a stickler for family dinners, and his German temper would flare if my brother and I were not seated at the dinner table nicely dressed.

"Throughout the day, we are scattered everywhere, but this is the only time we can be together," my father would say. "Dinner is a sacred ritual." When I met my husband, Gary, his late working hours prevented many early family dinners with my stepdaughters. The kids often ate before he arrived. But when we married, I found the echo of my father's voice ringing in my ears when I insisted that we have family dinners at least four times a week.

This is an example of what some therapists call concurrent benefits, a process where the interest of our loved one becomes our own interest.

Natalie Cole was a teenager when her father, Nat King Cole, died of lung cancer. In 1991, after releasing many successful albums, she recorded *Unforgettable with Love*, an album of her late father's songs. Using digital technology, the album's video juxtaposed father and daughter singing a duet, an indelible image of the link between families.

The multimillion-selling album won numerous awards, including seven Grammys, and became one of the most honored albums of the decade.

"These songs are a gift from my father. The best gift," said Natalie. "I feel like I'm sharing these awards with my dad. He would have been tickled that not only did I go on to sing, but that I recorded not one but twenty-something songs thirty years later."

Not everyone has the lyrical talent of Natalie Cole, but one can also summon the memory of a father by listening to the music he loved or humming the tunes he sang. Your goal is not to get a Grammy but to feel the connection.

Caretakers can also help kids connect to their loved ones by invoking values their parents cared about. For example, the surviving parent or sibling can say, "Your dad said . . . never cheat in school. Always be honest" or "Your mom said if you don't have anything nice to say, don't say it at all."

"When we remember the values they taught us, the dead are living and maintain their role of authority figure, helper, supporter or confidant," says Dr. Phyllis Silverman, a social scientist at Harvard Medical School and Massachusetts General Hospital and author of *Never Too Young to Know: Death in Children's Lives*. "When a child maintains such an active, two-way relationship with his or her dead parent, she or he has acknowledged the fact that the parent is really dead and belongs to another world in another form."

(4) The fourth strategy in keeping our loved ones alive is by symbolic representation, in which your loved one's possessions can link you to them. Keep a few objects that were routinely used by them close to you. These could be a watch, a hairbrush, a piece of clothing, a favorite book. Feel them in your hands. One woman likes to nuzzle the sweater of her husband because it still carries his scent.

These links can include having pictures of your loved one positioned throughout the house, as well as reviewing videotapes whenever your longing for him or her needs some form of relief.

When she misses her mother, actress Patsy Kensit will take the urn holding her mother's ashes into bed and hold it tightly and think about any important advice she may need. "It makes me feel close to her," says Patsy.

Sometimes, I'll touch my father's thick black glasses sitting near my desk, and it takes me back to a time when they rested by his bedside table. This memory gives me a sense of comfort that his presence is still near.

A study of bereaved children conducted by Dr. Phyllis Silverman and Dr. Steven Nickman revealed that many of the children devoted considerable energy to staying connected with their deceased parents in some way—even though therapies often discourage it. The children accomplished this by having dreams about their parents, believing they could talk to them and that the parents were watching over them and by keeping things that had belonged to the dead parents.

These linkages not only helped them cope but gave them comfort.

(5) Last but not least, try to create a special place for your loved ones during ceremonial times, the graduations, births, marriages and holiday get-togethers. Although her parents weren't alive to see her get married, one woman saved two seats in the front row for Mom and Dad to be symbolically present at her wedding. In many religions, it is believed that the spirits of your parents hover nearby for your special milestones and recognizing them only makes them feel more welcome. Another daughter took her tassel from her graduation cap and rested it on her father's grave site following the

ceremony. All these gestures are a ringing endorsement of how much your loved one holds an important place in your life.

Sometimes because death is believed to be a taboo topic, we feel apprehensive about making these ceremonial gestures to a loved one. But embrace your feelings of love. You'll be pleasantly surprised to see that most people find these efforts both tender and touching. I can't tell you how often I've heard, "That was so nice to mention your father in the service. I want to do that, too." In fact, these gestures inspire others to do the same.

Naturally, any of these suggestions can be taken to an extreme and a balance must be reached. "That's the paradox, finding the right balance," says Dr. Therese Rando. "It is perfectly healthy and even encouraged to maintain a continued connection with a loved one as long as it is not interfering with the continuation of life." Your goal is to integrate your memories while adapting to the changes in your life. Only you know what is the right balance.

There are times that it may hurt to remember. There are times when it's healing to remember. Grief follows no predictable course. You just have to go with the flow. There will be days that the painful aspects of these linkages can exceed the comforting qualities of them. In the early stages of grief, when the pain is so intense and overwhelming, we're often so busy adjusting to the loss in our lives that we haven't begun to think of how to keep these connections. Memories are more a bittersweet reminder of what we've lost rather than of what we still have. But over time, I promise, the bittersweet becomes more sweet and less bitter. It becomes very empowering for people to discover that grief can entail holding on as well as letting go.

Connie understands this paradox intimately. Her son Allen carried a small, shiny piece of quartz in his trouser pocket. When he died, she could barely look at it without welling up with pain. Now, however, she takes comfort in carrying it in her purse at all times. It makes her feel as though her son is close by. At one time, it made her cry. Now, when she rolls it around in her hand, it can actually make her smile.

"When we grieve, it is often very difficult to move beyond the realization that there is nothing we can do to bring our loved ones back to life and this thought breeds feelings of helplessness," says Dr. Craig Vickio. "Yet by relinquishing this thought and moving on to a consideration of our options, we can find considerable solace and empowerment in realizing the deceased can still be included in our lives."

As you realize and treasure your continued connections, simultaneously, you will find yourself suddenly thinking about planting your own memories. How will I be remembered? There weren't many pictures of Dad. Are there many pictures of me? What special events have we done together? Who will miss me and why? What have I achieved?

Therefore, discovering the many ways we can relate to the deceased also has the potential to help us reflect on our own mortality and focus our energies into creating lasting legacies for those who will survive us.

No one can say with certainty what happens following death—it still remains one of life's mysteries. Some believe in heaven, others in reincarnation. Some feel that earth is the final exit. But each of us can be certain of one fact. After we die, we have the ability to have an ongoing, enriching and lasting relationship with others. Our presence can continue to be felt and have an impact on our loved ones. Consequently, how we relate to others in life has the power to create a profound, lasting legacy that can survive long after our death. Even if that's all there is, it's a lot. The power of memory shouldn't be underestimated.

Within the Jewish religion, stories have been passed from generation to generation for thousands of years. In his book *The Bible for the Clueless but Curious* Nachum Braverman tells the story of how Napoleon was once passing through the streets of Paris when he heard some Jews crying inside a synagogue.

"Why are they crying?" he asked.

"They are crying for the Temple's destruction 1,700 years ago."

"A people that remembers the Temple's destruction for 1,700 years will ultimately rebuild the Temple," said Napoleon.

Remembering your loved one can have the same impact. It will ultimately help you rebuild your life. Yes, as mourners we must move on and find new sources for pleasure and companionship. Yet at the same time, we can achieve this by experiencing the past as very much a part of who we are, and by keeping our loved one nearby in our thoughts, our hearts and our actions.

3

⁓

Global Rituals to Keep Loved Ones Close

Intellectually, we all understand the necessity of death. If people lived forever and never died, the world would be hopelessly over-crowded. The lines at Starbucks would be miles long and rush-hour traffic would take days instead of hours. With so many people, we wouldn't feel the need or desire to have babies, nor teach them the lessons we have learned from our experiences. Hence, the promise of improving the human race with each passing generation would come to a screeching halt. Art, science, music, books, movies, TV shows, all that we know and enjoy, would stagnate. Yet emotionally, it's hard to look at it that way.

Instead of feeling powerless that we can't bring back our loved one, think of the power you do have to affect people's lives and to honor your loved one's memory.

In earlier times, keeping the memories of loved ones alive was so much easier. People coped with death more frequently. Children died often in infancy, young men were killed in wars, aging parents died at home with family instead of in the sterile, institutional setting of hospitals. Death was a routine part of life. But today, death is so often prevented that mourners have a far more difficult time accepting their loss and finding cultural support.

Although we are a tell-all culture, where the most intimate details of people's lives are revealed, death is the one topic that is still hidden behind a curtain of secrecy.

Yet some cultures live more openly with death and maintain rituals to free themselves from lingering grief. Any of these rituals can be applied to our own lives.

My friend Michael's family is from Ethiopia. "In Africa, anytime a family is celebrating a special occasion, the elder family member pours out a drink onto the floor before making the toast," explained Michael. "It is a symbolic gesture to bring up our ancestors from the earth and have them join the party."

"You do that for every special occasion?" I asked.

"Well, if it's outside, it's easier to do on the ground," laughed Michael. "But inside, if it's on the carpet, my father will only pour out a drop."

This ancient ritual is crossing the ocean to some pockets of urban cities. Grief counselors say that inner-city children, whose lives are so rocked by local violence, have incorporated this gesture to remember their classmates or relatives in an effort to not feel so helpless.

In ancient Rome, lavish feasts were held at the burial site on the anniversary of a loved one's death, including serving the favorite dishes of the departed. It was also a custom to create masks of the person's face to keep their presence always in the home. Family members would casually wear these masks whenever they thought of the person. On selected holidays it was a privilege to wear the mask to a party, especially if the deceased had status in the family.

"This tradition affirmed the ongoing nature of family," says Dr. Dale Martin, a professor of religious studies at Yale University. "We could also say that it helped overcome a fear of death because family members saw that the deceased family members were remembered in a concrete way."

Judaism has many ways of remembering loved ones, starting with the week-long mourning period called "shiva." No one goes to work, to the movies, or outside the home. Instead, the family gathers to tell stories of the deceased and reflect on their relationship with the loved one, each other and with God. King Solomon believed it was more meaningful to visit a house of mourning than a house of feasting because of the wisdom derived from a shiva. For eleven months following the death, a prayer called Kaddish is recited three times a day, and each anniversary a yahrzeit candle is lit. "The candle represents the soul of the deceased," says Rabbi Yitzhak Kalsmith. "Judaism teaches that though the body may die, the soul is eternal."

Huston Smith, the distinguished adjunct professor of philosophy emiritus from Syracuse University, told me about a story from his childhood in China, where his parents were missionaries. After someone had died, the family would build a paper house, complete with paper furnishings, cars, appliances and all possible worldly goods. A Buddhist priest would arrive and play the flute, creating an ethereal sound. He would then take a match, light it and burn down the house. "Some of them were even big enough to walk into," recalls Huston. "The belief was that every paper model of something they created would then be realized in the afterlife for the one who is deceased."

In Hong Kong, there are tiny stores that sell paper pictures of all earthly possessions. "If someone wasn't married, you could buy a picture of a mate for them," says my friend Yale Yang, who lives in Hong Kong. "If he didn't have a car, you could buy him one. Symbolically, this helped the griever. It's a way of feeling that the next life will offer even more than this, that life can continually get better."

During the annual Japanese summer festival called O Bon, families make paper boats and wax them to a stiff sheen so they can hold small candles. On the night of O Bon, these paper boats are set sail on the river to commemorate the members of the family who are deceased. To see the river illuminated with tiny boats, each representing special memories of loved ones, is truly unforgettable. Later, people have reflective discussions about those they love.

As Dennis Klass writes in his book, *Continuing Bonds,* prior to this celebration is a period of preparation. "Wildflowers are gathered, paths to grave sites are cleared, and graves themselves are washed and decorated. Fresh flowers, incense, water and lanterns are readied. After sunset on the first day, lanterns at the family site are lit and incense burned to invite the spirits home. The color of these lanterns varies: if a family has lost a member during the preceding year, the lantern is white, otherwise it is red or blue-green. There is one lantern for each deceased member still remembered by someone in the household. In some areas, the entire village forms a torchlight procession, singing and dancing through the village to those homes that have lost a member in the previous year."

The second day is the time to reflect on the family members. Families may either go to the grave site or to temple. On the third day the spirits depart, and a large celebration takes place so the spirits can be entertained and amused before their departure.

"At its core, ancestor worship is an expression of the human community that cannot be separated by death," adds Dennis Klass. "It is an important element in Japanese culture and the predominant feature of Buddhism."

In Mexico, as well as El Salvador, Colombia and Guatemala, *Día de los Muertos*—the Day of the Dead—is an honored tradition of celebrating the life of your loved ones. Families summon the spirits of loved ones with a personalized altar decorated with the most cherished possessions of the deceased. It could be anything from a favorite dish, a photo, puppets, masks or even a tall glass of Coca-Cola. Other families picnic near the graveside and even bring boom boxes with a loved one's favorite music.

According to writer Daniel Chang, *Día de los Muertos* blends both Indian beliefs in the afterlife and Roman Catholic traditions rooted in All Saints Day.

"Great attention is paid to prepare for the spirit's return and to ensure a safe departure," he says. "Candles light the altar so the spirit may rest following its long journey from the afterlife. And as with any guest, the spirit should not wear out its welcome, so the altars are erected on October 31, and are dismantled on November 2, after a feast of the departed's favorite dishes."

Some have created altars to celebrate a loved one's ideals. One family constructed an altar to women's rights and had pictures of people who were persecuted for exercising free speech as well as books on the subject.

Others created altars for their pets, complete with dog biscuits, pictures and a favorite water dish.

"American culture treats death as a surprise and as an unwelcome part of life," says Monsignor Jaime Soto, Hispanic vicar for the Diocese of Orange County. "Mexican and many other cultures see death as part of life and make death part of our understanding of how we must live."

Perhaps now it is time to reintroduce some of these rituals into our own lives. On Halloween, when making your homemade ballerina costume for your little girl, have the family also construct a small memento in honor of a deceased loved one. Or light a candle on his birthday as a remembrance and tell a story about him.

Indian cultures have similar customs. Chief Hawk Pope, the charismatic leader of the Shawnee tribe, told me about the Feast of the Dead, which takes place after the winter solstice, the gloomiest day of the year. The tribes gather to have a great feast. "A small portion of each dish is put in a traditional shell or in a wooden bowl and taken to the Great House, which is like our church," he explains. "We then put the food around the altar and fire and speak the names of each person who has passed to remember them."

At other times, whenever the tribes conduct a major ceremony, a bundle is constructed containing mementos from past great ancestors as well as possessions of those recently departed. "It can be a piece of crystal or clothing, anything that represents them in this life," says Chief Hawk Pope. "We then dance around it and sing a song, what we call our Howling Song, that invites the spirits to join us. It is our belief that our ancestors come visit us and we can ask them questions which they will answer in our dreams."

Many cultures believe our loved ones visit us most easily in dreams. I believe that if you want a question answered, speak to your loved one before you sleep. Jews say that when you sleep, your soul goes up to Paradise, where it receives wisdom from other souls. Since death is the separation of the body from the soul, sleep is the nearest replica of the experience. This explains why religious Jews awake each morning to say a prayer of thanks that the body and soul are reunited for another day.

A belief in immortality has existed for centuries. Prehistoric and primitive people had their "shamans" or healers who could make contact with the spirit world. According to writer Henry Reed, a research psychologist and former assistant professor at Princeton, and author of *Edgar Cayce on Channeling Your Higher Self*, the practices of shamans from around the world show a remarkable consistency.

"Dating back as far as 5000 B.C., the Egyptian Book of the Dead details the ability of the human soul to leave the physical body and communicate with spirits," he says. "Around 2000 B.C., the Chinese developed the prototype for the Ouija board. Later the ancient Greeks had their oracles, considered to be the mouthpieces of the gods.

"By 1000 B.C. monotheism became a strong religious force in the origins of Judaism. The Old Testament contains many descriptions of channeling, beginning with the prophet Moses, followed by Solomon, Samuel, Daniel, Elijah, Elisha, Ezekiel, Jeremiah and Isaiah. Perhaps the most profound example of channeling in the Bible is John the Beloved's Revelation."

Modern-day religions also have their roots in forms of channeling. In seventeenth-century England, George Fox's visions led to the founding of the Quakers. The book of Mormon is based on Joseph Smith's vision of the angel Moroni.

In the 1850s, the culture was particularly receptive to this type of thinking. "Prominent people, public leaders, and celebrities reported their conversations with the dead and helped establish credibility," says Henry Reed. In fact, Arthur Conan Doyle, best known as the writer of Sherlock Holmes, became the movement's historian with his two-volume work, *The History of Spiritualism*.

Although mediums still exist today, the practice is discounted by religious leaders or dismissed by skeptics. Yet millions of people still seek them out.

Another ancient communication form involved containers—bowls, cups or cauldrons—that were filled with liquid and then used for mirror gazing. Often these were polished to a sparkling sheen so that the shiny object could project a mirror image of a spirit. Some people would fast before looking inside, others just gazed intently in the liquid to put them in a meditative state. Dr. Raymond Woody, in his book, *Reunions: Visionary Encounters with Departed Loved Ones,* talks about this custom throughout history. "Tungus shamans in Siberia used copper mirrors," he says. "In their language the word for mirror was actually derived from the word for soul, and hence the mirror was regarded as a receptacle for the spirit. The Africans of Fez used a vessel of water in which to see visions, and in present-day Egypt a pool of ink is used in much the same way that Odysseus uses blood [in Homer's account]."

Later John Dee, a noted scholar and adviser to Queen Elizabeth, practiced mirror gazing. In one session he was given quite a prophetic message. The spirit told him, "The want of Science hindreth you from knowledge of yourself."

To researchers like Dennis Klass, modern society became the death knell for many of these practices. The culture's fascination with technology and speed resulted in ancient customs being discarded or devalued.

"Modernity is about freeing the individual from obligatory bonds, the family, the village, the church or someone's own history," observes Dennis Klass. "The modern individual sought autonomy and independence. This thinking naturally impacted how we thought of grieving. Grief too became the act of cutting bonds."

The advent of world wars also profoundly impacted death rituals. "There were so many deaths starting with World War I that the elaborate funeral rituals of previous eras fell into disuse because had everyone worn black for a year, as was the traditional mourning custom, or stayed at home to mourn, the impact on national morale would have been devastating," says Dr. Ken Doka, a Lutheran minister and professor of death studies at the College of New Rochelle. "People had to resume their lives not only for themselves, but for their country's sake."

Now, slowly but surely, the pendulum is swinging back. Battling isolation and alienation as they disintegrate through divorce, death and relocation, many families are aching for a sense of connection beyond the superficial and transient. We yearn for a sense of belonging and a revival of rituals that foster closeness and continuity.

Part of the solution is keeping memories of our loved ones alive as well as creating legacies and rituals that bond us to our friends and communities. Our ancestors have coped with loss by embracing, not denying death. We need to envelop ancient wisdom into our own lives and forge connections that transcend time and space and the material world. Fortunately, many of these clues our ancestors left us about how to cope have been with us all along, often buried in surprising places.

4

⁓

Our Cultural Mythology: A Hidden Healer

Do you remember when you were a child and your mother would wrap you in her arms and read you a bedtime story? Reflect back to that time. Now, remember the sound of her voice and the inflections she would use to make those stories come alive.

Many of the fairy tales and stories she would read were the same books mothers around the world were reading to their children. *Hansel and Gretel, Heidi, Pippi Longstocking, Little Red Riding Hood, Tarzan, Cinderella, Annie, Madeline, Bambi.*

A great deal of our cultural mythology is based on how loss—often of a parent—has been the driving force for change, growth and ultimately greatness. Yes, greatness. Think about it: Superman, Simba, Sherlock Holmes, King Arthur, Indiana Jones, Robin Hood, Batman and even Harry Potter are just a few of the icons who were struck a heavy blow but rebounded and transcended the experience to become heroic. A hero must be different. They cannot be like everyone else.

Bruce Wayne's parents were murdered, and he vowed to right the wrong. He became a crusading hero as Batman, along with his trusted aide Robin, who was also an orphan. After Superman's parents were killed, he had to adjust to a new life with new parents while harnessing powers that made him special and strong. The metaphor of being different also brought with it inner strength, strength strong enough to break down buildings and barriers. In *The Lion King*, Simba becomes a leader after his father dies. The movie's hit song, "Circle of Life," emphasizes the theme of how the spirit of our loved ones can guide us through life. Harry Potter is an orphan living with his abusive aunt and uncle. He discovers his parents left him the legacy of being a wizard, and this knowledge helps him develop secret powers that lead him into adventures and challenges, all of which test his leadership abilities.

Therefore, transforming loss isn't a foreign concept to us at all. In fact, it is a feat that is reinforced time and time again in thousands of ways throughout our lives. Let these characters inspire you. Look at them with new eyes. Observe how our favorite movies and TV shows are often about characters who have been crushed by a disaster and mustered the strength to build a new life.

When my little boy runs around the house in his Batman costume and pleads for us to put another *Batman* tape in the VCR, he wants to see how good can conquer evil. The evidence is there every day.

We already tell him why Batman is so determined to get the bad guy. I want him to be conscious that loss can be a motivator in making someone want to right a wrong. I want him to realize that life is filled mostly with good moments, but also with sad ones.

In one episode, Batman reveals that the Batcave is modeled after "The Gray Ghost." "I used to watch this show with my father," he reflects, summoning the memory of his parents. Another time he consoles a young Robin, whose acrobat parents were murdered. "Will this hurt ever go away?" asks Robin. "No," replies Bruce Wayne. "It never does. But it does get better with time."

In *The Prisoner of Azkaban*, Harry Potter believes his father helped him out of a jam, but he questions how this could have been possible.

"You think the dead we loved ever truly leave us?" his teacher Dumbledore asks. "You think that we don't recall them more clearly than ever in times of great trouble? Your father is alive in you, Harry, and shows himself most plainly when you have need of him."

In another book, *Harry Potter and the Sorcerer's Stone,* Dumbledore explains to Harry why he was protected from the evil of a menacing wizard. "Your mother died saving you," he tells him. "He didn't realize that love as powerful as your mother's leaves its own mark. Not a scar, no visible sign . . . to have been loved so deeply, [yet] even though the person is gone, [it] will give us some protection forever."

When a mother is stumbling to explain why her little boy's father isn't coming home, instead of using language he can't relate to, she can invoke the names of favorite characters. She can remind him that others have been guided by the memories of their mother or father even if we no longer see them.

For the little boy keenly aware of his father's absence at school plays, who enviously watches a friend playing catch with his dad, having someone who shares his loss and finds ways to overcome it can be tremendously empowering.

Barbara Hozinsky, a therapist at the Barr-Harris Center for the Study of Separation and Loss in Childhood, at the Institute for Psychoanalysis in Chicago, often encourages children to seek out figures who share their experience. "Making these connections helps combat a child's sense of isolation," she says. "When they hear about other kids who face the same challenge, they get some kind of objectivity about it. I treated a little boy who had been resistant to talking about his mother's death or its impact. We read a book about a boy who reacted to his father's death by losing his appetite and becoming sad. When this was addressed from a distance, with someone else, he realized that's what kids go through and was more responsive."

Finding a character to relate to in a book helped a young Peter Fonda cope with his mother's death when he was ten. The character was Stuart Little. "My father [actor Henry Fonda] never let me or my sister go to the funeral and told us that my mother had died of a heart attack, when in fact, it was suicide," he told me. "I felt so alone and confused. My family felt very bizarre and I felt like I didn't belong anywhere. What got me through it was that little book. Stuart was a survivor. Here was this orphan mouse that was different but he got it together. He had all this courage. I must have read it sixty times. Years later when I was thirty-five, my wife-to-be, Becky, gave me a present. When I opened it, it was a copy of Stuart Little. I cried because I knew then that she was the woman for me. That book really helped me. Stuart became a friend I needed."

You can also invoke the names of entertainment characters to hammer in a moral point and find it works far better than long dissertations. Entertainment provides me with a built-in Morse code. One day when Parker was having trouble accomplishing a task, I reminded him how Superman also has weaknesses—at least whenever kryptonite is around.

Rosie O'Donnell sometimes disciplines her kids by invoking well-known characters. "Do you know what Mufasa [from *The Lion King*] does to children who don't listen?" she scolded. Naturally she got quick results.

When seeing the movie *Madeline* or *Annie*, pose this question: "Why do you think Madeline or Annie is so much smarter than the other girls? Well, when you aren't given everything, you become more resourceful."

Perhaps try reading the original version of *Cinderella*.

"In the *Grimm's Fairy Tales* version of *Cinderella*, she depends on her mother's spirit to help her overcome obstacles. The character is a far more proactive person who relies on the wisdom of her ancestors and uses that along with her natural ingenuity to succeed," says Andrew Corsilia, who teaches mythology in literature at Horace Greeley School in Chappaqua, New York. "In the Disney-fied version, the character of Cinderella relies more on beauty and a fairy godmother."

Arthur, an orphan, pulls the sword out of the stone and becomes King of England and creates the knights of the round table. His earlier experience as an orphan taught him the importance of fairness, and his rule was marked by democracy, not tyranny.

Critics like to bash popular culture, blaming it for society's ills. Yet this isn't always true. Little attention is paid to the positive influences of the media and how many characters can be used to help inspire and heal.

"One thing that comes out in myths is that at the bottom of the abyss comes the voice of salvation," wrote Joseph Campbell, the late philosopher, author and professor of mythology at Sarah Lawrence College. "The black moment is the moment when the real message of transformation is going to come. At the darkest moment, comes the light."

Finding characters who may face similar challenges to you or your children can be therapeutic in reminding us that people are faced with all sorts of crises and find solutions to their problems. Grief is an isolating experience, causing such despair that often we feel paralyzed by our circumstances. However, comfort can be found in reading a book and being transported into someone else's life where similar anguish and uncertainties exist. Reading about these characters provides us with options of handling our loss and reminds us that we are not powerless.

Many therapists are finding that pop culture figures can be used to peel back the layers of resistance. "It is often much easier to have patients talk about issues that are happening to a character in a film or TV show if the situation is similar to what they may be going through," says Dr. Joe Rosenthal, a New York–based therapist. "They're less inhibited discussing someone else and can find truths from the character's dilemma and resolution. I'll often say, 'What would you have done?' and this can lead to a discussion about options and ways of thinking."

With teenagers, fitting in with the crowd is vitally important to their feelings of self-esteem, and anything that separates them from their peer group becomes a great source of shame and discomfort. Without friends to validate or relate to the experience, a death can make them feel isolated and lonely. Since teens often get their cues more from MTV than Mom, Dr. Linda Jordan, the director of the Unicorn bereavement center of the Triangle Hospice in North Carolina, uses music lyrics to show teens various options to express and view their grief.

One teenager was extremely tight-lipped about his brother's death. After repeated attempts to open him up, Dr. Jordan had him listen to Vince Gill's song "Go Rest High Upon the Mountain," and then questioned him about the way the artist explored his experience with his brother's death. This exercise reinforced that the teenager was not alone in his experience and showed that others he may admire also felt similar feelings of sadness and remorse.

"As therapists, you look for ways to relate to the child on their terms," says Dr. Jordan. "Popular culture offers many opportunities to open the lines of communication and then a therapist can help heal grief's wounds."

Since some teenagers gravitate to grunge and others to pop rock, Dr. Jordan has collected many songs that reflect the experience of loss in some way whether it's Elton's John's version of "Candle in the Wind" for Princess Diana, Eric Clapton's "Tears in Heaven" or Patty Loveless' "How Can I Help You Say Good-bye."

Others songs could be Dan Fogelberg's "Leader of the Band," Mike and the Mechanics' song "Living Years," Sarah McLachlan's "I Will Remember You" or the Beatles' "Let It Be." Pick any artist, and the likelihood is that they have once explored the legacy of loss.

In her work, Dr. Sandra Bertman, the director of Medical Humanities at the University of Massachusetts Medical Center, uses all forms of art—music, film, painting, books—to introduce characters who are not unlike the people she is treating.

"Visual and literary art enables us to appreciate the universality as well as the particularity of our own experience," says Dr. Bertman. "Drama and role-play are other ways to encourage children to examine their feelings and test their ideas against those of fictional characters. Role-play also provides an opportunity for children to work through their hidden concerns, beliefs and fears."

Aside from showing the universality of loss, entertainment vehicles can provide a comfort in linking us to the person we love.

As the survivor, we already know that it is our job to be our loved one's historian. Therefore, you can take the time to remind your child of the books that his father or grandfather read and how these lessons are meant to be passed on for generations. Knowing that his father may have read *Huckleberry Finn* or *Curious George* can help make the child feel that his father is looking over his shoulder and laughing too.

This is also a wonderful exercise to do at any age. One summer when I was particularly nostalgic for my father, I went into a bookstore and bought paperbacks of German authors. Transported back to Vienna in the 1920s, I could smell the smoke in the taverns, taste the Schnapps being clinked in glasses and hear the loud, roaring beat of the music as people waltzed until dawn. Another book took me on a historical tour through towns I knew my father visited before I was born, and I roamed through those streets imagining his face as a young man.

Years later on a European trip, I visited some of these towns and even searched for the home of Herman Hesse, in gratitude for providing such companionship when I needed it.

For holidays, many families take out dog-eared copies of books from previous generations that are read among family members. Sometimes it's *A Christmas Carol*. Or maybe it's the story of Passover. I also know families who have passed on copies of *Goodnight Moon* or *Eloise*, and each book is treated like a priceless jewel. Here's a suggestion to start a family tradition that can link your kids to their loved ones. Even if you don't possess the actual copy of your mother's favorite book, buy a new edition and declare that it will be passed on for generations. If your deceased son got an "A" for his book report on *To Kill a Mockingbird*, save a copy of the book so it can be passed on in the family. The significance of something is heightened by the importance we place on it.

This occurred to me the other day while watching *Mary Poppins* with my son. It is one of the few movies I remember my father taking me to, and it filled me with joy to be sharing this film with my own son.

"Grandpa took me to see this film too," I told him.

"Grandpa and Mommy see *Mary Poppins*," he replied, not knowing the emotional power of those few words.

Think about the films that your loved one liked. Remember the books or the TV shows he or she enjoyed. Revive those memories when you need to feel a connection. What made your mother laugh? What made her cry? What did your sister like to do on a lazy Sunday afternoon?

I really think *The Waltons* is a hokey show, but my father delighted in the family closeness, so now sometimes I find myself spending a few minutes watching the reruns. It brings me back to when we were all together lying on my parent's king-size bed watching it, long before we became a family of three place settings at the dinner table.

Music can also summon memories. Certain songs are forever frozen in time. Whenever I hear Billy Joel's "Just the Way You Are," I am carried back to when I was dating a boy named Richard and the song played nonstop on the radio. The same is true with Frank Sinatra. " 'My Way' is my song," my father would say and whenever I hear Sinatra, I think of my father dramatically imitating the lyrics—off key.

After my father died, I bought some of Sinatra's tapes to have on hand whenever I want to feel close to him, because the songs gave him pleasure. Yet, I will turn off the radio or walk out of the room when a song from the group Yes is played. The night before my father died, I went to see a Yes concert. At the time it was my favorite group. But now that music is forever linked to his passing, which conjures up sad memories for me.

It's funny how we associate certain shows or songs with specific times. Mystery writer Mary Higgins Clark was ten when her father died. "I was so petrified that my mother would also go that I made a deal with God," she recalled. "I said, 'God, if you keep my mother alive, I won't listen to the *Lone Ranger* on the radio.' That was a huge sacrifice to make because the *Lone Ranger* was the biggest hit on radio. I didn't listen to it. Now I realize how foolish this sacrifice was because it had nothing to do with whether my mother would be safe. It reminds me of my fear."

Even now, when she hears its theme music, Mary Higgins Clark is taken back to that painful time.

Reviving memories is a tricky business. We must sift through the hundreds that we possess and find the gems that sparkle brightest and whose gleam makes us happy and joyous. Otherwise we are left with an ache in our heart and a lump in our throat. Over time, you get better at it.

One of the tools that helps transport someone from isolation and depression is faith. Not only faith in yourself but faith in a higher being.

One of the best examples is *Touched by an Angel*. Although the pooh-bahs of pop culture predicted the show would fail, it attracted a devoted following and exposed an audience thirsty for spiritual themes.

The TV show, now seen in over seventy countries, doesn't sugar-coat life's traumas and disappointments. Mothers lose children, husbands get killed and relationships are strained by stress. The happy ending is not that people survive disease or accidents but that they are given the tools to accept life's challenges and find meaning in them.

In one episode, a gifted gymnast cuts herself off from emotion because she is guilt-ridden that she resented her father's terminal illness and avoided seeing him while he was dying. The angel, played by Roma Downey, consoles her.

"He knows you wish you were there, and he understands. He is with you right now. Feel him. Tell him how you feel. He is with you and so is God." Many find great solace in seeing this show week after week.

The show's executive producer and creator, Martha Williamson, believes that the show's appeal taps into the public's need for meaning. "We can download, fax, and e-mail in an instant," she says. "Yet our emotions still run at the same pace as always. It still takes the same time to fall in love, to grieve the loss of a love, or to have a baby." The show helps reinforce that although painful events occur beyond our understanding, life still offers possibilities.

When your emotional tank is on empty, search for life-affirming programs or films. If you can't find them channel-surfing, seek out films from the neighborhood Blockbuster. Some of my favorites are *It's a Wonderful Life*, *Field of Dreams*, *Frequency*, *Michael*, *Peggy Sue Got Married*, *City of Angels*, *See You in the Morning*, *Chapter Two*, *Ghost*, *The Lion King*, *The Land Before Time*, *What Dreams May Come* and *Star Wars*. They can inspire you and make you feel better.

Aside from a little spiritual renewal, laughter is good too. "God gave us an outlet from stress through laughter," says Dr. Cynthia Shelby-Lane, a Detroit-based doctor. "It helps us survive. It helps people cope. When you laugh, it focuses everything outward. It's like a shot of morphine. It releases endorphins, a natural substance released in the body like painkillers. It's happy juice to the body."

You're not dishonoring your loved one by finding a moment or two to laugh at someone's story or wisecrack. Your loved one wouldn't want you to suffer.

To prepare for those endless lonely nights, you might consider buying some comedy videos. I'm serious. Think of all the movies that made you laugh, and stock them right now. Keep some in reserve for those times, and they will come, especially when the pain overwhelms you. Laughter will be a welcome release. And it's good therapy.

Go ahead. Rent *City Slickers* or *Austin Powers*. Rent *My Cousin Vinny* or *American Pie*. Rent whatever movie you remember making you laugh.

While movies are a wonderful option, an often overlooked source for comedy are audio recordings. You may not know it, but most comedians have all their best material on tapes or CDs. You can buy Chris Rock, Bill Cosby, Bob Hope, Jackie Mason, Eddie Murphy, Richard Pryor, Rich Little, Don Rickles, Billy Crystal, Joan Rivers, Whoopi Goldberg, etcetera.

"I think audio recordings are actually far more effective," my friend Mark Simone says. "In movies, you may have to wait ten minutes for the belly laugh. With these, it's nonstop jokes."

Besides, you can listen to a tape in the car or soothe yourself to sleep with a little laughter to ease the sadness.

The entertainment we see and hear is all rooted in traditions from long ago, when our ancestors gathered together and told stories to make sense out of life. Now we can sit around the collective TV campfires, convene in movie theaters or visit bookstores to discover stories about how people coped with their struggles. In them we can find humor or wisdom, and be reminded that people not only survive, but they can thrive.

PART TWO

A Road Map Through Grief

"Change is inevitable. Growth is optional."
——Anonymous

"Happiness is not a station to arrive at,
but a manner of traveling . . ."
——Margaret Lee Runbeck

5

The Journey/It Hurts

In some small towns in Italy, when a woman loses a loved one, she wears black clothing for a full year so that anyone who meets her will immediately know that she is in mourning. In some Indian tribes, a similar ritual exists where mourners wear a black band around their arm for a year. The significance of these gestures is the same. People who are touched by loss are in a delicate state and need special handling.

In our culture, there are few symbolic gestures to let the outside world know our state of mind. After the death of a loved one, we are expected to spring back like a rubber band and resume our daily routines as though nothing has happened. A recent survey from the National Hospice Foundation revealed that most people think a month is plenty of time to recover. Nothing could be further from the truth.

It takes time, lots of time. If it takes the human body over nine months to make a baby, why should anyone think it takes less time to recover from losing one?

No one wants to suffer. We look for ways to make the pain go away. But where do we start?

In the beginning, everyone feels awful. It's as though you're riding a roller coaster with a hangover. The shock, disbelief and sheer agony of the death is so disorienting, so disruptive, that finding your way to the bathroom seems like a foreign experience.

This is normal. Allow yourself to feel the numbing shock. You are likely to have any one or several of these physical symptoms: a lack of appetite, nightmares, sweats, headaches, muscle tension, heartburn, unexplained desires to binge on a pint of ice cream and cookies.

Psychologically, you could be having a nice dinner at a restaurant with a friend and then blow up because the steak is too rare. Mood swings, feeling angry, sad, despondent and wanting to cry are all normal reactions. You may find yourself yelling at your kids or being impatient with a salesclerk. Even your thinking is sometimes impaired. It could take you two minutes to remember where you put your car keys. Confusion, forgetfulness and irritability are all part of the grieving process during its early stages.

"Late at night, you could be reading a magazine and then think, 'I can't remember anything I've read,' " says Barbara Johansen, a social worker at Greenwich Hospital in Connecticut. "This is part of the body's built-in defense mechanism. It can't bring in anything more. The person is on overload until she can decompress and allow herself to feel her feelings." Sometimes, you may not feel anything. It's okay to feel whatever you feel. This is your experience, no one else's.

Looking back, I was numb throughout my father's funeral, hardly shedding a tear. Because my mother was so consumed by her own grief that she never considered ours, I was forced to slip into the role of the adult. All the while, I distanced myself from emotions and resented my mother's weakness. It's not that I didn't think often of my father. But I intellectualized his loss and feared that if I gave in to the pain, I would crumble.

Months later, I was walking down the street and a stranger inexplicably reminded me of my father. My head jerked back, trying to see him again, but he had disappeared. Suddenly, for the first time, I burst into tears, my body shaking from my sobs. This emotional release felt like my pain was floating out of my body. At that point I stopped being scared of my feelings.

"Some people do have delayed reactions," observes Dr. Joe Rosenthal, a New York–based therapist. "Many of us who study grief responses are questioning earlier theories that documented the stages of grief—with the patient going from denial, to anger, to sadness and then eventually to acceptance. At any point along the way, you can backslide, depending on an experience that can trigger your loss. Someone could have felt acceptance for months or years and then suddenly be swept back to the initial pain. The secret is learning to go with the flow."

Like tides that have unexpected undertows, there is still some predictability to grief's ebbs and flows. I think Dr. Joanne Jozefowski's description of what to expect sums it up precisely and gives us a road map of what to expect on the journey.

A therapist in Massachusetts and author of *The Phoenix Phenomenon*, she breaks it down into the following five stages:

(1) Impact—The initial stage in which we process the reality of the death while sustaining our physiological needs like food, water and rest.
(2) Chaos—We develop order from the debris while needing outlets to express our emotions of grief.
(3) Adaptation—We learn to adapt to life without the loved one and seek connections to others through support systems, other grievers, work, school or our house of worship, as well as developing new roles for ourselves.
(4) Equilibrium—We attain stability and balance in life and are able to consider self-potential without our loved one.
(5) Posttraumatic growth—A resulting metamorphosis as the person emerges reshaped from the loss, developing more self-potential, greater spirituality, altruism, self-awareness and appreciation for life.

Everyone runs their own race in getting here. Some take baby steps. Others take big steps. Often you take steps backward. The only thing that really matters is that you are moving.

*   *   *

The only advice that everyone seems to agree on is that it's important to experience your feelings and express them. Reach out to a close friend you can trust or a family member. Talk about your feelings out loud. Don't worry if you become repetitive. This is healthy and quite normal. Dr. John Pelletier, a Massachusetts clinical psychologist, believes that speaking verbally about your pain helps "expel its toxicity" and this leads to healing. There's poison in your system and you should want to spit it out as you would if you swallowed turpentine. Don't hold it in. Talk about your anger, talk about the unfairness, talk about how much you miss your loved one. Punch a pillow if you have to.

Let your emotions rage as though a hurricane is ripping through your house. Feel your pain for as long as you need to. After the debris settles, you can start the work of rebuilding.

Carly, a forty-year-old widow, remembers getting up and feeling as though a thick fog was sitting in her bedroom refusing to budge. Often she would glance out the window and see daylight, knowing that behind the shimmering glass panes was a world functioning as though nothing had happened. Her neighbors were throwing Cheerios in bowls while hurrying to get their kids off to school. Traffic was jam-packed with commuters rushing to work. And somewhere, not far, husbands and wives were kissing each other good-bye as they started their day. For Carly, these daily rituals felt like a big slap in her face.

"How dare they go on with their life when I'm suffering so!" she recalls. "I remember feeling like gauze was wrapped around me, and I couldn't fathom how people were living their lives when I felt so numb. I felt like screaming out the window, 'It's not fair that you can be happy when I'm miserable.' "

Some days Carly just wanted to stay in bed under her soft down quilt, as though it was a cocoon to protect her from the real world, a world that had suddenly become scary and cold. Some days she didn't even get dressed and remained in her flannel nightgown. In her private moments, she wondered, Would she ever feel safe and secure again? Now she had to worry about supporting three children on one paycheck. How much insurance did Tommy have? Would she have to move? Other thoughts she didn't dare express. Who would she laugh with late at night while watching TV? Who would ever admire her slinky black dress with the scooped neckline?

"There were so many unanswered questions," recalls Carly. "It was so overwhelming. I just couldn't stop crying."

Like most people, Carly was too shell-shocked the first few weeks following Tommy's death to fully comprehend the loss. So many immediate tasks needed to be completed. The funeral arrangements. The eulogy. The surreal decision over whether to have red roses or white orchids at the church. The concessions on which music would be played during the service. Her kids opted for Sarah McLachlan's "I Will Remember You" while his mother insisted on "Amazing Grace." Even though the priest had suggested "On Eagle's Wings" because of its resurrection theme, she chose Bette Midler's "The Wind Beneath My Wings." That one is for us, she thought as she smiled at the memory of them slow dancing in Barbados.

After the funeral the phone rang constantly. Either it was her mother, her sister Debbie or friends from college or work asking how she was. "I'm doing okay," she would reply, although the thought of never seeing Tommy again would fill her eyes with tears. Soon each call would seem eerily familiar, as though she was following a script and the same lines would be repeated over and over again.

"Yes, I'm holding up as best as can be expected."

"The kids are doing okay. Yes, they're back in school, and Brian is playing soccer. Katie is busy with gymnastics practice."

"Yes, I miss him so much."

"Yes, I guess it was meant to be."

Aside from the phone calls, neighborhood mothers offered to carpool, and arrived with tins of ziti smothered in mozzarella, piles of homemade chocolate-chip cookies and enough meat-loaf casseroles to clog her arteries forever. However, the real loneliness hit her weeks later when the calls became less frequent, and she was left to put her life back together.

Even though it had only been a few weeks, she wanted to talk more about Tommy, about what he had meant to her, about how much she loved him, about a movie he would have laughed at, a song he would have enjoyed, about all the dreams they shared. Talking kept him alive to her.

Yet on the few nights she went out with friends, she sensed an uneasiness whenever she mentioned Tommy, so she instinctively kept her thoughts to herself. Not that it made her feel better. It made her feel worse. Only with her sister Debbie could she express her true feelings.

Karen can relate to this situation too well. It's been five years, but she is still disappointed by the insensitivity of many of her friends after her young daughter died. "For years, I would hear the same story over and over again about Susan's breakup with Mitch or Dana's divorce from Kevin. When I needed to talk, they would tell me how I had to get over it and move on," recalls Karen, blotting her eyes with a tissue. "It's very hard to find someone to talk to."

Indeed it is. In fact, psychologists and bereavement specialists say this is the hardest part of the mourning process—and the most important.

In the same way water builds behind the dam, pent up emotions need release. We must talk to people about what happened. About the change in our lives. About what we miss about them.

Sitting in his roomy leather chair, Dr. Gerald Koocher nods his head knowingly as he hears countless stories from those who have lost loved ones and find that their friends and family have let them down. As chief of psychology at Children's Hospital in Boston and an associate professor of psychology at Harvard, thousands of patients have walked through his door angered by their loss and miffed that their friends and family have not rallied behind them.

Gently, he reminds them to understand that most people aren't intentionally mean.

"I once had a patient who was talking about the death of her mother to someone whose mother hadn't died," recalls Dr. Koocher. "The conversation stirred up immense discomfort because it was something that brought out her friend's own fears. If this happened to my patient, the friend was wondering, will it happen to her? Will she lose her mother? The friend was thinking that she wanted to be supportive, but there was a limit."

Like many experts, Dr. Koocher gently advises that we must be very selective about with whom we share our thoughts. It has to be someone safe. His patient would have been better served if she sought the shoulder of a friend who had experienced a loss in her own family. By finding a kindred spirit, the friend would have realized that she needed an active listener who would have let her just talk. Instead, by choosing another person, the patient felt even more alone and isolated.

This is why Amy will never forget the kindness of her friend Melanie. Several weeks after her husband, Jeff, died, she was back at work as a magazine editor and went out to lunch with Melanie. They were talking about how Amy's son David had just reached a major milestone in his speech therapy when she burst into tears. "I wish Jeff was here to share this," she wailed, reaching for a tissue. "It would have meant so much to him." Melanie burst into tears with her, crying over Amy's loss, and silently comforting her friend, not with words, but with understanding.

"So many people want to stop you from crying and try to fix the problem," stammered Amy. "This is a problem that isn't going to be fixed. I don't want to hear that it's for the best or Jeff will always be with me. I want someone who will just let me cry."

Crying helps us heal. It's nature's way of releasing our anguish. We feel calmer and relieved after shedding tears. Sadness is emptied and you can refill yourself by welcoming the goodness that still exists.

We have been conditioned that crying is only for babies. We're told it should be stifled and repressed. Little boys are labeled "crybabies" if they cry. And this menacing, insidious message carries on into their adulthood, causing people to suppress their emotions often with disastrous results. For women, the message is almost the same, just packaged differently. Crying is socially acceptable but only in the confines of one's home or in front of a few cherished friends.

Sometimes, when a lump swells in the throat, we will have to stifle our tears. Just find another place where you can let go of your pain. Put yourself in a situation where you can have a good cry. At home. In the car. Sitting in the woods.

If we do not release our tears and let them flow, the pain within us calcifies into anger, hardening us in ways that create permanent scars and prohibit us from living life to its fullest. Only when we release our tears and expel our sadness can we begin to heal. Because along with pain also comes joy. Instead of trying to hold back your tears and saying to yourself, "I must be really weak if I can't stop myself from crying," reframe your conversation to your brain by saying, "I will be strengthened by crying because it is good for me. It will help me heal. It's good that I am connected to my feelings and that I can have this release that will make me feel better."

The ancients weren't wrong when they encouraged crying. They believed that crying delivers relief because "grief is carried off by tears."

6

⁓

A Friend in Need
Is a Friend Indeed

When I was a teenager, my father would always say that if you could count the number of true friends on one hand, you would be a lucky person. "Only five friends?" I said, shocked at the small number. "Well, Daddy, I have many more friends than that right now." Looking at me with an amused smile, he lovingly replied, "I hope that will always be true, sweetheart." Of course, he was right.

Most friends are like shadows, only appearing in the sunshine and then disappearing when darkness falls. In the early days following a loss, people are usually more patient with their friends' tears than later on. One school of thought says it is our job to reach out to friends and ask for support. Some believe that instead of being hurt by a friend's insensitivity, we should tell them not to be upset by our tears but just stick it out with us. These bereavement advisers say we should teach our friends not to be afraid of our despair.

I don't think this is good advice. When someone is in mourning and feeling vulnerable, how can they possibly have the energy or desire to educate people about friendship? This is the time that tests a friendship.

Sometimes when people are distraught, they push people away

right at the time they need them most. After I lost my baby, I didn't want to talk to anyone. I remained curled up on the couch with an invisible sign on the door that blared, "Do Not Enter." I remember someone sending me a big, umbrella-sized plant. I had received the same type of plant as a gift following Parker's birth. Then it delighted me. Now all condolence calls and gifts were painful reminders of what felt like my failure. I wanted to hurl the plant out the door. At that moment I realized how much of life is perspective. Although it was the same type of plant, a new meaning had been attached to it.

You may turn down invitations to go to the movies, to a restaurant, to a friend's house because you feel you're in no mood to be entertained. There will be times, especially early on, when you want to be angry and upset. Give yourself permission to let the pain travel through your body. Sometimes we want to be in our pain. It's okay to want to hold on to it. You'll know when you're ready to start letting go of it and focus on rebuilding.

When you feel lousy, it is okay to tell friends that you would prefer to stay home. However, give them positive reinforcement so they won't stop asking. It's just as easy to say, "I really appreciate the invitation. Can we make it next week?" Being abrupt or dismissive won't endear you to others. It's as simple as that. And now is not the time to lose any member of your support system.

Janet, whose sister died in a car accident, was inconsolable and shut herself off like a sealed vault to everyone except a handful of people—her mother, her husband and her best friend, Stephanie. She felt safe to share her despair with them only. Carol wasn't part of her A-team but showed tremendous insight. Every other week, Carol would send Janet a funny comic strip she tore from a newspaper to brighten her spirits. Janet would receive them week after week, but couldn't bring herself to call Carol. As her healing progressed and she felt more comfortable going out in public, one of the first calls she made was to Carol. "I was so grateful to her," says Janet. "Even though I couldn't say it then, I was so touched by her thoughtfulness. Many times, the comic strips did make me laugh, and it was a laugh I really needed." Now Carol is one of Janet's closest friends.

My friend Leslie would arrive at my house with chocolate cake and brownies to cheer me up. Other times, she would notice the pain I felt every time I saw a new baby. I will always remember her gentle, soothing presence and how much I needed it. These are the moments that forge friendships.

Yet don't be surprised if only a few friends come through for you. Susie, an art consultant, remembers a so-called friend visiting her after her brother died. "For about two whole minutes she asked how I was and then she launched into a discussion about her own problems," says Susie. "I couldn't believe it. This wasn't supposed to be about her." Mary, a mother of two, shakes her head in disgust when remembering a condolence card she received from a friend that said, "Mary, I know you must be upset, but you couldn't be as upset as me. You had your father for thirty-five years. I was forty-five when my father died so my pain is even worse." Dana, a computer programmer, still feels the sting of her colleague's words after her daughter died. "Well, at least you have another child." As though children are as interchangeable as CDs.

Take from this experience a heightened appreciation for the friends who stuck by you, and do not be preoccupied with the ones who did not. Train yourself to say, "Through this experience, I have learned the true meaning of friendship" instead of feeling embittered by those who let you down.

Many lessons can be learned on this journey and they are not only about our friends. Before you judge others, think about your own life. Sometimes the lessons we're about to learn are about ourselves.

Years ago, writer Nachum Braverman's daughter was diagnosed with cancer. His despair was overwhelming to him, and he yearned for people to involve themselves in his life and offer support. Yet few came to help. Most people were too preoccupied with their own lives to realize how a simple call or a little visit could have meant so much. Initially he judged those friends harshly until he looked at himself. Regretfully he realized that sometimes he had not done as much as he could have when others were suffering.

"Those qualities I had previously thought most precious and important—intelligence, ambition and creativity—were completely unimportant to me in my crisis, useless to help my baby or even myself," he recalls. "It didn't matter whether I knew more or less than others or who was more successful. I realized how often I had failed others with my preoccupation with my talent, so much less important than the ability to care.

"These simple lessons seem to me so important, so close to the heart of life, that I have come to embrace my own pain with a kind of tenderness. I think that through it, I may have gained what is best about myself. Eventually the pain recedes, and then looking carefully, we may find that tragedy has left behind gifts of insight into the meaning of our lives."

Let this experience help you become a better friend and a more compassionate person. You'll now know what someone needs when it's their turn on the roulette wheel of life and how much true friendship and simple kindness can mean.

7

⮎

The Internet Connection

With families now scattered like seeds across the globe, it's not like the old days when aunts, uncles, cousins, parents, sisters and brothers all lived on the same street and could provide a shoulder to lean on. Yet even in our hectic, hustle-bustle culture, a new outlet has emerged for those who need to talk and cry: the Internet.

"It has been my lifeline," says Shari, whose husband Jimmy died a few years ago after a car accident. "Here are people who understand. I have someone to talk to because I don't have family members with whom I can share my true feelings."

For Gina, who's mourning the loss of her baby, having the Internet provided an opportunity to vent her emotions without the pressure of being judged. "Sometimes my true feelings scare me. But on these chat rooms, people understand. I don't feel as though I'm so alone," she says.

Giselle, who lost her sister, says the Internet was a huge help to her because she could plug into it whenever the need arose. "I now have four kids, including my sister's twelve-year-old, and I have no time to get to support groups," says Giselle. "I don't think I would like that anyway, as I don't like getting emotional in front of strangers." And there was another advantage. "Grief doesn't come on certain days of the week." She adds, "A support group meets at a set time. That's why I like going on-line. I can go on it whenever I feel I need it."

Although the Internet is a form of free therapy, professional help is also attainable. Many sites invite bereavement specialists to chat rooms at designated times that are advertised on the site. This means you can get their expertise gratis.

However, the best part of the Internet chat rooms is the camaraderie. They provide the ability to find kindred spirits who can listen, offer advice and provide a cyber shoulder to cry on. More times than not you can find someone who will respond to your message and relate to your pain and loss 24 hours a day.

Most major Internet sites have chat rooms for those who are grieving. Along the way, when you interact with enough people, they will lead you to other sites that are tailor-made to your own needs. Sites often specify what type of loss someone is struggling with and then an SOS is sent for others to join and share their experiences.

Well-known and helpful chat rooms and sites

Search Engines—AOL and Yahoo can lead you to sites when you type in the subject "bereavement."

www.ivillage.com—click onto "find section" and type in "bereavement," which will lead you to a section on support groups and chat rooms.

www.momsonline.com—search for sites on bereavement, which include more chat rooms.

www.webhealing.com—site for mourners, which offers sites for specific types of loss.

www.letterstoheaven.com—here people write directly to loved ones, which allows people to maintain an ongoing relationship with the deceased. Some share family milestones ranging from the birth of a baby to a graduation. Others explore unresolved issues of anger or disappointment over the deceased's behavior. Many have just apologized for whatever they may have said to their loved one and now regret. This site is considered a cathartic outlet for those who are grieving and offers a thorough, helpful directory dealing with all aspects of loss.

Another Net trend is the creating of memorial sites for your loved ones. One reporter from the *San Diego Union Tribune* called these sites virtual graveyards, and in a way he is right. Instead of having to travel, one can simply click on to The Web Memorial and read a tribute to a loved one. In the same way you may prune the weeds growing around a grave, families are invited to add updates to their site as well as offer messages to the loved one.

"I think it's a psychological need," said Charles Wilkes, a partner in a San Jose design firm that operates The Web Memorial. "They want to somehow preserve the memories of their loved ones, and they really don't have any other way to do it. This helps people recover from grief."

This trend has been evolving for several years. In the past, there have been sites for the famous such as Elvis Presley, Princess Diana, Kurt Cobain. Then sites started being launched for victims in news stories. The public would collectively assemble around the Internet campfire to grieve together and share their shock and sadness. Thousands of people would click on, reflecting on a need to make sense of the senseless. As the Internet became as much of a staple in people's homes as a carton of milk, people started creating memorials to give their loved ones a special place in cyberspace.

Perhaps Sheri Snively, a chaplain who launched the Forget-MeNot.net site, sums it up best. "People have a desire to be remembered and thought of as being special."

Sites to visit for remembrances

On AOL, type in "memorials" for a vast index of sites, including some for pets (some may charge a fee).

Forget Me Not (www.forgetmenot.net)

www.memorials.com

www.webmemorials.com

Pet resources

www.Petloss.com—To honor his beloved beagle, Ed Williams started the site in 1992 with just 16 names. Now there are more than 49,000 tributes as well as a Monday Pet Loss Candle Ceremony to help grieving pet owners. Williams, who receives more than 250,000 visits on the site per year, says people appreciate meeting others who understand how deeply pets are loved by their owners. In fact, for many people living alone, pets become cherished companions who offer love and never complain. This site offers many resources for these people.

General resources

www.adec.org—Run by the Association for Death Education and Counseling. Although used by professionals, this site has a resource section that is extremely helpful in finding support groups and therapists.

www.ubalt.edu/bereavement—Directory to support groups provided by Bereavement and Hospice Support Netline.

www.teencentral.net—Run by KidsPeace. Best chat room for young people and offers all sorts of information concerning kids and adolescents.

www.griefnet.org—Provides directory for bereavement chat rooms.

8

≈

Writing and Art Therapy

Writing can be a welcome release from our troubles. Some people tell me they like writing to loved ones because they don't like talking to friends about the truly intimate details of their lives. Sarah, a seventy-year-old widow, missed telling her husband the mundane details of daily life, whether it was complaining that her friend Mildred cheated in bridge or finding a TV program funny. Now she writes to him and maintains the dialogue that sustained her for years. Vicki's mother died when she was seventeen. Since mothers are a child's most enthusiastic cheerleader, Vicki felt compelled to write a letter after she got an "A" on her college biology exam. In the letter, she wrote, "I wish you were here for me to tell you. No one gets excited like you did. I miss you so much. I know you are guiding me through, but I wish you were here with me where I could see you. Until we meet again, Your daughter, Vicki."

Others have unresolved issues of guilt that they need to expel. Sometimes the reason we have trouble letting go of our grief is that other emotions are connected to our loss. Maybe we didn't like the person who died, or said something we regret, and now we feel guilty. Healing requires coming to terms with what you liked about the person and what you didn't. One daughter vented on her father's favoritism toward her brother. Raymond, a thirty-five-year-old mechanic, regrets fighting with his wife before she was killed in a car accident. "Even though we had fought over her credit card bill, I just wanted to write and let her know that I loved her," he says. "I feel horrible that our last conversation was so heated."

Another mother, whose daughter committed suicide, initially felt overwhelming shame that she had failed to see her child's mental anguish. In her letter, she wrote, "I went through your drawers and boxes and read all the notes searching for some clue. I couldn't find any, and this has only compounded my grief. Why? Why? I do see other options. I could follow your lead. I could remain here crying in your room. But, Samantha, I want to live. I choose the option I wanted for you. I am setting myself free to go out into this day and feel the sun, see the spring flowers and to truly live. It is a gift I give myself. I wish you could have found that gift in your life. With all my love, Mom."

Whatever the motivation, writing produces results. It clarifies our thoughts, sharpens our focus and addresses all the messy emotional layers of loss. And it feels good. In fact, researchers found in a 1990 study that expressing inhibited emotions through language helped individuals to understand and absorb the event. Articulation of the facts is crucial to the breakdown of denial, one of the key roadblocks to grieving. It also leads to the other stages of grief, which involves acceptance and finding alternative ways to keep your loved one close by.

Many write letters on the Web. Others write in journals. A journal is a more permanent record of your journey. It is also a map showing how you've progressed through the healing process. As writer C. S. Lewis observed, "Grief is not a state, but a process. And that is the value of putting thoughts on paper—one can look back and see that progress is being made."

Barbara Baumgardner, author of *A Passage Through Grief*, sees many other benefits.

"Journaling is a safe way to discharge anger that might otherwise be directed toward someone still living and helps you come face-to-face with the harsh reality of your loss," she says. "It can help diminish any guilt feelings and be a more comfortable way to unload the sorrow you are not willing to share with another human being. Perhaps one of the most compelling reasons of all to write is that it preserves the memories, and that can be a very special love gift to family and friends."

Around the country, Barbara Baumgardner teaches journaling workshops. She emphasizes that there are no right or wrong subjects. Any idea that pops into your head is worth recording. It can be a whimsical thought. "Aunt Margaret, I'm wearing the nightgown you used to wear. It makes me feel close to you. I'm so glad you're not suffering anymore. I see your smile and it's making me smile." Or it can be a serious thought. "Darling Steve, I miss you so much. I feel a wave of pain hitting me again. We're all going to Thanksgiving dinner at Donna's, and I know how hard it will be without you. I am trying to be strong. Will I ever not hurt?"

Here are some ideas offered by Barbara Baumgardner as well as other experts to get you started.

First, find a place to be alone without distractions. In the early stages of grief, it is helpful to write often because your body needs a release from the shock. Make it a habit and commit to writing once a day for two weeks. You can write in the early morning when the sun is rising and the family has not yet awakened. Or you can write in the dark hours when loneliness creeps in. Just make the time to do it.

Before you begin, say a prayer. Ask God to direct your journaling and your healing. I found a prayer from Rabbi Naomi Levy's book, *To Begin Again,* particularly helpful.

Please, God. I am feeling sad, help me to find my way. Give me the will to rebuild my life in spite of my suffering, to choose life, and see its many gifts, even in the face of death. When I feel lost and empty, teach me to see that I am not alone. Show me that You are with me as is my loved one. Kindle within me the flame of hope, God. Help me write and cleanse my soul.

Here are some suggested questions you can answer. Do as many as
you feel comfortable with.

1) What are you feeling? Make a list of the things that come to
your mind.

> I am sad . . . that you are not with me.
>
> I am afraid . . . that I'll never love again.
>
> I am angry . . . that I do not have you and now am alone.

2) What do you miss most about the person in your thoughts?

> I miss . . . having someone to hold in the morning.
>
> I miss . . . cooking dinner together on Sunday evenings.
>
> I miss . . . going with you to the movies.

3) What do you wish you'd said or hadn't said? What regrets do
you have?

> I regret . . . that we never went on the fishing trip you
> wanted to take and instead went to the beach.
>
> I regret . . . that I didn't lend you the sweater you wanted
> to borrow.
>
> I regret . . . I told you to leave me alone that day.
>
> I wish . . . I didn't yell at you when you didn't do some-
> thing I asked.
>
> I wish . . . I didn't resent your sickness and sometimes
> wasn't as patient as I should have been.
>
> I wish . . . I hadn't hurt your feelings when I dismissed
> your advice.
>
> I wish . . . I'd talked to you instead of reading magazines.

4) What are the things your loved one did that made you thank-
ful they were part of your life?

> I am grateful . . . that I learned love through you.
>
> I really appreciate . . . how we would hold hands and
> take walks.
>
> I really liked . . . your sense of humor and how you made
> me laugh.
>
> I really admired . . . your sense of discipline and how you
> worked so hard.

> I am grateful . . . that you taught me about loyalty and
> how family always comes first.

5) What piece of knowledge or wisdom did your loved one give
to you? How has it impacted your life? How do you intend to
use it in the future?

> You always said . . . to look at the bright side. I didn't al-
> ways do that. I'm really going to try to have a better
> outlook.
>
> It doesn't matter . . . now that I didn't get the china set I
> wanted. It seems so unimportant now.
>
> I know how important . . . it is to follow through and
> finish tasks.

6) What gave your loved one a sense of deep and lasting pleasure? How was it sought? What was his or her most meaningful pleasure? How will you be connected to it?

> I don't like golf . . . but bought a golf print because it
> reminds me of you.
>
> I'm reading . . . all the detective novels you liked, and it
> makes me feel closer to you.
>
> You wanted me to . . . spend more time with the kids,
> and I'm reading to them every night.

You can also buy prepackaged journals to help you along. *The
Simple Abundance Journal* by Sarah Ban Breathnach includes uplifting anecdotes and inspiring quotes about the importance of cultivat-
ing gratitude.

These writing exercises also provide another benefit. "They help
to alleviate some of the powerlessness people feel about a loved one's
death," says Dr. Joanne Jozefowski, a Massachusetts grief therapist.
"Mourners feel the need to do something with their frustration and
pain, and these rituals promote a physical release that decreases the
intensity of emotion."

Actress Mary Tyler Moore may be best known for turning the
world on with a smile, but behind the scenes, she suffered the loss of
her only child and younger sister.

Yet writing about her losses in her autobiography, *After All,* helped put all her feelings in perspective. "As I wrote, attitudes I thought I had, feelings I thought I had, no longer existed. I didn't know I had changed until I was forced to look back at myself while I was writing. So it was very enlightening for me," she told me. Pausing for a moment, she then added, "Writing opens up chambers that aren't well lit otherwise."

Not everyone needs to write in a journal. Letters work just as well. Joanne Jozefowski told me how one of her patients wrote letters to her mother and put them in a mailbox with no address on them while another tucked messages into the earth by their beloved's grave.

This ritual also gives the mourner permission to think about the person in a way that is vibrant, and very much alive.

When bringing a pen to paper, the end result need not only be written words.

At the New York University Hospital's oncology unit, Dr. Robin Goodman, a therapist at the facility, softly talks to ten-year-old Jenna, whose brother, Alex, has recently died.

"Can't I just play?" she asks defensively.

"How about making a drawing?" suggests Dr. Goodman.

In a calm voice Dr. Goodman asks Jenna to draw a picture of her family on one of her favorite days. The project appeals to Jenna, and she busily begins drawing her mom, her dad, her dog and herself in the house. Then she draws a cloud in the sky with a stick drawing of a little boy with a smile on his face holding on to a Pokémon figure.

"Who's that?" asks Dr. Goodman.

"It's my brother," says Jenna. "He's now in heaven."

With this opening, Dr. Goodman has the opportunity to discuss what heaven means to Jenna and how she feels about her brother. Dr. Goodman talks about the importance of remembering Alex, and Jenna reveals that when she misses her brother, she can feel his presence, though she can't see him. Dr. Goodman continues the conversation by asking Jenna how she feels about crying.

"When you miss him, does it make you cry?" asks Dr. Goodman.

"I try not to because Mommy was upset when Alex was crying in the hospital. I'm not in the hospital. It's not okay if I cry."

Here again, Dr. Goodman gently guides Jenna into conversations on how tears help us release our troubles. She also tells the little girl that her parents will be happy if she shares her feelings with them.

This is an example of art therapy, a growing trend in hospitals. While writing therapy is effective for children as well as adults, sometimes children aren't as expressive with words or don't have the ability or maturity to process their emotions. Art therapy can often reveal the subconscious more clearly than words and open up a dialogue.

Adults can also take advantage of art as therapy. Many artists ranging from Michelangelo to Leonardo da Vinci used painting as an outlet to bring their loved one back by transferring their memories onto a canvas or fantasizing how they wished their loved one could be. Clearly, not everyone will be a Michelangelo, but that doesn't mean you can't derive the same benefits. So often what we miss most is the ability for our loved ones to share in our daily events. Try painting a picture of the spirit of your loved one, whether he's by your side playing tag or smiling up above while your family is having supper.

Also visualize a new form for your loved one that reflects the change in your life. This exercise is important, for it is designed to move you forward, not backward. However, you may find yourself drawing a pleasurable memory that you had mutually shared.

Since death is so often tackled within the confines of the internal mind where abstract thoughts must be sorted and stored, drawings or journals become tangible objects to observe a life change and can help someone adjust to the person's altered position in their life.

9

Silence Is a Sound

One day I found myself talking to my father and stopped myself in midsentence. I worried that someone would find this behavior a bit odd. Luckily, I shared this story with my friend Ted Menten.

Ted is a compassionate, gentle giant whose friendly face is framed with a thicket of white hair. His towering figure is often seen in hospitals dispensing teddy bears to terminally ill children. The children call him Mr. Silly because he makes them laugh. But he's not really silly. He's just very wise.

"Oh, everyone talks to the person who died," Ted reassured me. "It's perfectly normal. Did you speak to him out loud?" he asked.

"No, the conversation took place in my head," I replied.

"Well, here's my advice," said Ted. "Speak out loud."

"Out loud? In public?"

"No, not on the street but in private. Children seem to do this naturally—until they get caught by a parent and are discouraged from continuing," he said, frowning with disapproval. "But it isn't crazy to do this; it feels terrific. When you speak in your mind, there is no tone to the words. Sound gives it the richness of tone. The spoken word has color and texture."

A twinkle in his eye, Ted gave me another word of advice. "Go for a walk somewhere quiet, in the woods or by the ocean," he urged. "Talk out loud about your hopes and sorrows. Then listen to the wind's response. Who knows? You might even get a message back."

As Rabbi Naomi Levy observed in her book, *To Begin Again,* "Moments of true inspiration are rare in life, but when they do come, they are most often found in solitude. The power to produce exquisite art or great writing, the ability to make new scientific discoveries or to experience God is intimately connected with a capacity to be alone. Naturally, people have a fear of silence. It unveils an intensity that we are not used to facing. Our inclination may be to seek noise and distraction to cut the force of our solitude. But we must also realize that silence can help heal us. Most great insights arrive when human beings are by themselves searching for answers. It is in solitude that we can receive the answers that have the potential to change our lives."

In her book Naomi tells a story about a young boy who goes out to the woods day after day. His father, puzzled, asks, "My son, why do you go out to the woods each day?" The son responds, "I go there to find God." At this his father gently reprimands his child. "Don't you know that God is the same everywhere?" The son replies, "Yes, Father, but I am not the same everywhere."

In nature, the cyclical rhythms of life and death are seen more clearly. With no phones ringing, no music blaring, no kids running in and out of the house, the lessons of birth and rebirth reassure and inspire. Buds swell into luminous flowers only to wilt and die in the winter, then are reborn a few months later in the spring. Seeing the expanse of the ocean or the stars stretched across the sky is both humbling and soothing, and restores faith in beginnings. Nature also teaches us about how random life can be. The wind can be calm and peaceful, a gentle breeze softly caressing the skin. Another day, a gust of wind can build strength from invisible forces and turn into a menacing hurricane, leaving destruction in its wake. In my hometown, one side of the street was ravaged by a hurricane and the other left alone. Why is one family struck and another ignored? Rabbi Levy eloquently explains that these times remind us there are forces in this universe greater than we, which we must trust serve their own purpose.

Nature can also be a refuge. After a loss, familiar surroundings seem foreign, irrevocably altered by the death. Many people return to the house they shared with their husband or child and report how they find it strangely empty, as though something besides the person is missing. A change of scenery can often be restorative, even if it's for a few days. Being immersed in nature can help you ease into this transition, and give you needed perspective. As my friend Ted Menten reminds me, this doesn't mean that grief won't be your traveling companion. It just means you're making a move to help yourself, to gain deeper wisdom and understanding.

In his book *The Seven Spiritual Laws of Success,* Deepak Chopra discusses the therapeutic benefits of sitting near nature. His theory is that the universe listens in quiet. I agree.

The word *meditation* actually comes from a Sanskrit word, *medha,* which means wisdom. Meditation means doing the wisdom, getting in touch with the wisdom inside oneself. It becomes a guide to help us deal with our problems, release our tensions and understand our connection to God and the universe.

When you breathe slowly and deeply, your nervous system relaxes and becomes calmer. Slow, deep breathing alleviates anxiety and diminishes despair and anger. As you breathe slowly and deeply, the mind clears and you will be able to gain a broader perspective that is helpful in dealing with your distress.

Cheryl Aiello, an earthy, effervescent yoga teacher, believes it is an ideal activity for grievers because unlike aerobic activity, it is not stressful or overwhelming. "It's a more relaxing form of exercise, needed when someone is depressed," she explains. "By combining breathing exercises with movement, it creates a therapeutic release that is both spiritual and physical. It's about letting go." Furthermore, when you are mourning a loved one, the intense emotions churning inside become like toxins that need to be expelled from the body. The stretching exercises flush the body of grief's poisons by activating the lymph system—which is like the dirty dishwater of the body—and helps prevent blockage that can lead to disease.

As *Time* magazine reported, hospitals, including New York Presbyterian and Cedars Sinai Medical Center in Los Angeles recommend yoga for recovering heart patients. Those who practiced yoga showed "tremendous benefits," says Dr. Noel Bairey Merz, director of Cedars Sinai Preventative and Rehabilitative Cardiac Center, including lower blood pressure and cholesterol levels, and in some cases a reversal of artery blockage. Isn't loss a wound to the heart?

I remember going to her class when I felt very low. It wasn't only the soothing music of Windham Hill but also the calmness that oozed from Cheryl that helped me relax.

Instructed to sit up straight in a cross-legged position, I rested my hands on my legs with my palms open to the sky. "Breathe in and out," Cheryl said gently. Then she talked us through the exercise.

"I want you to think of the clouds floating in the sky. From the sky, think of particles of light beaming down, warming your body, washing over your eyelids, smoothing out any fine lines and wrinkles. Let the particles of light continue washing down on your nose, your chin, your chest and over your legs. . . .

"You are starting to feel relaxed. Take a few moments to allow attention to gather within the even rhythm of the breath. Notice the breath coming and going all by itself deep within the body.

"Now when you exhale, draw energy up from the earth, and let it move up through your stomach, up through your collarbones, up through your mouth. Exhale deeply. Now let your next breath be full of your angst. Let it stream out of you like a gust of wind."

"Now," Cheryl continues, "it is time to focus on the breath we take in. Inhale deeply. Feel the breath fill you deeply. When you inhale, think of taking in new ideas, new creativity, new ways of being and doing, new ways of experiencing yourself and the world you live in. Now exhale your new breath of life."

This little exercise did indeed make me feel better—far better than a pint of Häagen-Dazs rum raisin ice cream or even a pair of decadently expensive shoes. To this day, it still works like a charm.

Sometimes Cheryl uses other exercises. Words can conjure images that make it easier to travel deep within yourself. She used the idea of floating in a hot-air balloon. "With each breath, you might float a little higher. Imagine the feeling of the gently swaying basket. Notice how relaxed you feel. The air is soft and warm against your skin. The breeze is very gentle. Notice the colors of the landscape, the variety of green in the trees, the grasses and plants below. Notice the birds floating along the air currents. Acknowledge the feeling of joy and contentment. Allow yourself to continue basking in the comfort and contentment of this moment where all things seem possible."

Thanks to Cheryl, whenever I have a particularly stressful day, I use these images of the particles of light washing over my body from the sky or the hot-air balloon floating through the clouds to help center me and ease the day's distress.

Although women are more likely to seek it out, therapists have been recommending yoga to their male patients. Men are conditioned to contain their emotions, to keep the proverbial stiff upper lip. Finding someone to talk to is harder for men than women. Yoga becomes an acceptable way to let go of emotions because it is a physical activity, which is socially acceptable.

"The variety of positions also teach students of any gender to detach themselves from their bodies and see themselves in a new way," says Maryland-based Shelly Greenberg. "In some cases, you are literally turned upside down, which is how loss often feels. But in yoga, being turned upside down builds control. You see life from many perspectives. Yoga also helps people access their inner strength and power, providing a support system through ups and downs."

Although doctors recommend a more relaxing form of yoga during the initial stages of grief, you may try more athletic forms ranging from Kundalini to Ashtanga later on. Dr. Jack Miller, a former priest and hospice worker who founded the Center for Education on Death and Dying in Chicago, insists that patients take at least one yoga class a week. "The breaths become like gusts of fresh air, which cleanses the system," he says. "It is an invaluable healer."

Yoga works for all age groups. "Many young people don't have the maturity to sort out the intensity of their emotions," says Adriane Goldstein, a teacher for troubled students. "Yoga can be an outlet to express anger and resentment in a positive, helpful way. Even the breathing exercises, the slow breaths in and out, are a calming exercise they can easily do anywhere. These kids need to feel a sense of control when they have been struck by a loss that was out of their control." Yoga is like a windshield wiper to the heart, clearing away the pain and letting us reflect on the wisdom and goodness within.

10

⁓

Pleasurable Pursuits

When chimps want the comfort of contact, they groom each other. This story was told to me by Dr. Rita Freedman, the author of *Overcoming Loss*, and speaks to an often overlooked point. It is so easy to give in to depression and spend the day in your bathrobe and slippers, never showering or combing your hair. In time you look like a mess, which also mirrors how you may feel. If you want to feel better, start looking better.

Try to invest in some personal grooming. This can mean a manicure, a pedicure or a relaxing massage with aromatic oils. After a shower, smooth on some floral scented lotion to feel refreshed. Get a few blond streaks to brighten not only your head, but also your spirits. Part of the beauty of looking good is how good it can make you feel.

Although bereavement specialists stress that this is not the time to make major life decisions—such as selling a house or changing a job—that doesn't mean you can't be proactive in making yourself feel and look better.

One of the added benefits of these services is that they are a great way to enjoy the touch of another human being. We are meant to have skin contact with other people. This does not have to be an inti-mate touch from a lover. Instead, it can mean a masseur's gentle rub to reinvigorate the body, a big bear hug from a grandchild or a sweet embrace from a friend. It is no secret that preemie babies who are touched and caressed grow far stronger than the ones who are not. Orphanages report that children who are not touched develop men-tal handicaps. As human beings, we need to connect to others, and grooming provides opportunities for heads to be washed, hands to be pampered and bodies to be kneaded like dough into total relaxation.

Annette Blaustein, a former nurse, oversees a grief support group in California. A sweet woman with a radiant smile and Shirley Tem-ple curls, she looks twenty years younger than someone in her sev-enth decade. At the end of each session, Annette encourages a ritual that may be frowned upon by academics but is certainly welcomed by those in her group. She has everyone give each other a hug.

"You have no idea how much people miss the simple touch of an-other person," says Annette. "It helps make people feel not so alone, that there are others in the world who care for them. Touch is a very important healer." Take Annette's advice. Try to find places to con-nect to other people who can help combat loneliness.

Another helpful healer is music. My friend Samantha found mu-sic to be a balm to her troubles when her husband was diagnosed with cancer. One day she felt compelled to visit Borders and rashly bought fifteen CDs from her college years when life seemed so care-free. "I would play this music nonstop," recalls Samantha. "I would sing at the top of my lungs in the car to and from the hospital with tears streaming down my face. The music was a huge release. It felt great belting out the songs and the words came so easily, pouring out of my brain. It forced me to be consumed with something other than my crisis." The music also lulled her back to another time and place, which reinforced how life is full of possibilities.

Rita Freedman also recommends music as therapy. "Babies are naturally soothed by lullabies and also by being rocked or rubbed," she says. "Many such childish pleasures can reduce stress and ease pain. The sound of recovery has a special beat. If you tune in to your body's messages, you can pick up the beat of life and learn a basic step in the dance of recovery."

Another tip is to beautify your surroundings. Buy fresh flowers once a week. It can be one daisy sitting inside a simple vase or a big bunch of dreamy daffodils.

Paint a room a bright, sunny yellow or a calming blue. Stencil a wall with a whimsical design. Rearrange the furniture. Buy aromatic candles and light them depending on your mood—lavender is known to soothe while lemon or vanilla scents can energize you. The more pleasant the surroundings, the easier it is to heal.

After some time has passed, and the wounds aren't as raw, it may be time to think about how to build your new life. You're in control now. You have the freedom to choose what you want to do. Think of ways to keep busy because physical action often diminishes anxiety or sadness. Here are some things you may try:

Take your kids or a friend's children to an amusement park
Visit a museum or aquarium
Have tea with an old friend
Start a new hobby
Volunteer for a charity
Bake a pie and give it to a neighbor
Take a cooking class
Take dance lessons
Learn a new language and plan a trip
Try gardening
Attend concerts, plays or any social events where you can meet
    new people
Have a slumber party with girlfriends—you're never too old
    for this
Plan a weekend in your hometown with old classmates
Join a book club

A friend of mine found making chicken a l'orange extremely helpful in dealing with her grief. "It surprised me how gratifying chopping and grating orange rinds can be," she said. "It totally absorbed my mind and the hours flew by."

Ashley Davis Prend, a social worker and author of *Transcending*

Loss, believes that the successful griever engages in many activities to emerge from the crisis a new person.

"I was looking for the linkage as to why loss made some people bitter and frozen and stopped them from growing while others took this pain and channeled it into ways that have meaning," she says. "I found that transcendence isn't one act but dozens of acts, thoughts and beliefs that combined bring about a metamorphosis."

Out of necessity you will have to fill the time once shared with your loved one by finding new companions and pursuing new projects. As hard as it is, try to focus on your possibilities and not your limitations. You are alive. You have choices. You are entitled to be happy. It just takes some effort, but anything good usually does.

Yoga, music, grooming, talking, drawing and reflection all help us build stronger selves. However, none of these activities will work effectively unless you have the right attitude.

Rabbi Zelig Pliskin, a psychologist who lives in Jerusalem, is the author of many books including *Happiness: Formulas, Stories and Insights*. His achievement is showing people how to see more clearly. He does this by teaching students about the importance of what he calls "reframing," which in effect is the art of positive thinking. His wisdom is profound and his joyful nature is contagious.

Rabbi Pliskin points out that we constantly choose what our brain will focus on. "Some people habitually focus on what is not to their liking, what is disappointing and what is distressful about their situation or what they are doing," he says. "They have done it so often that they can mistakenly think this is their basic nature. It is not. It is just habit that has become automatic."

Rabbi Pliskin believes that a true commitment to achieve happiness requires mastering the attitudes and actions that create it. This involves study and repeated practice. Like swimming, riding, writing or playing tennis, he believes that happiness can be a learned skill.

He begins by asking students to train their brains to become more mindfully aware of all that they can appreciate and enjoy. Be mindful of your ability to see, he says. Of your ability to hear. Of your ability to move your hands. Practice being mindful about each of your senses and basic abilities. Choose one a day. On the day you are focusing on sight, take in the various colors of the flowers in neighbors' gardens. On the day you are focusing on hearing, take note of the various ranges of sound that emanate from people's voices, from the cooing sound of a ten-month-old to the gravelly voice of the grocery clerk. Be grateful for hearing music or hearing birds chirp.

Next, notice all the possessions you own or can use. Be grateful for the pretty plates with the floral design. For the crisp cotton sheets on the bed. For the family picture from a summer picnic. Literally say to yourself, "I am grateful for . . ."

Now start focusing on all the people who are involved in making your life better and express gratitude.

Then make time to ask yourself, "What can I focus on now that is enjoyable? What do I like doing?" Make a list of the things that give you pleasure and find opportunities to do them whether that means taking an exercise class or dining at a fine restaurant.

At this point you may find yourself feeling better because appreciation enhances every aspect of our everyday lives.

Now try another exercise. Dr. Elisabeth Kübler-Ross showed how each of us has had "little deaths" to prepare us for facing larger losses. Little deaths, such as not being picked for the baseball team in grade school, breaking up with a boyfriend in college, being rejected from a job, losing a crush to your best friend. She suggests going back and remembering how you solved each loss. "We are better equipped than we think to handle our losses," she says. "The little losses are what teach us to handle our current situation."

Here are some things to think about:

Remember falling down off your bike and getting back on.
Remember getting the flu and then feeling better.
Remember getting rejected by a friend and then finding another.
Remember feeling overwhelmed by a deadline and then making it.
Remember making a mistake and learning from it.
Remember when someone had what you wanted and how you lived without it.

Remember when you were stuck on a problem and eventually figured it out.

Remember when you reached out to someone for help and got it.

Remember winning an assignment or a spot on the team.

Remember having someone tell you how much you are loved.

As Kübler-Ross points out, we have survived other crises. That's how we grow as people.

However, the most crucial step in surviving the loss of our loved one is training our brains to react a certain way to particular events. Even when the event is unpleasant, it can be experienced many ways. "You can say, 'I'm grateful my life isn't usually this way.' " Or instead of saying, "I'm sad that I only got to spend ten years with my friend," Rabbi Pliskin urges people to reframe their thought pattern and say, "I'm grateful and glad that I had ten years with my friend." You have the choice of whether to view yourself as a victim or survivor.

Of course, many people initially ask how they can change their focus to a positive thought when a negative one springs into the brain. Here the rabbi suggests saying to yourself, "Next," or maybe, "Time to move on," as a command to shift gears to another thought. This is not denying your feelings. Instead it is a discipline to create an environment where negative thoughts have no place to fester and destroy your potential for happiness.

Let's say it's Thanksgiving and you say to yourself, "I'm going to miss my mother this Thanksgiving." Experience this feeling and then find something to be grateful for such as . . .

It's wonderful that . . . Aunt Susie is cooking Mom's favorite stuffing recipe . . .

It's wonderful that it's not raining.

It's wonderful that I'm going to see a movie with friends . . .

It's wonderful that my child will be in a school play next month . . . etcetera.

Words are powerful. Like chemicals, they change your body's inner chemistry. Happy people use happiness-producing words.

"We can minimize the intensity of the words we use even in bad situations," adds Rabbi Pliskin. "For example, you might say, 'I would have preferred that things were different.' This is a far better approach than saying, 'Isn't it terrible what happened?'

"After consistently choosing thoughts conducive to happiness for a long enough time, it will become your second nature to do so. By choosing joyous and enjoyable patterns for your brain, your brain will repay you with unending series of enjoyable thoughts."

Not enough people reinforce this message. It seems so simple. Yet most truths are simple. As Mark Twain said, the funny thing about common sense is that it's so uncommon. Although we can benefit from the help of others, we ourselves are most responsible for our happiness. It is in our interest to try all methods available to live life free of the handcuffs that grief can put on us. Remember: Change is inevitable. Growth is optional.

Most authorities on grief don't believe we can just sit and wait for happiness to return. This is why it's called grief work—it's work! "Mourners need to work on grief rather than have grief work on them," says grief therapist Dr. Joanne Jozefowski. "How we use the opportunities and challenges of bereavement determines whether someone is transformed in their relationships with themselves, others, the physical world and the spiritual world, or spirals into despair and depression."

Even the Bible tells us this story. Jesus didn't pick up and carry the people he healed. He told them to throw away their crutches and start walking on their own.

This is why counselors like Diane Rosenstein at New York University Hospital are proponents of putting the responsibility of healing firmly on the patient.

As she points out, in everyday life, those who are grieving need to function alongside people who are not aware of or as sensitive to your state of mind. But the more joyously you approach life, the more enthusiasm you ooze, the more people will want to be around you, which will diminish the feelings of loneliness you may have.

Diane Rosenstein takes the example of a widow. "Aside from the grieving wife, she is a sexy woman, a neighbor, a friend, a mom, a daughter, an employee, maybe an employer," she says. "She has to redefine her new role, and the onus is on her to make a new life and identity. It's a process, but one that must be done. Your life doesn't finish because one of those roles no longer exists. Her job now is to find another door and reinvent herself as this new person. We talk about ways to redefine the person, and then a transformation can take place where she also rediscovers herself."

In Chinese, the word *crisis* is composed of two characters. One represents danger, and the other represents opportunity. The same can be said of the grieving process.

11

~

Professional Help

Sometimes you don't feel better despite the best efforts, and it may be time for some form of therapy.

"It is normal for the behavior, emotions and thinking of children and adults to be different when they are grieving, and therefore it is important not to be concerned too soon," says Harvard's Dr. Gerald Koocher. "When considering the need for professional help, the most important factors are the intensity and duration of grieving, and the extent to which those and other changes interfere with your own functioning or that of your child at school, home or work."

The following list compiled by Dr. Koocher are some warning signs that professional help may be necessary. Remember, though, that many of these symptoms can also happen on an occasional basis during the normal grief process. If, however, these symptoms persist over time and do not decrease in frequency or intensity, it is appropriate to seek professional help.

- Staying withdrawn from family and friends
- Patterns of aggressive behavior

- Persistent anxiety, especially when separating from parents and surviving children
- Persistent blame or guilt
- Wanting to die and having suicidal thoughts
- Becoming accident prone
- Acting as if nothing happened or acting even happier than normal
- Unusual and persistent poor performance at school or work
- Physical complaints—feeling pain or sickness a lot
- Extended use of prescription or nonprescription drugs, and alcohol

There are several ways to seek professional help if this situation applies to your state of mind. You can contact a local hospice center, a local doctor or family friend or plug into the Internet.

Even though you may have several names at your disposal, it is in your best interest to ask questions before choosing a therapist, since you are about to embark on a very personal relationship. Better to shop around until you find the right person. Dr. Koocher reminds patients that because they are grieving, they are "especially vulnerable to the mistreatment of a therapist." Visit with at least two therapists before choosing one.

Before you confide in a therapist, you need to know what manner of person that therapist is. You can ask questions. How long you can expect to be in therapy. How much it costs. What your mutual goals are. Investigate what insurance will cover. Ask about the therapist's training and experience.

Make sure that the person you call is listening to your individual needs. A person who lost a husband from cancer will have different issues than someone whose spouse was murdered. Dr. Koocher offers this clue to determine if you're with the wrong person. "If you have someone telling you what to do in the first half hour of spending time with you, you know there is a problem," he says. "You need someone sympathetic who will listen and can hear from your perspective." The doctor refers to this first type of therapist as "procrustean," the types that are like cavemen living in the dark ages.

Often, these therapists offer a one-size-fits-all type of therapy. "Some people are very set in their ways and have been doing this for so long that their minds shut off to what you need."

You may think that any therapist can work with your grief, but therapists also have specialties. Just as a fine French restaurant wouldn't hire a short-order Greek cook, you wouldn't benefit from a bereavement specialist who had no experience or training with your particular reason for grieving.

Be wary of the doctor who immediately prescribes drugs to ease your pain. "One mom came to me after her young son had drowned," recalls Dr. Koocher. "She had gone to see another doctor telling him she was depressed, had headaches and couldn't sleep. Almost immediately he pulled out a prescription pad and started writing prescriptions for tranquilizers, antidepressants and headache pain medicine. She left the office with enough medication to kill herself." While drugs can be helpful in combating sleeping disorders and severe depression, moderation is obviously the best approach.

Keep in mind that each individual responds differently to a given therapist. "Some people do well with a gentle person who holds their hand and listens and has a certain bedside manner appropriate for them," says Dr. Eve Rosemarin, an Australian doctor who now practices in New York. "People who are angry and resentful and are shutting themselves off need a strong person who may be more dogmatic and challenges them. Personality types need to be matched."

However, at the same time, do not expect the therapy sessions to make you feel good. If the therapy sessions fail to provoke any thoughts at all and you don't think about the issues discussed between sessions, then the therapy isn't working. A therapist shouldn't always agree with you—you need a therapist to sometimes challenge the way you have handled things, and then explain at least one alternative way of handling your problem.

"If a therapist is gentle and soothing and makes you feel that your life is not your fault, run for your life," says Dr. Frank Pittman, a California-based therapist. "Stick with the therapist who sometimes pisses you off by insisting that you take more than your share of the responsibility for your life and your relationships. Hire the one who cuts through your defenses, your pessimism and your rationalizations and one who offers optimism, who believes life is worth living to the fullest so you can come to feel that way too."

A personal therapist is like a customized suit tailored to fit your measurements. Sometimes grief can't be resolved easily because of another underlying issue complicating the healing process. Therapists can probe your individual experiences and stitch together personal profiles to help treat loss. For example, Dr. Koocher had three patients who had each lost a child to leukemia, but each needed a different therapy.

One mom had a pet cat that she didn't want to put to sleep. On television she had heard a report that cats transmitted deadly viruses. Afterward she became overwhelmed with guilt that she was responsible for her son's death. By finding an expert to prove that there was no link between the cat and her son's illness, the woman was able to start the gradual and slow process of healing.

Another mom had an affair with an old boyfriend and never told her husband. When her son died, the mother consulted a priest, worried that God was punishing her. The priest confirmed her worst fear. She fell apart from the burden, yet couldn't confide her secret to her family. Finally, after revealing the problem to Dr. Koocher, he found a Catholic priest who didn't have "the blaming sort of mind-set" to counsel her.

The last mom didn't require as much internal digging. Discussions centered on how to rebuild her life following her loss. Although a housewife for many years, she decided to go to nursing school to help others. Helping others made her feel more useful.

"Here you have a similar situation, but the meaning that was attached to the event and the coping styles were completely different," he says. "This is one of the primary advantages of individual therapy."

In group therapy, the focus is more on the relationships and shared dialogue between the members. The advantage of group therapy is that you meet and talk to others who intimately understand the depth of your loss. Often the group consists of people who shared similar losses—widows gathering together, parents who lost a child, siblings who are missing a brother or sister. Sometimes people are grouped together by disease, such as cancer, or by the nature of the death, such as a sudden heart attack, car crash or murder. Finding others who can empathize and sympathize with what you're experiencing is the strength of this therapy.

Typically a doctor or therapist opens the discussion, asking participants about their week. Each person then talks about their week, their progress, their stumbling blocks, and conversation ping-pongs back and forth. Aside from the therapist peppering the discussion with provocative questions, the group is also encouraged to comment on what the participants are saying, often sharing advice and empathy.

Annette Blaustein says group therapy provides "reality checks" for people who are going through this unsettling and unfamiliar experience. "You don't know what's normal because many of us have never been in the situation until it happens," she explains. "One group member asked about sex. He hadn't been with anyone new in thirty years and was overwhelmed by the 'casserole brigade' trying to date him. This is all new territory for these people, and here is a safe place to discuss it."

Widows are at particular risk for a variety of reasons. According to the *Handbook of Bereavement*, more than 50 percent of all women sixty-five years and over and 12 percent of men that age have become widowed. "The grief reaction can be devastating because the bereaved are often required to deal with the simultaneous disruption of their financial security, social stature and primary support networks," wrote Dr. Margaret Stroebe, Dr. Wolfgang Stroebe and Dr. Robert Hansson.

Carla Fine, author of *No Time to Say Goodbye*, says group therapy was a salvation. After her husband Harry committed suicide, she was treated as a pariah. "There were no flowers, no condolence cards, no one bringing over noodle pudding," she recalls. "It was as though I was to blame for Harry's death and should have kept him on the Stairmaster or made sure he was on a low-fat diet. People who knew me for twenty years never even mentioned his death. When I joined Samaritans [a support group specializing in suicide deaths], I met others who were just as confused as me. Many of us became friends because we had gone through so much together. Healing meant we had to give up this idea that our love could have kept them alive."

When the subject of dating came up, the group was also helpful in maneuvering this emotional minefield. "Men think you're damaged goods or potentially dangerous. When someone dies this way, it becomes a reflection on you," says Carla. "By talking about all the issues surrounding suicide, we helped each other."

Battling social stigmas is clearly a different challenge than recovering from the death of a loved one from cancer. Here, the lingering effects of prolonged care can be discussed without the worry of being judged. "Grief can often be a delayed reaction," says Katherine, a recent widow. "I was still recovering from spending so much time in a hospital, and it felt good to admit it."

Mark, a thirty-year-old man whose wife was killed in a car accident, remembers visiting a group therapy session filled with widowers. "I walked in and everyone could have been my grandfather," he recalls. "I was worried about raising two kids. Completely different issues than these guys. Luckily, the therapist referred me to a group of young guys like me."

Some groups meet once a week; some require a commitment of more time. Psychologist Jack Miller is the founder of the Center for Education on Death and Dying in Chicago. A former priest and hospice worker, he has developed what he calls "The Phoenix Project." While not exactly a boot camp for grievers, it is a demanding program that has produced great results.

Participants must be willing to initially spend a full day in therapy, then meet weekly in group sessions for three months. They also meet with Dr. Miller once a week. Although talking is an important component, Jack emphasizes the healing power of action. Each person is required to be altruistic once a week. Some visit an elderly, homebound or dying person or they can visit a day care center and spend time with children. Members also present three creative expressions that capture the deceased's environment or the feelings they have for their loved ones. Examples can include poetry, paintings or intricate collages. Some write songs. One made a quilt. "Art creates a permanence," says Dr. Miller. "Even if the person isn't here, you have the memory you made of them close by." This therapy can also unearth underlying issues. A grieving mother made a large collage of photocopied family photos and then colored them in. "While I was coloring them, I got to really look at the images of my parents and at us as a family," she says. "It made me reflect and allowed me to better understand who I was." She came to realize that she wasn't only grieving the loss of her son, but also of her childhood.

To help people sort through their grief, Dr. Miller also has participants create a half-hour presentation on how loss impacted their life using pictures enhanced with written words.

Furthermore, each person must meditate daily, commit to exercising a half hour a day at approximately the same time and never smoke or take antidepressants.

I like the program—which travels around the United States and now across the globe—because it is not a passive process. One must be proactive and recognize that grief work is a battle and a fight. Being prepared and engaged in a planned-out strategy is required for optimal results.

But Dr. Miller's subtle hand is always visible. A woman who lost a mother would be required to visit an older woman as part of her therapy. Someone who lost a spouse and has little hope for the future may be matched with a child who feels immortal and can show that life offers promise and possibilities.

"Each piece of the puzzle serves the healing process," says Dr. Miller. "Meditating and yoga is important because your body carries the trauma. Group sessions help people realize they are not alone. Helping others helps you have a different perspective, and by reviewing one's history, you reconnect with your roots and the progression in your life. Going back and reconnecting what you got from Mom, Dad, your mate or your child will recharge you with all the values and energies these people gave to you."

Under the umbrella of grief, there are many permutations. Death to homicide. Death to leukemia. Sibling death. Parental death. Child death. Age of the deceased. Age of griever. However, one thread knits together all therapies. Most people find it both restorative and reassuring to have a safe haven to talk about their loved one as they work on building a new life. It is often at these gatherings that the words of George Sand ring true. "One knows what one has lost, but not what one may find."

12

~

Male and Female Differences in Grief

Very few people dispute that men are from Mars, and women from Venus. As John Gray reveals in his immensely successful books, gender distinctions do exist. Not only in how we love, but also in how we grieve.

Men often have the hardest time coping with loss. This is no secret. We live in a culture where boys are given fast-and-hard rules about what is expected of them. From an early age boys are told to be "tough" and are forced to wear what some have called a mask of masculinity. They are discouraged from showing emotion and called "sissies" if they cry. They are rewarded for aggressiveness on the sports field and displaying a stiff upper lip. Parents often reinforce this message by limiting emotional affection in the misguided effort to make their boy "strong." In his book *Real Boys*, Dr. William Pollack from Harvard Medical School describes this phenomenon as a gender straitjacket.

Research has revealed that male infants are actually more emotionally expressive than female babies. However, by the time boys reach elementary school, much of their emotional expressiveness has been submerged by social conditioning. In one of his case studies, a grieving fifteen-year-old boy said, "With girls, everybody expects they'll go off and talk to somebody. When you're a guy, you're really not allowed to do that. I guess it's pretty hard being a guy because there are so many things a normal person would probably do, but you're just not expected to do."

Diane Rosenstein, a social worker at New York University Hospital, sighs deeply after hearing this story. Men, she says, are often taught that being taken care of is a weakness so they resist coming for therapy. She remembers one case where a man's wife had died and he began drinking heavily. Finally a concerned relative intervened and brought him in.

Diane avoided asking how he felt. "Men respond differently to the question," she explains. "Instead, I said, 'You're not doing well, are you? Look at yourself. You're not sleeping. You're not shaving.' With men, you define the experience. I often use action words, focusing on what they are 'doing' to deal with the death. Women like to talk and can relate to conceptualizing. Men rarely do."

After further probing, Diane realized the core problem. He was a cop used to saving people. "You couldn't save her. You tried but you couldn't. No one could. You need to grieve and let go of the pain."

At first the man was silent, but after a few moments elapsed, he bowed his head and started sobbing like a baby, crying loudly and deeply. Once he gave in to his feelings of grief, he began the healing process and eventually stopped drinking.

This also supports Therese Rando's findings. "Men have more superficial buddy relationships that usually are structured around activities, not feelings," she observes. "If a man yields to the natural and necessary processes of grief, he will be confronted with an overwhelming conflict. He will want to focus on managing and controlling his feelings, when what he needs to do is to identify and express them. In grief, he has failed in all his roles."

To help a man through his grief, Therese Rando suggests appealing to behaviors that will give him a sense of productivity and physical relief. Suggest a hike in the woods, a trip to the ballpark, chopping wood for a fire. Sign him up for a computer course. Rather than discussing the grief associated with his wife's absence if he's a widower, give advice on how to manage the household and tips on housekeeping, which will appeal to his affinity for fixing things. Still, don't stop reinforcing the importance of experiencing our emotions. The advice can be packaged as a method to achieve relief rather than being presented as something that will make him feel better. Also remember that even though a man may not be overtly emotional, it doesn't reflect a lack of depth or pain. Often men carry more unresolved grief, because intense emotions reside inside and are never released.

Women are far better equipped to grieve. Their social structure revolves around sharing feelings. They are encouraged to rely on others for support and ask for help if needed. A premium is placed on their sensitivity and openness. "The helplessness and powerlessness of grief is not incompatible with their role," adds Therese Rando. "They have intimate relationships that afford them sources of consolation. Since they do not have to hide their feelings, unlike their male counterparts, it will not be inappropriate or difficult for them to admit to their problems."

These gender distinctions can prove problematic when the couple is grieving together. Women have accused men of being unsupportive and unfeeling during their time of need while men complain that their wives are too needy. Each becomes further isolated in their grief, believing that their partner has abandoned them. Furthermore, the stresses of grief can tear apart a relationship and even lead to divorce.

This often happens when the death is of a child. A little baby is imbued with all the hopes, dreams and desires of parents, and when a child dies, so does a part of the parents' future. It also triggers intense anger because the death is a slap in the face, a violation of the natural order of things. Often exacerbating the pain is the reaction of friends and family. Because a child's death is every parent's worst fear, their support group tends to avoid being around the couple, making the nightmare even more of a dark and isolating experience.

"What often happens is a variation of this exchange," says therapist Ted Menten. "The husband says to his wife, 'Why are you crying so much? It's time to get on with your life.' The wife will feel, 'Why isn't he crying enough? How insensitive can he be?' He'll bury himself in work; she'll be so paralyzed by grief that she can't leave the house. Men internalize. Women externalize. This is why many need therapy. Their pain blinds them to what's happening. They are both experiencing the same thing but expressing it differently. If you don't speak the same language, you don't have communication, and that's when the breakdown happens."

As with any situation, understanding is the underpinning to a successful relationship. The couple must come to realize that they are both in the same boat, and to reach shore, they must paddle in the same direction, even if that means using different oars to get there. If one member paddles in a separate direction, the boat will spin and you go nowhere. They must work as a team.

To help them work as a team, they also must find simple pleasures to enjoy together. Kindness and warm hugs are great healers. Also find rituals or small gestures that show you care, whether it's brewing a cup of your husband's favorite coffee or buying your wife flowers. Perhaps start a foundation or program that benefits a loved one's passion or interest. If your child or sister loved dance, create a ballet program or scholarship at a neighborhood school, or sign up for a course for the two of you to enjoy. When someone dies, it is important to realize that there is still much love to be given and received.

13

A *Child's Grief*

Have you ever watched a baby cry? Infants cry with gusto. They do not attempt to stifle their tears or apologize for feeling bad. Some people assume that babies don't comprehend a loss, but their finely tuned antennas can sense the discomfort of others and the absence of a loved one, especially the nurturing of a mother. As a result, the baby may have trouble eating or sleeping. Providing physical care isn't enough. Like any child, a baby needs to be comforted too.

A child's grieving pattern is often hard to recognize because it is not like an adult's. Children grieve in bits and pieces. They do not absorb the grief in one fell swoop. They can't. It would be too much for their undeveloped psyche to handle. They are simply too immature.

"Often, they will show no reaction for a long time, which is bewildering to parents," says Dr. Ava Siegler, the director of the New York Child, Adolescent & Family Institute. "Instead of being sad, they'll laugh and giggle when the parent's name is mentioned. This isn't a disregard for the situation. Quite the contrary, their defense mechanisms are kicking in and it's easier for them to be in denial."

In a game of hide-and-seek, the three-year-old child who happily scurries under her mother's canopy bed may be also crying out for her parent. It can be the reason for the six-year-old boy's unexplained temper tantrum in the supermarket, or when a ten-year-old girl starts wearing her deceased mother's red lipstick. Their actions are speaking louder than words.

Researchers have found that many children don't start to grieve until six months after the death, around the time the household returns to some form of normalcy. After a death, daily routines are disrupted, meals served late, dishes piled high in the sink and laundry sits in bins. Surviving parents often are so consumed with their grief that the child's care suffers, so a child's delayed reaction has its roots in practicality.

"Children need the surviving parent's permission as well as help with mourning," says Erma Furman, a clinical researcher. "I am not thinking of verbal permission, although that can be of some help, but of the many nonverbal ways by which adults convey their wishes and attitudes and which children sense, respond to and comply with. When the surviving parent is not able to mourn, the child is implicitly not expected to do so either."

The role of the surviving parent or surrogate caregiver is vital to the child's development. Providing a loving environment where the child can discuss their feelings openly ensures that the pain won't destroy them. However, the kids who confront difficulties—an unstable home life, stepparents who reject them, financial upheavals—have a far harder time in recovering from the loss.

Children from the ages of two to four will often repeat questions over and over again in an attempt to dispel their confusion. They understand that the person is no longer there but are uncertain what that exactly means. Caregivers should discuss that the loved one can't come back now but that the child is safe and protected. Don't be surprised if the child is impacted developmentally and may revert back to thumb-sucking or bed-wetting.

From five to eight, a child understands the permanence of loss. Telling a child that terrible things don't happen all the time helps relieve his fears that his loved ones can disappear or be taken.

"Children of this age think that death is someone or something that comes and gets you. They think they can get it," says Joy Johnson, who founded the Centering Corporation in Nebraska. "Here it is important for the caretaker to explain the difference between an earache and cancer. Kids may be satisfied with an explanation like Aunt Liz's heart was very weak. It finally stopped. It was not at all like yours."

Morbid fascination with death is often seen in kids from eight to twelve. Questions about what it's like to live underground and what happens to the body should not be dismissed but dealt with in a sensitive manner.

Don't be surprised if children repeatedly ask the same questions, over and over again. Although your tendency may be to say, "Enough already, Jake. I explained it to you," try to be patient and soothing. One of the benefits of therapy is that the psychologist has more patience because she isn't suffering from the loss simultaneously.

As the child grows, the loss will continuously be evaluated. "Every time the child makes any cognitive leap, the loss is reprocessed so they can try to make sense of it with a new set of skills," explains Andre de Lisser, the director of the Den for Grieving Kids, in Greenwich, Connecticut.

Therefore, the loss will never ever be far away. "I think when you lose a parent as a young person, it takes away that dreamy quality of life that kids should be allowed," observed actress Julia Roberts, whose father died of cancer when she was ten. "I think you are still able to be a child and be frivolous, but I think that you are forever changed. I can remember specifically a whole phase of time where internally I did feel a lot of confusion, which was just really being pissed off. It had a profound impact on my life. Sometimes I think, Wow, how remarkable I must have been. And a lot of credit goes to the fact that I had a sibling close in age, so we were able to really lean on each other."

In those days, therapy wasn't often prescribed. But now therapists have various methods to help kids sort through this confusion and anger—especially when they are not emotionally mature enough to compartmentalize it. At the Den for Grieving Children, de Lisser has a "volcano room," a room filled with pads and punching bags and blown-up bouncing balls. For a designated amount of time, she invites the kids to express their anger and frustration in this room. The kids rip up newspapers, punch the bags, sock the balls with all their might while one supervisor watches. "Afterward, they often emerge giggling," she says. "We have found this room to be very effective in helping kids explore what their bodies may be feeling and giving these emotions an outlet." Unlike psychologists who work with anger management, these expressions do not reflect latent problems because the source of the anger is already identified.

Adolescents may appear to have more coping mechanisms, especially when you're looking at a six-foot-two-inch linebacker or a Madonna look-alike with mile-long legs. But, in fact, teenagers who lose a loved one have a different set of difficulties. Although they are more mature and can understand the finality of death, they are also left with a deep sense of guilt and isolation. This is an age when the child is breaking away from the parent and staking claim to their individuality and independence. Yet if the parent is suddenly ill or dies, this natural progression is interrupted and the teenager may feel guilt that he was remote or unavailable. Complicating matters, teens are so impacted by peer pressure that they often shut down their emotions, especially since they rarely have any friends who can validate or relate to the loss. Boys often suffer more than girls, as girls are more apt to discuss their feelings with their friends in contrast to boys, who are sent the signal to be "strong" and unemotional.

Sibling loss creates another set of challenges. Aside from missing their sibling, kids confront other feelings. In many cases, the deceased brother or sister may have been ill and getting most of the parental attention, and the surviving child may be relieved that the long ordeal is over. Furthermore, the family and community at large showers the surviving child with more attention out of compassion. "Sibling loss can create what we call a 'secondary gain,'" explains Dr. Sandra Bertman, director of Humanities in Medicine at the University of Massachusetts Medical School. "The book *Death in the Family* tells the story of how after a boy's father died, suddenly the bullies are kind to him. Now the child is getting attention he craved but along with these gains he feels guilt and worries that the attention isn't caused by his own merit."

To combat the guilt, which often can be transferred into destructive behavior and a deterioration of school performance, Bertman first asks the kids to answer these questions: How is your life different without your sibling? What do you miss most? And then she asks them to ponder what they have gained from the writing experience. She believes that too often therapists focus entirely on the distress of loss and don't help patients identify and connect with the positive gains that may result from the trauma.

Dr. Bertman also says the caregiver should reinforce these growth gains. "Chloe, how independent and self-sufficient you've become. What a great dinner you made. I'm so proud of you," or "Chloe, this painting is beautiful. It shows such sensitivity. Your skill has really improved."

There are also instances where the eldest son has been groomed for greatness and when he dies, the second child then becomes the leader, often surpassing anyone's expectations. Examples include India's Rajiv Gandhi and U.S. President John F. Kennedy.

"The positive side is that the younger sibling has had an opportunity until the death to develop his own personality without expectations and pressures placed on him," explains Dr. James Feldman, national director of public education at KidsPeace, which is based in California. "Usually in powerful families, the family invests its emotional energy in one child. Now this other child has the best of both worlds. The surviving child has had the opportunity free of pressure to develop his own internal strengths and likes and takes those with him along with integrating the most positive aspects of the deceased."

To honor their deceased sibling, they become the best leader or person they can be.

The other side of the spectrum is that children are saddled with a feeling that it should have been them instead of the sibling.

"Survival guilt is a real problem with grieving kids," acknowledges Dr. Feldman. "I had a child who had survived a fire but was unable to rescue his sister and became suicidal. Our psychiatric facility worked on reinforcing how he had been heroic in trying to save her. We also highlighted positive traits that he liked about his sister that could be part of him. He had been a discipline problem unlike his sister. The child then can adopt some of the valued qualities of the deceased along with their own personality traits which have been strengthened by the grieving process."

By reflecting on their loss and looking for meaning, growth can be found. This does not minimize the loss or ignore the prevailing feelings of longing. Instead, this philosophy focuses on the potential of still living with their loved one versus a gloom-and-doom approach. Furthermore, the child usually sees a personal growth himself. Whether it's a loss of a parent or sibling, many children are forced to become more independent during the crisis. Parents are so consumed by the emotional gale force of taking care of an ailing loved one that the remaining children inevitably take on more responsibilities—cooking dinner, entertaining themselves, doing their homework without supervision—and they inexorably will emerge from this experience changed people.

One study found that the growth-producing aspects of sibling loss included the bereaved sibling's appraisal that they have become more mature with their friends, been able to cope more successfully with stress, become closer to other family members and experienced an increased empathy, compassion and tolerance toward others and themselves. But this only happens with time.

Be aware that sometimes kids withdraw. Sometimes they act out. Whether the loss is of a parent or a sibling, the child feels abandoned and will test the parent to make sure they'll stick around.

Early on, parents should not mistake silence for disinterest or severely punish bratty behavior. The caregiver must be understanding and give the child or teenager an opportunity to grieve and reflect on the person they loved. This also provides an opportunity for a closer relationship with the surviving parent, since peers will not serve this role.

One fifteen-year-old told me how much he liked it when his mother talked about his dad.

"Did you tell her that you liked it?" I asked.

"No, but it's what I felt."

This pretty much sums it up.

Discussing death is never an easy topic, no matter what your age. However, it is a task that must be done. The manner in which it is discussed can have an impact on a child's development. Counselors discourage using euphemisms such as "gone to sleep" or "lost" when describing a death. Saying that the person has gone away or is alive in heaven leaves an impression that the person will come back. Kids have vivid imaginations and take things literally.

I read a newspaper story about how a little girl was crying over the death of her cat. Trying to comfort her, the little girl's mom said, "Don't worry, honey, your cat is with God in heaven." The little girl looked at her mother, her eyes widening in horror. "What does God want with a dead cat?" This story illustrates a vital point.

"It is not God who took away a loved one, it is death," says Ted Menten, an author and grief counselor. "And this is an important distinction to make. Often I tell parents to be very careful in how they describe death to their children. If God is the one who took away Mommy, the child won't want to go to God for help and comfort. God should never be portrayed as a parent snatcher or kidnapper of siblings or pets."

One mother explained the death of her husband by taking her child for a walk on the beach. A broken shell was in the path. "The shell is like a body, it can break, and we never know when it will happen," she said. "But the spirit of what's inside lives in the air and will always be around us."

I find that explanation quite comforting.

Years ago, adult and child therapy was lumped together like oatmeal. Since the grieving patterns of children are so varied, child therapy has now developed into its own discipline with many practitioners in the field.

Many national and global centers cater to the special needs of kids, such as the Dougie Organization, Den for Grieving Children and the Barr-Harris Center for the Study of Separation and Loss in Childhood at the Institute for Psychoanalysis in Chicago.

KidsPeace, based in California, is the largest and most comprehensive organization helping kids face and overcome emotional crisis. Their Web site has become the equivalent of a blockbuster hit with over two million kids worldwide visiting it every month. Although the chat rooms on www.teencentral.net are confidential, experts do monitor exchanges in case teens are in obvious danger of self-destructive behavior and need direction.

"We give kids positive suggestions on how to cope with loss," explains Dr. James Feldman, the national director of public education at KidsPeace.

By not visually seeing that the moderators are adult psychologists, kids are far more receptive to their advice—and the center is savvy enough to package it in hip, user-friendly language. The site enables kids to talk to others from around the world who suffered similar losses and they create a support group, which is difficult to find at home since so few of their peers can relate to their loss. Conscious of pop culture's influence on kids, the site also provides news bits on others who, like them, have suffered a loss. "Look at how 'N Sync dealt with this blow" was one banner headline that provided an interview with the band.

In Durham, North Carolina, the Triangle Hospice has a wonderful weekend program to help children cope with loss, and many of their methods can be used by anyone. Their Camp Releaf is one of many bereavement camps now in existence around the United States. Approximately thirty-five campers arrive each session. Most are referred by local hospice programs, schools or counseling centers. Scholarships are available and the fee is nominal.

When they arrive at Camp Releaf, the kids are divided into groups based upon age. Each group has its own facilitator.

Typical camp activities are tailored to the needs of the grieving. A scavenger hunt takes on added meaning in this rustic setting when the clues kids are asked to search for reflect the metaphors of life.

"Find something from nature that represents birth, death and renewal," the children are asked before they scurry off into the distance. And then they come back, faces flushed with accomplishment, showing off their discoveries. Flowers, clovers, a brand-new egg are proudly displayed as representing life. A crumpled leaf fallen from a maple tree becomes the metaphor for death. Dandelion seeds and an empty bird egg, as thin and light as a feather, becomes a triumphant symbol for renewal.

After collecting their bounty, the kids are told to create a collage, representing all these cycles of life.

During one session, a little boy bursts into tears. Thinking about his sister has made him cry. The other children instinctively let his tears fall and later gather around him. A little girl gently takes the clover she has found and starts stringing it into his hair without a sound. Soon he stops crying, and they all continue to play.

"Part of the therapy here is to let the kids help each other," says

Beth Sorenson, a therapist who works at the camp. "Here, they don't feel alone.".

Like most camps, there's an arts-and-crafts program, but here it's called "Cool Tools for Coping." Sometimes kids are asked to look through magazines in search of pictures that represent what they enjoy, everything from watching Pokémon to riding on a carousel. Counselors use this activity, called "A Collage of Life" to emphasize the importance of having fun, even though they have suffered a loss. Fun, they are told, is good for them and doesn't disappear just because someone is no longer there.

Often kids are so confused by their conflicted feelings that they don't know how to react. A young child will momentarily forget about his loss and then feel guilty for enjoying a ride on the playground slide. However, therapists are prepared to take away the guilt.

Other times, they make T-shirts or baseball hats with slogans that reflect what they're feeling or what they want to say. One little boy wore a hat with "Bro Forever" scrawled in childlike print in honor of his deceased brother. "I remember one girl. She created a hat with pictures of mountains, streams and flowers from a wooded area," recalls Beth Sorensen. "It represented an activity she loved doing with her father. While making the hat, we discussed how she could still enjoy this activity and be reminded of her father too."

All the games are expertly crafted to encourage the kids to discuss their feelings while therapists give helpful advice to help them heal.

For the younger kids, a silly clown shows up and becomes a favorite friend.

"Janie, what face is this?" asks the clown.

"A sad face," replies Janie knowingly.

"Do we know anyone who has this face?"

"Sometimes my mommy," she replies.

"What face is this?" asks the clown.

"A happy face," cries Max.

Soon the clown pretends to be holding in an emotion. His cheeks inflate like balloons. His eyes bulge, and his face looks as though it's going to burst. "This is what happens when we hold in our emotions," he says, sparking laughter from the kids. "See why it's good to talk about things?" Throughout their stay, the clown acts out all the possible responses of grief—anger, sadness, confusion, loneliness— that could be occurring to surviving members of the family as well as the kids. He also tries to teach them that laughter and humor can be good medicine when you're not feeling well.

In another workshop, a facilitator teaches the kids to cope with their anger by using handmade puppets to play out various roles. "Make a puppet who is like you," the counselor tells the kids. Each boy and girl is given a sock, and then uses a glue gun to decorate their puppet with sparkling glitter or a mishmash of buttons, sequins and colorful yarn.

"These puppets are your friends," says Beth softly. "They can listen when no else is around. So talk to them if you want to anytime." Sometimes Beth tells me that children who have difficulty talking to adults will have the puppets speak for them, especially when they're worried they're saying something that the adult may not like. Beth encourages this role-play.

Toward the end of camp, each child is asked to make a memory board using pictures, cards or even ticket stubs from a trip, which they were asked to bring to camp. Sometimes the child will sift through books and magazines trying to find the right image. Then the child writes words to express their feelings about their loved ones.

"I loved going hiking with you," Oliver wrote to his father.

"You were always my best friend," Zachary wrote to his sister.

"The memory board not only provides counselors an opportunity to talk about the loved one so the child doesn't repress their feelings, but later, when the child returns home, the board is an ideal instrument to spark a conversation about the loved one and what the child got from their camp experience," says Beth.

One time a twelve-year-old boy couldn't bring any pictures because his house had burned down, destroying all the family's pictures as well as causing the death of his young sister. So the camp counselor suggested they look through magazines to find pictures to illustrate his memories. Using yarn, he started braiding a border to the board as well as on the pictures of a little girl from a magazine. Thanks to the expertise of the counselor, a conversation ensued that unlocked some of the boy's secrets and helped with his therapy.

"His role in the family was to braid his little sister's hair," says Beth, her voice quivering slightly. "He still enjoyed this connection, and doing it on his board brought back this pleasant memory and allowed him to think of his sister."

The last ceremony could be implemented in any family as an annual ritual. Each person—child or teen—is given a piece of rice paper on which to write messages to their loved ones who died. If they're too young to write, staff members help out. The rice paper is then attached to a helium balloon.

The director of the camp stands up in front of the campers and starts to talk to them about the meaning of rituals.

"Rituals are ways to take care of yourself," says Dr. Linda Jordan. "There are the rituals with a little *r*, like brushing your teeth, combing your hair and taking a bath. Then there are the rituals with a big *R*, and these are the rituals you create. These are the special moments like birthday parties and putting a tooth under your pillow. Today is a ritual with a capital *R*."

"Your balloon stands for the person you love. This ritual is a special way of saying, 'I love you,' of saying good-bye and helping make you feel freer from your pain. Sending up this balloon is saying you will never forget them and they will be part of your life. Remembering them is very important. You will always miss them and wish they had been with you longer. This is a way to celebrate the special times you had, the happy times. We use balloons for birthdays and parades. They remind us of gladness, love and thankfulness. Sending up your balloon says you can experience a broken heart and still go on with your life."

Since many children are denied a final deathbed farewell, this symbolic good-bye creates what we know as closure. "Too often kids are excluded from the memorial services," says Beth Sorensen. "Children also need to say how much they loved someone, and they want to say good-bye."

A counselor from each cabin calls out the name of each child's loved one and the child's special name for that person, such as "MeMaw" or "Daddy." As the balloon drifts up and away, Collin Raye's song "Love Remains" is played. Campers and staff spend time then talking, hugging, consoling and silently learning the importance of acceptance and creating new ways of communicating to their loved one.

There are many other nurturing programs throughout the globe that are specializing in helping people live with loss.

At the Den for Grieving Children, jagged stones are given to each parent and child when they arrive to symbolize their grief. In time, through talking and workshops, they then are given smooth, rounded stones to carry with them as a tangible reminder that pain can be eased through remembrance and activity.

In Europe, the Age Exchange program is a community-based theater group that has workshops exploring life review and reminiscences for older people.

Another solution-based therapy that is gaining in popularity around the globe and is widely popular in Germany is Neuro-Linguistic Programming (NLP), the study of the structure of subjective experience. Founded by Richard Bandler and John Grindner in 1976, it studies the mental patterns or "programming" between the brain (neuro) and the language we interpret from our senses (linguistic). "We all filter information that comes through pictures, sounds, tastes, smells and feelings and make patterns from them," explains Myra Beals, an NLP practitioner in California. "By altering the images coded in the brain, we can alter how we feel about the experience."

Think of someone you know and picture her in your mind. Now think of the person who has died. Notice how your image of the person who died is most likely in the distance, a transparent, faded figure. The image of the person who is alive is nearer, has more density and can be seen in color. Consciously move the deceased to the foreground where your friend was previously standing. What mood is he in? Now concentrate on hearing your loved one's voice. What smells are in the room? Really concentrate. Can you smell your loved one's perfume? Can you smell a familiar scent from the kitchen? Now if your image is in black and white, put it in color. Soon you will feel a physiological reaction and the person will feel closer to you.

"Quite often, people will have visual memories of someone they have lost but are unable to experience the positive feelings associated with those memories," says Dr. Robert Dilts, coauthor of *Tools of the Spirit.* "Instead, they focus on what they are missing now, rather than feeling gratitude for what they used to have and still have." Since most people's goal is to still feel their loved one's presence, NLP becomes extremely helpful.

Practitioners say that NLP is particularly successful with post-traumatic syndrome, where the griever keeps reexperiencing a terrifying event, such as a homicide or sudden death. The horror of seeing a loved one's face ripped apart by a sniper's bullet completely violates any sense of security. The event becomes a recurring nightmare, causing deep depression and despair. Physical sensations like a burning in the chest, anxiety attacks or shortness of breath are common reactions.

Dr. Robert McDonald, a world-renowned NLP teacher and author, says traditional therapies have produced few results for these cases and NLP is far more effective.

"When a person has memories of trauma, traditional methodology tries to work through the issue by identifying the problem," he explains. "It's the 'you experienced this and that's why you're suffering' theory and through cathartic expression, we'll work through it. NLP doesn't look at the problem but the goal. What does the person want to accomplish? I'm like a taxi driver. I start by asking where do you want to go and then I take you there." Dr. McDonald gives the example of one woman who accidentally killed a small child in her care and was racked by guilt. Her goal was to imagine the child without feeling terribly guilty.

In these cases, NLP practitioners often will have the person project the image of the trauma in their mind and show the patient ways they can diminish or enhance various details by shifting the images of the event, which ultimately empowers them.

One daughter couldn't erase the image of her mother's murdered corpse. An NLP practitioner asked her to identify her goal. She wanted to feel close to her mother. The painful image became a way to hold on to the mother. The therapist discovered that one enduring memory she had was of sitting on her mother's lap while her mother sang. Now whenever she thinks of the painful image, she inserts the memory of being on her mother's lap and consciously moves the painful memory to another corner of her mind which helps her minimize the painful memory by enhancing the positive one.

When I went through a session, Dr. McDonald took me on an amazing journey. Through these exercises, he helped bring my father closer to me and identified what was the source of my deepest pain. Aside from missing his laughter and companionship, my father's death left me feeling as though I wasn't protected. I missed the safety he represented. This forced me to realize that the issue I needed to address was how to become more self-sufficient so I would build my own force of protection. He also showed me that I could accomplish this feat with my father's image and wisdom as a guiding force.

I have sampled many therapies, both conventional and unconventional, and have come to this conclusion. Therapy is a worthwhile endeavor because ultimately you learn more about yourself—and the more you learn about yourself, the stronger you become.

14

The Shadow of Grief: Emotional Scars

Sometimes I find myself reading the obituary column in the same way others read the sports pages. I check out the scores. How long did they last? Did they make it to the seventy-year-old line or only to forty-four? Was life a marathon or did the Grim Reaper tackle them before they could get to the finish line?

Of course, this is rooted in fear. Fear that I won't make it past the age of my father's death. Fear that at any time, despite all my Nutri-Grain breakfasts and spin classes, my body will betray me. Maybe cancer isn't like catching the chicken pox, but anytime I get sick, my anxiety level soars.

I know I am not alone with these fears. My friend's mother battled Alzheimer's, and whenever she forgets the name of a street, her face takes on a worried look. "I am petrified that if I forget the street, my keys or where I placed a shirt, it means that I'm getting it," says Lauren. When a parent or sibling dies, the surviving children will have worry festering in their stomachs. Jeff's father committed suicide, and he worries that a light will go off sometime in the future and lead him astray. Rachel's sister died of breast cancer, and she worries it will happen to her. The mother of my mother-in-law,

Joyce, died of lymphoma at forty-nine. "When I turned forty-nine, it was the hardest year of my life," she recalls. "I must have gone to the doctor thirty times worrying that every little ache meant doom."

My friend Molly's brother died in a plane crash. Her husband Mark knows that whenever he arrives at a destination, he must call immediately. Otherwise, she panics.

With Parker's birth, my fears grew exponentially. I was convinced that every sniffle was a life-threatening disease, every tumble would mean a hospital trip. I've come to terms with the fact that while I squeeze every drop of juice from each day, I also carry a nagging fear that catastrophe is looming. It is my residue of loss.

"What you learn from a catastrophe is that you can't control it or prevent it from happening," says my friend Leslie. "It's the oddest lesson. On one hand, you learn to loosen your grip in believing you have control and then you are put in a position of being more protective than ever."

Others face these fears by becoming defiant daredevils. After his father died, eighteen-year-old Paul started to push the limits. He went skydiving, raced fast cars and took drugs.

"It is not unusual for someone to want to tempt fate, thinking, 'Oh, you just die anyway and you can do whatever you want,' " observes Dr. Robin Goodman. "The loss has empowered them, and they feel they are already dodging a bullet every day. This often results in people becoming great risk takers. However, sometimes that confidence can turn destructive, and the patient needs to be aware of these possibilities during their recovery."

Aside from reckless behavior, another common response is a reluctance to connect to someone. "I never believe that anyone is going to stay, so I never give of myself fully," says Zoe, whose mother died of breast cancer when she was fourteen. "Because I worry that someone will leave, it becomes a self-fulfilling process. If you tell a guy you're worried about him leaving all the time, eventually he does."

Self-protection is an understandable reaction for anyone who lost a parent or loved one. Having experienced the devastating pain of a parent's death, and the domino effect the loss has on all aspects of one's life, the motherless or fatherless child wants to avoid ever feeling so vulnerable and sad again. Love, as this child already knows, brings with it a huge risk.

"When a motherless daughter fears loss so much that she believes it inevitable, she avoids forming relationships that might lead to the deep intimacy she craves," says Hope Edelman, the author of *Motherless Daughters*. "This daughter either dodges romance, chooses aloof partners or bolts each time a relationship shows the first sign of long-term commitment. It's as though she's telling her mother, 'See, I can leave you too!' " This syndrome can also apply to men.

Brian finally realized after ten years that he had an intimacy issue. After his father died of cancer, Brian was hit with another loss. The family business he had expected to run one day fell apart, and he was left to fend for himself. Additionally, like many young men, he became the male figure to his sisters and mother, becoming both financial adviser and confidant. After becoming a successful stockbroker, he married a woman named Julie, who seemed the perfect match for him, quiet and accommodating.

On his first anniversary, he insisted on going to his mother's for a barbecue instead of a planned dinner for just the two of them. Julie's birthdays were hardly acknowledged by Brian, nor were special holidays. Clearly he did not make Julie a priority in his life, and she complained about his lack of sentimentality. Only after he had a child did Brian confront himself and his inability to get too close to someone.

"I couldn't let go and truly love someone," he says. "I just couldn't. I felt like I lost control. I hated that feeling. It made me feel powerless. In therapy I realized my inability to let go was really about my fear of abandonment. I didn't want to go through another loss. My therapist reminded me that I had already survived a loss, so what made me think I couldn't survive again. He let me see that I had more to gain from loving than from holding back. Confronting these issues saved my marriage."

Others have trouble finding anyone as good as Mom or Dad. The deceased parent becomes mythologized, and no one else can possibly measure up. The person they seek must be perfect, and any little flaw becomes an excuse to break away. Because they were too young to see their parent's faults, their expectations become impossible to meet.

With such an intense experience, it shouldn't be surprising that loss produces extremes. Some survivors become overly needy of a relationship, almost clinging to the person in the way a child does to a parent.

Fay is the president of Mode Works, a New York–based graphics design company that paints large murals often displayed in restaurants and stores.

"My mother died when I was nine, and then my father died six years later," she says. "When I was a teenager, I was so sure of myself. 'Hey, I'm doing all this without a parent. I don't need anyone. I'm fine without parents.' But then I realized that wasn't true at all. I have this emptiness that never goes away, this neediness that I call my genetic flaw. I'm like a computer with a missing chip. I can't let anything go in my life because I was stripped so early of any security. I feel so attached to everyone, trying to create a family, that I hang on much too long to bad boyfriends and even at work, to horrendous employees who should have been fired.

"Still, I know this and it doesn't help. I know I'll be eighty years old and still feel this hole inside me."

Sam Klagsbrun, a noted researcher, psychiatrist and director of the Four Winds facility in Katonah, New York, says that the child who loses a parent often ignores warning signs of a troubled relationship. "They want the relationship to work so much that they become blind to someone's faults," he says. "Even when abusive behavior occurs, they will go into deep denial because they want to prevent another abandonment."

"Clinging to a dead relationship or pleading for a last-minute change of heart is less an adult's attempt at reconciliation than a child's cry for the parent to remain," adds Hope Edelman. "They often bond with partners quickly and approach adult relationships with a child's expectations."

Not surprisingly, the parentless children whose surviving parent was supportive and emotionally attentive found it easier to form warm, healthy relationships as an adult. Research also confirms that children also benefited from a strong network of family members—

whether it was grandparents, aunts, uncles, cousins or siblings—all of whom can become role models for the benefits of close bonds.

When Becky's father died, the eighteen-year-old started spending time with an uncle who hadn't any children. They would occasionally go to museums together, and he exposed her to his love of Renaissance paintings and Rembrandts. Her uncle didn't replace her father but provided a link to him. "If you don't have what you want, then your survival instincts lead you to someone who can provide it," says Becky. "I think this is done both consciously and unconsciously. Someone makes you feel good and you may not have the analytical skills to understand why at the time, but later you can see why it all happened."

Keith found solace in a camp counselor after his father died. "John was only a few years older than me but became someone I could talk to," says Keith, now a media executive. "I think I needed a father figure, and as an only child, he wanted a younger brother." Now like brothers, John was Keith's best man at his wedding.

However, that doesn't mean it's hopeless for the child who doesn't have this support system at home. My mother was so dependent on my father—she had never even balanced her own checkbook—and so self-absorbed in her grief that she was incapable of giving me a secure sense of the future. I remember her yelling, "Your father is dead, and your life around here is different now." As if I didn't already know. Like many other children, my loss was aggravated by the inability of the surviving parent to function, which was exacerbated by the financial constraints my father's death created.

In retrospect, this experience has made me very self-reliant. I think our parents teach us not only who we want to be, but also who we don't want to be. My mother's isolation partly stemmed from her having no safety net, no professional career or family close by. As a result, I have sought both a career and a husband who is part of a close clan.

My loss also forged a closeness to my brother that many of my friends lack. We only had each other. A study by Anna Freud following World War II found that children from concentration camps created families from their peer group out of necessity and need. I understand this. Normal rivalries are obliterated when your common goal becomes emotional survival. Clearly some crumble from

the pressure. Yet others cobble together a sense of family and closeness even when little exists.

So why do some people rebound, and others do not?

Within grief literature, the profile for a successful griever consists
of several factors. First, the mourner must address these questions.

What have I lost?
What do I have left?
What may be possible for me?

The successful mourners look at possibilities for themselves.
They allow themselves to experience all phases of the ordeal while
looking for ways to find meaning from their loss.

"One's perception of grief is a key factor," says Dr. Joanne Jozefowski, a Massachusetts therapist. "Beliefs often lead to self-fulfilling
prophecies. If grievers believe the process of grief can only have a
negative outcome, they will be disheartened rather than helped. On
the other hand, the belief that grief can lead to a positive outcome
may give the griever enough courage to begin the journey. The
knowledge that strength and growth can be gained by fully experiencing grief can encourage a bereaved person. It gives purpose and
meaning to the pain. Suffering should not be in vain."

What is surprising is that this research is rarely publicized. "That
may be because scientists are more interested in the pathologies,
and the problems associated with loss," says Dr. Richard Tedeschi, a
clinical researcher and author. "Growth is not only possible but a
frequent occurence." According to his research at the University of
North Carolina, two-thirds of people who go through traumatic
events find some kind of benefit.

He gives an example of a widow. "Although the pain persisted,
she found herself becoming more independent," says Dr. Tedeschi.
"Her husband had always paid all the bills, taken care of fixing the
car, mowed the lawn. Now she was left with these chores and found
to her surprise that she was more capable than she ever thought."

This heightened self-awareness also encouraged her to try new
things—take a cruise, meet new friends, learn bridge, join a charity,
which all helped her adapt to a new life.

Aside from gaining independence and a reshaping of goals and ambitions, grievers often take away from the experience a heightened appreciation for life. They see its value more vividly. They don't sweat the small stuff. In separate studies with both cancer and AIDS patients, participants said their relationships with their loved ones were enhanced as was the enjoyment of daily tasks.

This is the continuing paradox of loss. You can gain as well as lose.

PART THREE

Finding Meaning from Loss

≈

"I merely took the energy it takes to pout and put it into writing the blues."

——Duke Ellington

15

The Link Between
Loss and Greatness

When you lose a loved one, suddenly you become part of a club you never wanted membership in but one that marks you for life. My friend Dennis, now a successful editor, told me that when he was growing up, he wanted to start "The Dead Parents Club" except he couldn't find enough members in his neighborhood. Yet little did he know what an extraordinary club it really was, filled with some of the greatest leaders, thinkers and artists of all time.

George Washington, a man so determined to set democracy in motion despite overwhelming obstacles, became fatherless at the age of eleven. Thomas Jefferson, the author of the Declaration of Independence and such democratic ideals as the belief in "life, liberty and the pursuit of happiness," was fourteen when his father died. Lincoln, who fought the Civil War to preserve the mother country and keep the United States intact, was a mere nine years old when his mother died. Franklin D. Roosevelt, the president who expertly navigated the country through the Depression and World War II, lost his father at nineteen, while his wife, Eleanor, whose father died when she was nine, having already lost her mother the year before, was a crusader for social causes and champion of the underdog.

Other U.S. presidents who fit this profile include Grover Cleveland, Benjamin Harrison, James Monroe, Herbert Hoover, Andrew Jackson, William Harrison, James Garfield, John Tyler, Rutherford Hayes, Andrew Johnson, Calvin Coolidge and Theodore Roosevelt.

President Bill Clinton's father died before his birth, and he subsequently lived with an emotionally withholding stepfather, inspiring, many say, an insatiable desire to be liked and respected. Historians will credit him for guiding the country through the biggest economic boom of all time as well as weathering blistering attacks during the Kenneth Starr investigation that most men would have been unable to endure. Like many survivors, he developed an innate ability to compartmentalize his emotions and single-mindedly pursue his goals.

"Early on, I learned that I had to fight for myself," President Bill Clinton told me. "It makes you extremely resourceful and independent because you have no one to lean on."

As a young boy, Clinton is said to have endured the chaos of his turbulent childhood, a childhood marked by an alcoholic stepfather and loving, but hell-raising mother, by focusing on the snapshot of his biological father, Bill Blythe, that he kept near his bed. One writer speculated that by staring at this shrine to a father about whom he knew next to nothing, "he dreamed up an idealization to fill the empty place where others had fathers." This might explain what Clinton meant when early in his career he said, "The violence and dysfunction in our home made me a loner, which is contrary to the way people view me, because I'm gregarious, happy, all of that. But I had to construct a whole life inside my head."

In his research, Dr. Pierre Rentchnick, a former professor at Geneva University, found that boys who lost their fathers made up the great majority of revolutionaries and political leaders. Ten of the twelve Caesars lost a parent. Other world leaders who suffered early losses include Simón Bolívar, the liberator of northern Latin America, German Chancellor Willy Brandt, Aga Khan III, Augustus, Chiang Kai-shek, Peter the Great, Alexander the Great, Aaron Burr, Henry VIII, James III, Benito Juárez, Kagawa Toyohiko, Henry Clay, Francis Bacon, Oliver Cromwell, Jefferson Davis, Robert E. Lee, Lenin, Khrushchev, Napoléon, Pierre Trudeau, Zhou Enlai and Gamal Nasser. Research also reveals that almost 60 percent of all British prime ministers lost a parent in their formative years. Yet this is a situation that only affects a small minority of the population. According to Harvard social scientist Phyllis Silverman, the percentage of kids who lose parents early in life can range from 2 to 15 percent, taking into account such variables as era, culture and class of the deceased. Whichever way you slice it, this is a very small percentage of the population.

Why do so many of these people grow up to become leaders? Dr. Rentchnick believes that political power becomes a form of compensation and even overcompensation for the emptiness, the abandonment and helplessness the child once felt. To defy his sense of weakness, he will identify with the strongest of leaders and then adopt these qualities into himself to gain an edge over others. Furthermore, unlike his peers, the young man will often seek out the advice of older successful men who subsequently become loyal mentors and role models. "Since he has not had a father, the fatherless son will be the father of the group, the guide, the chief from which is derived this conscious or unconscious will for political power," says Dr. Rentchnick. "Facing the father's empty place, the parentless child must fill the void, struggle against the anguish by sublimating his aggression into creativity and a need for political power."

This great motivation and insatiable lust for power has not always contributed to the enhancement of mankind. Many despicable dictators also lost a parent, including Joseph Stalin, Genghis Khan, Eva Peron, Ivan the Terrible, Ho Chi Minh, Adolf Hitler and Bosnia's Slobodan Milosevic.

"The reaction of rage at being abandoned can be transformed into a sense of social injustice," explains Dr. Marvin Eisenstadt, who for twenty-five years has studied the link between loss and achievement. "This system of thought can be manifested into either outstanding achievement or outstanding antisocial achievement. It can go either way."

A death makes the child an outsider, different from his peers, and this often fuels an ability to see things in a nontraditional way. Visionary means seeing something that is not there. After a parent dies, a child must develop a relationship with someone whose physical presence is not there but who still exists. This I believe develops introspection and abstract thinking, which are the foundation for all visionaries who build empires by seeing what others may not.

In modern times global power is not only derived from elections but from the electronic media that provides the ability to vastly influence the general population. Many of the giants in this field also lost fathers.

Rupert Murdoch's beloved father, Sir Keith, died when he was nineteen, forcing him to leave Oxford and return to Australia. When his father's executors tried to convince his mother to sell their remaining paper, the fledgling *Adelaide News*, Murdoch went into battle mode, moving into the remote town of Adelaide to turn the paper into a success. "Being mad is a great motivator," said Murdoch. "It made me angry. I thought they were trying to take advantage of my mother. They certainly wouldn't have dared do it in my father's time. I said, 'To hell with the idea, we'll fight 'em.' " And fight them he did, turning the paper into a success and then subsequently launching his communications empire. In his will, Sir Keith had written that he hoped his son would have "a full life in newspapers and broadcasting activities and of ultimately occupying a position of high responsibilities in that field." And indeed he has, with newspapers and television stations around the globe.

Before he committed suicide, Ted Turner's stern, emotionally withholding father wouldn't leave him the family billboard business. This fueled the twenty-four-year-old's unrelenting ambition and desire to prove himself. Acquiring his father's troubled billboard company and borrowing heavily to save the company, he then used the profits to not only purchase divisions of the billboard company his father had sold off before his suicide but to buy a small local TV station that would become the first piece of his cable empire. The station beamed signals to cable customers nationwide and became the prototype for what would eventually revolutionize the future of television by becoming CNN. Later, he again risked his company's profits by buying MGM studio and its film archives. Because of his determination, he built his entertainment empire, which now includes such cable channels as Turner Classic Movies, Turner Broadcasting Systems and the Cartoon Network.

Turner acknowledges that his early motivation was activated by wanting to prove his father wrong. "When he died, it left me alone because I had counted on him to make the judgment of whether or not I was a success. It also taught me that I had no time to waste." Only after winning the America's Cup, building his TV empire and getting on the cover of *Forbes* did he say he began to "lay the ghost of paternal judgment to rest."

Gary Winnick's father died when he was eighteen. The billionaire founder and chairman of Global Crossing, the company that created a state-of-the-art worldwide fiber-optic network, believes there is a link between loss and greatness.

"I don't look at failure as others do," he says. "To me, it's part of the process, part of the cost. What is failure if you are testing out your dreams? As long as it's not fatal, so what? The difference between failure and success is the difference of trying versus not trying. What's the impact if you lose? Nothing. You're still alive to try again. So go for it. Ted Turner, Rupert Murdoch, all these guys like me have ultimately hit a wall but the only ones that knew it was everyone around us because we always are in motion. We look at those hurdles and walls that get thrown at us, and we get turned on. Nothing can be as bad as losing a parent at a young age, nothing can ever be as painful, therefore any obstacle thrown in our path is a challenge and another hurdle to climb over. No professional adversity can ever reach the pain I suffered when my father died. I remember the incident of his dying as if it were a second ago. It's an image and vision that never changes."

Winnick remembers turning from a young fresh-faced kid to an adult overnight. "When I was eighteen, I wasn't thinking of my future and thought I'd go into my father's restaurant supply business. But that moment changed me, changed who I was. Responsibility became the sole focus of my life."

Following the death of a father, the son is often turned into "the man of the house" on whom the surviving parent now relies for both advice and counsel—and often financial support. "The death of a parent gives the child an unfortunate but critical developmental push," says Ken Doka, a Lutheran minister and professor of gerontology at New Rochelle College. "They are forced into roles not normally absorbed by their peers where they are looked upon as the leader in the house. Some will be crushed by the responsibility while others will integrate this role into their personalities and be spurred on."

For many achievers, the added responsibilities were empowering and liberating. Although the emotional loss was painful, the ability to chart their own destinies enabled them to take risks and try different tasks.

After his father died suddenly when he was fifteen, Malcolm Glazer, now the billionaire businessman and owner of the Tampa Bay Buccaneers, was left with the responsibility of supporting his mother and siblings by working in his father's store, which sold watch parts. "We were two steps away from welfare," he recalls. "Shortly after his death, I decided to take a Greyhound bus and traveled fifty miles to try to sell watch parts. This was so crazy and bold. But I felt I could do anything I wanted. I did sell more watch parts. This gave me initiative then to try other things, which I've been doing all my life. I never think I can't do something."

"Guys who lose a parent are forced to make their own decisions, which can actually help you," he adds. "If all your life, you went to your parents to ask them what they think, when you grow up, you think you can't do things on your own. But when you're on your own, you say, I got no one to help me but myself. You learn to develop and trust your instincts." A textbook case of this thinking was when Glazer purchased the Tampa Bay Buccaneers for $192 million, a sky-high amount at the time for a team that was under-performing. "I realized that forty-five thousand people were still coming even though they didn't expect the team to win," he said. So Glazer invested in top-notch performers and then savvily negotiated a deal with the stadium where he would get more high-priced box seats than other owners had asked for, which gave him a steady stream of revenue. The team is now one of the most successful franchises, and the investment is worth over a billion dollars.

Seeing opportunities where others do not is the formula for success. This ability to look at a situation from many perspectives is fostered by the grieving process. The child or adolescent is forced to examine life and its mysteries with an urgency unlike their peers. Furthermore, because the child was faced with an uncontrollable situation, the way to deal with chaos is to create as much control as you can.

Chase Manhattan Bank Vice Chairman Jimmy Lee believes his command control personality was forged after the loss of his father when he was twelve.

"There is this anger, this sense that you got shortchanged, a raw deal, and you say, 'Why me?' You feel cast adrift," says Lee. "You realize you have no cushion, no fall-back, and I knew I had to reach manhood right then. At boarding school, through sheer force of personality, I became the captain of the ice hockey team even though I wasn't the best skater. This reinforced the notion my internal drive could get results. It energized me to win people over and become my own poster child for overachievement. Unlike my friends, I felt incredibly mortal. My friends didn't have that sense and weren't as focused on achieving. Since I didn't have a role model, I created the perfect one. I worked nonstop.

"Your loss develops a philosophical competence as well as a need for control. I'm a control freak. I would be known for structuring every detail of a deal when others in my position would let junior people do it. I would be told to let other people do some of this work, but for me, it's hard to trust people. Once control was taken away, you always want to be in control of what you can control and you end up only trusting yourself."

This hard-driving micromanaging has resulted in Lee being asked to structure the financing for headline-making deals for General Motors, Kmart and R. J. Reynolds as well as for baseball and football teams, work that has rewarded him with $20 million paychecks annually.

"Grief is not only an emotion," adds Dr. Ken Doka. "Some people respond to grief by not so much feeling but by doing and thinking, which often results in achievement. One's energy goes consciously or unconsciously into creating an identity or legacy that honors the parent. Basically, the child is saying, 'I'm no one you should feel sorry for. I've learned well. I've done well.' And in this society, the best way to do that is to become a success."

Seeking achievement from all sources becomes the way to fill the hole left by the loved one. "Since you never got all the love you needed, you look for external support and confirmation," explains legendary First Amendment lawyer Martin Garbus, whose mother died when he was three. "The way you get that confirmation is by either making lots of money or standing up for something and getting public recognition. I call it the need and greed syndrome. You need so much to have that hole in your heart filled up but it can't be refilled. Nothing can plug it up so you keep on trying and pursue more successes. You also think that your success will make your loved one proud."

In his research on grieving kids and adolescents, Dr. Benjamin Garber, the director of the Bar-Harris Center for the Study of Loss and Separation, found that following the death of a parent, the school grades of many children improve. "So the question is, why does it happen? We have seen it over and over again. The child feels that in a sense they are doing what the parent expected them to do. This particularly happens to girls. She feels the parent is watching over her, and in order for her to please him or her, she studies hard," says Dr. Garber. "But eventually you have to make it your own. If there's enough positive reinforcement from the academic performance, then you will make it your own."

Linda Shostak, one of the first female partners at Morrison and Foerster law firm in San Francisco, understands this response intimately. Her mother died from cancer when she was thirteen. "I just immersed myself in work so I didn't have to think about it. I remember my father telling me to sit down and get enough Girl Scout badges to get the curved bar. I then proceeded to read books, each with at least a thousand pages, so I would be consumed by something else. I took on all sorts of projects. I developed habits which have positive and negative sides. On one side, I developed an incredible work ethic. But I also compartmentalized my emotions. Yet I know I am not alone. When I went to Harvard Law School, there were only a handful of women graduates and the majority only had one parent. I never believed that was a coincidence."

It was an effort to please her mother that activated the academic ambitions of Supreme Court Justice Ruth Bader Ginsburg, who was seventeen when her mother died. Her mother had urged her to strive for excellence, be independent and be a lady. Justice Ginsburg now says that she is what her mother would have wanted her to be, and she derives comfort from the fact that her accomplishments went beyond her mother's wildest dreams. "She would have been very proud of me," said Ginsburg, who keeps a picture of her mother on the wall in her chambers.

This looming shadow of the deceased does not have to be haunting but can actually be a loving, inspiring guide. As Justice Ginsburg told me, "Thinking of my mother's death when I just turned seventeen, I have often written to people who have lost a parent, sibling or another deeply loved person: 'May you carry on, thriving in your life, and work, just as _____ would have willed.' "

The concept of a spiritual guide can be a powerful, motivating force that is frequently discussed by children of loss.

Real estate executive Lauren Muss, whose father died when she was seven, says that she chose her profession because being around construction sites and the smell of sawdust made her feel connected to him. "I feel like we are sharing a mutual interest. I sometimes feel sad that I can't call him or get free advice. When my friends' fathers call them at work, and I hear them become Daddy's little girl, it stirs up the pain of my loss all over again. I just wish I had him. There's this hole that never gets filled up. But I console myself knowing that he must be very proud of me, and I feel certain that he has been with me when I've had to make important decisions."

This striving to connect to a loved one is deep rooted and transcends all fields.

Henry James described it as a deep-rooted need when he transformed his sorrow over his father's death into prose, poetry and other artistic forms of expression. Art, for many, is therapy.

As Hope Edelman observed, Virginia Woolf was haunted by the death of her mother from rheumatic fever when she was thirteen. In her autobiographical essay, *A Sketch from the Past,* Woolf explained how writing her book *To the Lighthouse* became a cathartic release.

"I wrote the book very quickly; and when it was written, I ceased to be obsessed by my mother. I no longer hear her voice; I do not see her.

"I suppose that I did for myself what psychoanalysts do for their patients. I expressed some very long felt and deeply felt emotion. And in expressing it, I explained it and laid it to rest."

In 1953, researcher Mark Kanzer studied the influence of early loss on creativity. Among the historical authors who were orphaned during childhood were Baudelaire, the Brontë sisters, Dante, Dumas, Rousseau, Henry James, Edgar Allen Poe, George Sand, Tolstoy, Voltaire, Byron, Keats and Dostoyevsky.

Mark Twain, considered the preeminent American writer, suffered the loss of his father when he was twelve, which later made him reflect that "the source of all humor is sorrow."

After his father died, Sam Clemens, a rebellious boy and never much of a student, was sent off by his mother to apprentice as a printer, making him feel like an orphan. Like the other famous orphan characters he would later invent—lads known as Huck Finn and Tom Sawyer—he set out for new territories and adventures and made a success of himself.

Dr. Eileen Simpson, herself an orphan and the author of *Orphans*, wrote how many biographers rarely looked at the link of loss to greatness because people were so conditioned to bury their feelings, which explains the dearth of material on the subject.

In a 1987 study researchers discovered that the creative individual's ability to venture off into fantasy and the possession of thin ego boundaries may serve as a buffer against stress rather than as a consequence of it. Many children retreat into a dreamworld to help them sort out their changed environment. The act of dreaming, creating new worlds in your mind, is a vital component to the creative process. Art becomes an outlet to control their hopes and fears, and enables them to design a way to transform reality to their liking.

Writers who fit this profile also include Edward Albee, Tom Stoppard, Joseph Conrad, Somerset Maugham, Robert Louis Stevenson, Hans Christian Andersen, Robert Frost, Jean-Paul Sartre, Emile Zola, Elie Wiesel, Orson Welles, William Wordsworth, James Agee, Steve Allen, Albert Camus, E. M. Forster, Joseph Heller, Friedrich Nietzsche, George Sand, William Saroyan, Aleksandr Solzhenitsyn, Jonathan Swift, William Thackeray, Isak Dinesen, H. L. Mencken, Edith Wharton, Theodore White, Victor Hugo, Aldous Huxley, Herman Melville, Thomas Mann, James Michener, Truman Capote, Dean Koontz, Margaret Mitchell and Eugene O'Neill.

In another study, researchers found that intelligence and creativity are useful resources for coping with stress. The ability to see things differently from other people and to regress when warranted is a necessity for those who become brilliant trailblazers in the scientific or creative fields.

To many, achievement is a form of escape. Researcher Sam Silverman discovered in his study that many of the world's greatest scientists—ranging from Copernicus to Isaac Newton—lost a parent in childhood. Since the child's emotional psyche has been bruised, he believes they veer toward fields devoid of human contact. Science is also a field where the need for control can be exercised.

Dr. Marvin Eisenstadt, a researcher and senior supervising psychologist at St. Mary's Children and Family Services in Syosset, New York, looked at eminent people worthy of at least a page in the American and Britannica encyclopedias and found the vast majority suffered early losses. This led to his landmark research, which found that those who suffered early losses were three times more likely to be achievers than others. To Eisenstadt, the mourning process is where achievement ripens, since grievers learn to be adaptive, resourceful, philosophical, and independent. They also must devise a way to find meaning in their loss.

"In the mastery of these personal problems creative expression may find its deepest roots," says Dr. Marvin Eisenstadt. "The creative effort is thus seen as a restorative act. I believe that the intensity of emotions caused by grief causes sufficient pressure on the psyche to create a burst of productivity and creativity." By not accepting the loss of something so important, artists find ways to replace it, with words, art or music.

Early drawings in caves reveal how primitive man needed ways to express his sorrow, and this has been consistent throughout the ages. "Civilization," wrote Dr. Geza Roheim in a 1943 study, "is a huge network of more or less successful attempts to protect mankind against the dangers of object-loss."

Consumed with the fear that his days were numbered, Michelangelo worked feverishly around the clock to create masterpieces like the Sistine Chapel and *David*. His fear was fueled by the early death of his mother when he was six. Psychoanalyst writer Dr. Matthew Besdine believed the artist's unresolved Oedipal problem "created an unusual attachment to his mother," but by seeking to be connected to her, he created transcendent art that still inspires awe today.

Adds Dr. Andre Haynal, a psychiatrist at the University of Geneva, "Raising a statue in the image of the one who has disappeared, using art to breathe life into the image, trying to understand or avert a bad destiny, that is the cradle of our culture. Art reunites, restores and conserves the lost objects; its ultimate goal is to triumph over death. Confronted with the painful sense of limitation, the individual seeking reparation may turn to art or science for a certain promise of immortality."

Nothing is taken for granted by the motherless or fatherless child. Artists often give objects eternal life as a way to fill the void left by their parents' absence. Art, observed Picasso, is a lie that shows us the truth. Picasso didn't lose a parent early in life, but other artists who fit this pattern include Francis Bacon, James Whistler, Helen Frankenthaler, Edgar Degas, and Eric Fischl.

Classical music geniuses such as Beethoven, Liszt, Tchaikovsky, Schubert and Bach all lost parents early in life and found music to be their salvation. Irving Berlin lost his dad at five. His songs "Putting on the Ritz," "No Business Like Show Business," "Easter Parade" and "White Christmas" all evoke a tenderness and memory of love.

Often sadness triggers a gushing fountain of creativity that Eisenstadt believes is a physical response to grief. The pressure of sadness actually elicits a chemical reaction that sparks a creative burst. Vince Gill says that writing songs about the death of his father and brother helped him find a way "to celebrate, to grieve, to laugh . . . all those things. Creativity helps me deal with those emotions; it's a sweet gift to be able to sit down and write a song about what your dad and brother meant to you. I have a tendency when I'm singing those songs ['Go Rest High on that Mountain' and 'The Key to Life'] to think of a much lighter side of my brother or my father and not go to the saddest place while I'm singing it. Another thing about those songs, as sad as they are, there's some real celebration in those songs, and I lean on that side of it much more so than the morose and sad 'death' side of things. Thinking about them that way, the interesting thing in both of their passings is they don't feel gone. Because of the memories, they're always there, and there's comfort in that."

Is there any song that illustrates this better than Eric Clapton's "Tears in Heaven" whose haunting lyric of questioning if his child would remember his name touched people deep in the core of their being? On a late afternoon in 1992, four-year-old Connor Clapton was running around in his New York apartment and, in the throes of frenzied activity, fell out an open window, tumbling to his death. His father, singer Eric Clapton, was shattered and wrote "Tears in Heaven" for consolation.

Professionally, his child's death awakened what critics called, "a new sensibility" in his writing. Another wrote that Clapton has "since put a lot of emotion into very bare personal songs." These songs move people profoundly and the raw, heartfelt emotion connected Clapton to the largest audience of his career.

"I was advised after his death to live my life in honor of his memory," Clapton said. "It was in honor of his memory, to do things that he would be proud of, and that immediately gave me somewhere to go."

Loss has been the inspiration for many other contemporary artists. Many have wondered what connected John Lennon and Paul McCartney together and how, like modern-day alchemists, they changed the direction of popular music with the Beatles. Yet most have missed one obvious link: Both lost their mothers as adolescents.

Following the death of his mother when he was fourteen, Paul asked his father for a guitar. Music became his companion. Paul's father remained a strong, caring presence, and Paul had many support systems that had impact on his development. His mother, by all accounts, doted on her son. As a result, Paul's songs were marked by a sweet sentimentality, optimism and a longing for perfect love. In the song "Let It Be" he tells how "mother Mary" visits him, giving him words of wisdom, which shows how the deceased can still inspire.

John had a far angrier relationship with his mother. She had abandoned him, sending him to live with his aunt and uncle. His music was infused with the disillusionment of an outsider, someone who felt like a loner and wanted a connection to something or someone.

However, whether the child was embraced with love and affection or felt isolated and alone, the loss still activates the creative process. "The loss will spark creativity to alleviate the feelings of apartness and prove to the world the person's essential goodness and worthiness," said Dr. Marvin Eisenstadt.

Is it any wonder that the children whose parents weren't at the school plays now seek careers where a large audience publically applauds their accomplishments? In explaining her close bond with Madonna, Rosie O'Donnell said, "She was the only other woman I had met who had lost her mother when she was young and had the same sort of fantasy that fame would heal those wounds, and then did anything she needed to do in order to get there."

Jerry Lieber, the lyricist of the world-famous award-winning songwriting team of Leiber and Stoller, wrote "Jailhouse Rock," "Hound Dog," "Love Potion Number Nine," etcetera. After his father died when he was six, the family was forced to move from their modest home in a middle-class neighborhood into a poor area of Baltimore, where his mother owned a tiny general store. Because most of the neighborhood couldn't afford electric heat, Jerry's job was to deliver coal for the neighbors. While he was there, many invited him over for sweet-potato pie while listening to some down-home music. The scrawny Jewish kid learned the exotic rhythms of jazz and blues music, which later infused his own writing.

"Out of necessity, I had a very strong work ethic very early," says Jerry. "I didn't worry about rejection. Rejection? A parent's death is the biggest rejection. Nothing compares. A parent's death, it's such a shock, such a loss, but it plays both sides of the coin. On one hand, you have this trauma and sense of loss; on the other hand, there's this sense of liberation and freedom. You do what you want. There was no one around to inhibit me or tell me what to do because my mother was so consumed with trying to get food on the table. How else would I have been hanging out listening to this music, which later made my career?"

Without the bosom of a strong traditional family, these children are also willing to take risks and leave their communities in hopes of a better life. Conversely, people who have had happier homes, homes that represent safety and security, are sometimes loath to move away or endure hardships with long stretches of time on the road.

To a child of loss, there is no such thing as "women's work" or "men's work" in this radically altered family paradigm. As a result, the children aren't handcuffed by traditional gender expectations and can become extremely competent.

Singer Shania Twain understands the growth experience of loss intimately. When her parents were killed in a head-on collision with a logging truck, the twenty-one-year-old college student was forced to quit school and return home to take care of her younger sister and brother.

"I was so overwhelmed with decisions," says Twain. "I had to deal with my parents' mortgage, and I didn't even know what a mortgage was. But what I learned through all of that was how strong I was, how strong I was capable of being. I didn't fall apart. I kept it together, paid the bills, took care of the kids, did the groceries, cooked and cleaned and still kept a job. I always had a feeling things would work out. I still feel that way about life."

Madonna also wasn't muzzled by the expected female gender roles reinforced by a traditional two-parent home. Since her mother died when she was five, Madonna didn't have a mother saying, "Dear, you don't talk to people like that." Instead, she grew up in a home where she could define her own role of what a woman should be without the shadow of her mother's expectations. That's why I was so intrigued when Madonna was asked what her mother's death had done for her.

"In a way, it has made me very motivated," she said. "Her death fueled my ambition."

Unlike their peers, the music of Madonna and Shania is infused with a profeminist sensibility, where they love men—or leave them— on their own terms.

Another example is Marie Curie. Her mother died when she was a child, leaving her to be raised by her father. The father's influence became the dominant force and his love of physics, math and biology were all passed on to his daughter. Marie Curie would later become the first woman to win two Nobel prizes. Yet when she decided to pursue science, it was not as bold a move as it would have been for someone reared in a traditional home where feminine roles were narrowly defined. Nor was she locked into one way of thinking because she had already witnessed different approaches to the family structure.

This also applies to men.

Tom Monahan, the billionaire founder of Domino's pizza, was placed in an orphanage by his father after his mother's death. Growing up, he describes himself as "a dreamer" who would play out all sorts of scenarios in his mind of how life could be. Later, when he worked in a pizzeria, he realized that customers wanted delivery but companies were resistant because it was considered demeaning drudge work. Not for Tom. "I thought of how it could work and made it happen," he said. "I got rid of all the tables and chairs to make room for the delivery system. I did everything. I just had this inner belief it would work. And the determination to make sure it did."

Research reveals that loss is often a springboard for careers in public service as children who suffered the deaths of a loved one validate their anger by wanting to right the wrong, or change destiny. They are determined not to feel powerless ever again.

Florence Nightingale transformed her feelings of helplessness caused by her father's death by taking charge. She changed her lot in life by becoming the person who eased suffering and gave comfort to soldiers during the Crimean War. Many believe it was the death of her little boy, Charley, that fortified Harriet Tubman and gave her the strength and passion to start the Underground Railroad during the Civil War era, which gave slaves a route to freedom. After living through the loss of her child, no risk seemed too great. Years later, Carolyn McCarthy's story echoes the same theme. Carolyn was a surburban housewife. After her husband was killed and her son wounded by a crazed gunman, she became an outspoken advocate of gun control. Her relentless campaign led her into politics, where she won a congressional seat from Queens, New York. She is now one of the nation's leading voices against the powerful NRA and has been instrumental in legislating gun control.

Persistence, patience and a willingness to endure discomfort for a greater good are all skills developed from the bereavement period, which later can be summoned to help build empires of lasting influence.

This fraternity of grievers also includes many philosophers and poets. Fyodor Dostoyevsky, who lost his mother at fifteen and his father two years later, came to believe that "suffering is the sole origin of consciousness."

Indeed, naturalist Charles Darwin's theory of "survival of the fittest" may be rooted in his ability to adapt to loss and disappointment, which according to psychologists is the time that someone is tested and their true character is revealed. Darwin's mother died when he was eight.

The saying goes that to be a philosopher, one must have graduated from the school of hard knocks. It is no secret that suffering ignites reflection. Someone whose world remains tranquil is not as likely to ponder the mysteries of life and death passionately for answers.

Gandhi, whose father died when he was fifteen, preached pacifism and helped liberate India. Both Mohammed's and Confucius' fathers died when they were babies, and Buddha's mother died in childbirth. Sartre, whose mother died when he was two, became a leading exponent of existentialism.

Transformative growth can happen at any age. Howard Rubenstein, the czar of public relations and the man known as Mr. Fix-It for clients ranging from George Steinbrenner, Sarah Ferguson and major hospitals and universities, endured four long years of his son's terminal disease. Diagnosed with an inoperable brain tumor, Howard had to cheer up the young child and remain stoic while his heart was breaking. "After David's death, I buried myself in work. Work can be a salvation," he recalls. "In my business, it has been helpful to remain calm in a crisis situation. This experience may have been what taught me to do this." Donald Trump's late brother Fred Jr. struggled with alcoholism. "Because my brother had this problem, I don't drink," Trump told me. "In fact, Fred told me not to drink and I never have." To combat the silence and stigma attached to suicide, Nevada Senator Harry Reid spoke in front of Congress about his father's death, opening the floodgates for others to share their stories and turning him into a role model.

Time and time again, survivors have also spoken about how loss has given them an iron will to pursue their own interests without worrying about social conventions or peer expectations. For example, many people questioned Pulitzer-prize winning author Anna Quindlen's decision to give up a coveted column in the *New York Times* to become a novelist. "Lots of readers couldn't understand why I would give up a public forum for a quieter, more private one," she said. "The answer was simple. I wanted to. I knew to do what I wanted, when I wanted, because I know today is the only certainty I possess. I'm pretty sure I'll be a woman who'll die without regrets. My mother left me that along with her engagement ring."

Yet for some, loss is not always redemptive. Many artists, scientists, writers, business and political leaders never seem satisfied and continue to pursue their grand ambitions at great personal sacrifice. Nothing is ever enough.

Dr. George Pollack, who also found a link between loss and greatness in his study, suggests that because their art never quite fills the void of the loss, the artist must continually "begin again" and rebuild empires. "New failures accompanied by feelings of incompleteness will follow new attempts at restitution and re-creation," he says. "The failures cannot be canceled except by the product of a new creation, and it is thus that work always continues, without respite, in that quest for immortality which creation promises." But it never delivers.

As a result, many become workaholics, people who are consumed by their art or business, often at the expense of their personal lives, which inevitably take a backseat to this unrelenting desire to achieve at all costs.

"The command control quality is not that healthy in the long term," acknowledges banker Jimmy Lee. "I worked eighteen-hour days for most of my career, but have missed many of my children's school events. What I have learned now is that I need more of a balance."

What is also spurring this reflection is Jimmy Lee's age. He is now forty-seven, the same age at which his father died. To him, he's beaten the odds. The scorecard of his success was always gauged by the mortality of his father. Could he achieve before he reached that goal post? This is a common occurrence in those who have lost a parent early in life. A study by Columbia researcher Veronika Denes-Rag, whose father died in her childhood, confirmed that children of loss believed they would die several years before their parent's age at death. "People whose parents die young fall into two categories," says Denes-Rag. "One child says, 'I will die young, therefore I have to do everything that is important to me in a shorter period of time.' They become high achievers and very assertive toward their goals. The other says, 'I will die young, so why bother?' Very few fall in between."

Malcolm Glazer says he cleans off his desk every day because he's never sure if it will be his last. This lingering concern over his mortality has motivated him to teach his six children at a very young age all aspects of his business. "I've always lived with the knowledge that you can go tomorrow and I don't want any unfinished business," he says. "I didn't want them to ever wonder what I would have done or thought about anything." Furthermore, his loss gave him the impetus to groom his successors, which many successful businessmen often avoid to disastrous results.

It is not only loss that sparks greatness. Ultimately, a child's internal wiring will create their future calling. "My father's death when I was a child had a profound impact on me," said playwright Tom Stoppard. "But my brother can't write a lick. How do you explain that?"

In the same way that fireworks explode and light up the sky, a loss can ignite the psyche to expand and do things we otherwise never would have dreamed of doing. However, this doesn't mean that someone who can hardly draw a stick figure will suddenly become Michelangelo or that severe loss means one is destined for the White House. All three Brontë sisters became acclaimed writers, but their brother Patrick was a ne'er-do-well who died of alcoholism. "The latent talent must already exist deep within," says Dr. Eisenstadt. "But what the loss does is trigger it and give it life."

As the next chapter will explore, this burst of activity can be highly meaningful, even if it's not channeled in the political, artistic or scientific fields.

16

⁓

I Will Remember You

In Peoria, Illinois, in the year 1982, thirty-three-year-old Nancy Brinker sat vigil by the bedside of her thirty-year-old sister, Suzy, who was wasting away from breast cancer. "I remember her looking at me and saying, 'Nancy, when I get better, help me find a cure for this disease so others won't have to suffer. Promise me.' Suzy never did get better, and I was left with this promise to keep," sighs Nancy, recalling the moment so long ago that inspired her to start the Susan G. Komen Breast Cancer Foundation in her sister's honor. Now a world-renowned grassroots organization with 35,000 volunteers in 117 affiliates across the United States, South America and Europe, it has raised millions for breast cancer research.

Echoing the sentiments of many, Nancy says pouring her energies into the foundation helped turn her sense of helplessness into empowerment. These results happen so often, and are so restorative, that therapists are now recommending charity work as a form of therapy because it helps people turn from victim to helper.

In fact, such pursuits are actually good for your health—yet another bonus. Many studies confirm that the immune system—which often suffers from intense, agonizing grief—is actually boosted by altruism.

Scientists at the University of Michigan studied 2,754 people for twelve years. They discovered that men who did volunteer work at least once a week are two-and-a-half times more likely to live longer than those who didn't. Other research by Dr. Paul Pearsall, author of *Super Joy*, found that when a person helps other people, he experiences an immediate biochemical response that enhances his immune system. "Pay attention to how your body reacts when you help someone," he says. "You will feel actual positive changes taking place in the body."

So where does someone begin to help others?

For Nancy Brinker, her first step was to research the disease that had ripped her life apart. Because only a fraction of cancer research money was funneled into breast cancer, she knew there wasn't a possibility for a cure. Her mission, she decided, was to highlight how this silent killer affected millions.

Late at night, surrounded by legal pads and coffee cups, she began calling up friends, acquaintances and colleagues to build a database to help raise money and outrage. During the day, she got blisters knocking at the doors of corporations to donate funds, often getting doors slammed in her face. "If you want to change the world, prepare for rejection and failure," advises Nancy. "It takes the two p's—patience and perseverance. But loss and anger are great motivators. I just got up and kept going. You have to quantify what you're going to do and take it step by step."

Among the many fund-raisers she devised was the annual Komen Race for the Cure run, which has grown from eight hundred participants to over a million people across the country.

When Nancy was in the trenches, other more high-profile people were joining the ranks. After surviving breast cancer, cosmetics queen Estée Lauder readily agreed to the suggestion of her friend Alexandra Penny that she distribute pink ribbons at Estée Lauder counters to raise awareness. Lily Tartikoff, widow of the beloved TV executive Brandon Tartikoff, emerged from her ordeal a cancer activist. Thanks to her bulging Rolodex and popularity with big-name stars, she raised enough funds to support the research of

Dr. Dennis Slamon, who developed the life-saving breast-cancer drug, Herceptin.

Breast cancer awareness truly hit the jackpot when Rosie O'Donnell started her own crusade. "October is Breast Cancer Awareness month, and I want women to go out there for a mammogram," the talk-show celebrity urged her audience, sounding both like Ma Barker and Mother Goose. "Send me a receipt, and I'll send you a 'Don't be a Boob' T-shirt." Each day throughout October, O'Donnell, whose mother died of breast cancer, devotes a segment to raising awareness. Behind the scenes, she also funded a store in New York Hospital to provide state-of-the-art wigs for women undergoing chemotherapy, since the emotional pain of losing one's hair is often more difficult than the physical treatments.

Thanks to all these layers of activism, the National Institutes of Health has devoted $475 million to breast-cancer research, a supersonic jump from years ago when breast cancer was hardly funded.

However, don't forget that plenty of people, people like Nancy, started many a foundation sitting around the kitchen table. You, too, can make a difference. If you want to start a foundation or charity in your loved one's honor, here's where to start.

Getting your event noticed

For grassroots organizations, radio stations are the first line of attack because they are more receptive to community-based concerns. Most stations have public affairs directors who collect fund-raiser information. John Bell of New York's Z-100, says, "It's important that people have the event already planned. Radio stations are not great organizers of events. We can, though, be very helpful in publicizing an event and getting folks to it."

Although some take information over the phone, the best approach is to write a brief description of the event containing the five w's—who, what, where, when and why—and then fax it, calling a day later to follow up. Most stations will tell you whether your pitch will be picked up.

A sample press release could be as simple as "Dear John, My

brother died in an automobile accident, and we are hosting a fund-raising dinner in his honor on February 21. The money is going for a scholarship program at the school (name the school). Could you mention something on the air? We'd really appreciate it." Other press releases are more elaborate with detailed information on how many people may have been killed in car crashes due to drunk driving and how this fund-raiser is designed to educate students on the perils of drinking and driving.

Generally, deejays want to promote events whose funds are funneled into scholarships, day-care centers, local baseball teams or a recreation facility. "A cause to help defray funeral costs won't get as good of a response," adds Bell.

Newspaper columnists usually answer their own phones so you can also call up local columnists and make a pitch. If a reporter isn't interested, he may direct you to someone else who would be more receptive. Even if he takes a pass, don't give up. Keep up a relationship. Ask him what would make him more interested in the story.

Gimmicks also work. Come up with a clever concept. Offer to cook dinner in a different house each week for radio listeners who will donate money to your cause. Ask a school to create an art project—a painting, sculpture or collage—and hold an auction. Covering the launch of the David Letterman show, I remember one publicity-seeking woman stood outside with an enormous sculpture of Letterman's head—carved out of butter. All the news stations picked up on it. These kinds of enterprising ideas can be applied to your charity.

Bring an oversize cake to city hall with a sign that says, "It would be sweet if you would give funds to cancer research so my brother didn't die in vain." (Call all the news stations and newspapers first so the event can get covered.)

Or make a tape with an impassioned plea, " 'Tis the season to be good, we'd be so grateful if you would . . ." Send a letter with your grandmother's favorite recipe and then say, "I'm giving you one of my family's most treasured possessions. In return, could you help me . . ."

Journalists are far more receptive if they can feel the passion behind the cause versus receiving another form letter. "There's a charity event every day of the week," says Richard Johnson, the editor of the *New York Post*'s Page Six. "We usually only write about an event that stands out from the crowd."

Maintain your creativity and enthusiasm, but also be prepared for rejection. This is an uphill battle, especially if your cause doesn't impact millions of people. Audrey Lewis, head of Families of Spinal Muscular Atrophy, once had her family, including her seventeen-year-old son who suffers from SMA, climb a mountain in Colorado, and walk across the state of Illinois in the rain. Tom Duffy, the father of a nine-year-old with the disease, sat on a billboard (Beep if you care! Fight Spinal Muscular Atrophy Now!) for twenty-four hours in Scranton, Pennsylvania. The publicity stunt raised $28,000 but would have raised far more if a celebrity were involved. It is no secret that celebrities raise the profile of charities.

This is why some resourceful fund-raisers often besiege celebrities at stores, restaurants and even movie theaters asking them to donate coats, clothes and even a piece of paper with "a celebrity kiss" for a charity, which are used as items for an auction. Another option is a call to the star's publicist. Looking to contact Lisa Kudrow? Call up NBC and ask for the publicist for *Friends*.

"Celebrities, like everyone else, are more apt to help a charity which has touched them directly, or someone they know," says veteran publicist Nancy Haberman, executive vice president at New York's high-powered Rubinstein Associates. "It's a very human reaction to reach out and connect with a cause that affects you directly."

For example, following the death of her nineteen-year-old sister Heather from lupus, former *ER* star Kellie Martin became the national spokesperson of the American Autoimmune Related Diseases Association and is lobbying Congress to pass a bill to create an institute to find a cure.

"I can't imagine anything worse that losing a sister, because that person is supposed to be your best friend all your life," says Martin, explaining her commitment. "I want to make sure that what happened to my family doesn't happen to anyone else."

There are L.A.-based companies like the Entertainment Industry Foundation, which links stars with causes. However, you can also pay attention to news reports, tune in to entertainment programs and read *People* and the gossip pages. For example, Mary Tyler Moore helps juvenile diabetes, while *Frasier* star David Hyde Pierce and Angie Dickinson help Alzheimer's causes, because a family member was afflicted.

Also monitor what is taking place in the news. I'll never forget working at *Nightline* early in my career when a little girl named Jamie Fiske was looking for a kidney transplant. Her father held a press conference to make an appeal. Because it was a slow news day, the story got immense coverage. If a major news event is taking place, your story will become low priority. So be strategic. Timing is everything when you make your pitch.

If a news report reveals that a news maker is suffering from a disease, also call the media and offer to speak as a regular citizen who is impacted by the disease. Journalists often want to round out coverage with more than one person who's affected.

Overall, radio and newspapers still produce more bull's-eyes. Deejays have endless hours of airtime and newspapers have empty pages to fill, so these outlets are better options than television, which rarely covers local charities.

Sometimes, but not always, a noncelebrity story does receive coverage from both the national and international press, especially when the story reflects the best of the human spirit and touches the public in a profound and lasting way.

When Reg and Maggie Green's seven-year-old son, Nicholas, was shot and killed by would-be robbers during a family vacation in Italy in 1994, the California couple donated his organs to Italians in need of transplants. In a country with one of the lowest organ-donation rates, the gesture touched the nation deeply. The story made headlines all over the world.

"I remember saying to someone at the time that I wanted to squeeze the last drop of good out of this miserable affair," recalls Reg. "I was advised to think of it as a trickle turning into a stream. And that is how I do think of it now. We never expected one act of love could have such an impact."

Yet, it has. In the years following Nicholas's death, organ donation in Italy has quadrupled. Reg, a publisher of a mutual-fund newsletter, and his wife, Maggie, have now become international spokespeople for organ donation, giving lectures around the world. Their Nicholas Green Foundation now helps train Italian doctors in transplant surgery.

"The loss of Nicholas doesn't go away; it's there always, a kind of weight in the heart," says Maggie. But what they've also learned is that the act of giving in the face of grief brings other rewards.

People write to tell Maggie that if it wasn't for her generous example they would have died without a donor organ. Others send her paintings, sculptures and gooey homemade chocolate cakes, which the couple views as a testament that the world is still populated by good and decent people.

"Nicholas's death brought people all over the world closer and saved thousands of lives," says Reg. "I remember afterward, one of Nicholas's teachers told us that he was the most giving child she had ever met, that he would probably have done something quite remarkable. On the other hand, he did."

That's a sentiment John Walsh shares. In the summer of 1981, Walsh was a partner in a hotel management company in Hollywood, Florida. "You would hear about horrible things on the news, but you never thought it would happen to you," recalls John.

However, the horrible happened, shattering his family's comfortable carefree life. In July of 1987, their son Adam was abducted and later murdered. Frantically searching for him, the Walshes were stunned by the bureaucratic ineptitude at finding missing children and the lack of resources available for the search. "We were normal people who were anguished by the injustice of it all," he says, his voice tensing at the memory. The loss invaded every pore, ripening thoughts of unspeakable revenge and causing scorching pain that literally melted thirty pounds off his body. Yet instead of remaining victims, the couple channeled their rage into launching the National Center for Missing and Exploited Children, and their efforts later resulted in the Missing Children's Act.

"What was needed at the time was a nerve center to track down people because often all an abductor had to do was cross a state line, and they were free and clear," says John. "There was no cooperation between all the police forces." Soon Walsh's crusade attracted national attention and mounting public support.

Later he started *America's Most Wanted*, now seen in forty-five countries, a show that he describes as "the public's last resort." Since the inception of *America's Most Wanted*, almost six hundred criminals have been caught, making him the favorite friend of law enforcement agencies around the world.

"All this is for the love of a little boy and because of the hurt we were feeling," says John, now the father of three children. "People like us used to be invisible. Now we're not. More and more people are standing up. My son didn't die in vain. For our own healing, we had to make sense of it somehow, and find some way to right the wrong."

However, Walsh wisely advises that starting a charity is not always the best course. Because launching a charity often requires a full-time commitment of round-the-clock work, he suggests joining an existing charity, testifying in front of Congress or simply marching in rallies. Many people have also effectively started charities on a smaller scale.

After his daughter died, Chris Lacey wanted to help neighboring families defray some of the expensive hospital costs of their children. The owner of Side Street Saloon, a Staten Island, New York, restaurant, he spoke to other restaurant owners to help organize events to help raise funds, ranging from baseball or basketball outings to in-house dinners for families in need.

"We're not the high earners of the world but little by little, each donation does add up," he says. "The community has been so generous, and we've been able to raise $20,000 for each family."

For a good cause, many stores may offer discounts on T-shirts, graphic artists can donate their time for posters and community members can send out faxes or call other people in the neighborhood. Because there's so little overhead, all the money does go to the families. "I can relate to what they're going through," says Chris. "I would have really appreciated this help." Furthermore, because it's a local effort, Chris doesn't have to concern himself with the bureaucratic headaches of starting a national organization.

Experts say the biggest mistake well-intentioned people make is failing to figure out whether a new charity is really needed. You will save considerable headaches and bureaucratic hassles by joining an existing charity that could benefit immediately from your help. To give you an idea of how many already exist, in 1995, more than

67,000 groups applied to the IRS for charity certification, a clearance that enables the charity to solicit foundation grants.

If your cause isn't already championed elsewhere, and you still want to start a national organization, here's what to do. First, you must certify your charity, and create a mission statement before your organization takes the legal steps to become a charity. The mission statement should explain the group's goals, by which means donors, watchdog groups and government oversight agencies will measure the charity's performance.

To gain legal authority to operate a tax-exempt charity, you must become legally incorporated and apply to the IRS for charity status. Charities that solicit donations are often required to file forms with state and local entities. And after a charity has been operating for a year, it needs to file an informational tax return describing its activities and finances to the IRS.

You'll also have to draft a business plan and have experienced people advising you. A board of directors—from four to twelve people—must also be organized.

And last, but not least, you'll need a steady stream of funds to support your cause and the upkeep of an office.

"Nonprofits don't fail because they didn't have a great idea or they weren't trying to do good in the world," observes Jude Kaye, senior staff consultant at the Support Centers of America in San Francisco. "They fail because they ran out of money to pay their bills or they didn't file the proper forms."

To use your time efficiently, contact these organizations, which can help beginners maneuver many minefields.

- www.nonprofits.org/library/gov/urs
- American Association of Fund-Raising Counsel
  212-354-5799 ext. 3007
- National Council of Nonprofit Associations
  202-833-5740
- National Federation of Nonprofits
  202-347-0929
- National Society of Fund-Raising Executives
  703-684-0410 ext. 458

Some people's involvement in charities turns into a lifelong project, while others become involved for a shorter time. Any effort enhances the healing process. After Candy Lightner's daughter was killed by a drunken driver who had been accused of three other drunk-driving accidents, she turned her rage into action and formed Mothers Against Drunk Driving, (MADD), a nationwide network of activists who lobbied federal legislators to change the drinking age from eighteen to twenty-one.

Her work ignited a movement that has evolved into a public consciousness of drinking and driving, seen in TV shows and movies, public service announcements and news reports. Drunk-driving deaths have dramatically decreased since the group was launched. But Lightner decided to leave the organization in 1985, tired of dealing with "victim's issues" because it can be "sad and depressing."

A similar situation occurred with Gene Wilder, the husband of the late Gilda Radner. After the *Saturday Night Live* star died of ovarian cancer, Wilder and a group of Gilda's friends started Gilda's Club, a meeting place for those with cancer. The multilayered program, says executive director Joanna Bull, incorporates everything from "the camaraderie of a potluck supper or the silliness of a joke fest with a first-prize rubber chicken, to information about body relaxation workshops to radiologists visiting to give lectures."

Started in 1991, the wellness program at Gilda's Club has been such a comfort to so many that there's now interest in it from Europe, the Middle East and the Carribean. However, having left a legacy for Gilda, Wilder no longer works with this very special program. "He says he retired from medicine," explains Joanna Bull.

Both Lightner and Wilder did what was right for them. You have to know when your own emotional tank is on empty. They both channeled their anguish and produced glorious results that honored the memory of their loved one. Sometimes, long-term involvement fills up the soul; other times, people need to pursue other interests.

Mentoring is another option, because helping someone else gives the griever a new perspective on their loss, and this doesn't have to be as time-consuming as starting a charity.

"When survivors speak out, they must go back and relive the experience, although on a different level, with a new sense of perspective," observes Massachusetts therapist Dr. Al Siebert. "They no longer feel emotionally wounded when their minds go back. Thus, they are able to willingly help others so that what they went through has meaning and purpose."

Heidi Snow, whose boyfriend was killed in a plane crash, started ACCESS (AirCraft Casualty Emotional Support Services), a grass-roots organization where people who lost a loved one in a plane crash counsel others facing the same crisis.

Serving as a grief mentor enables someone to turn from victim to helper. ACCESS, like other grassroots organizations, helps victims deal with shock, anger and the anguish of waiting for exhaustive searches and recovery efforts, which rarely yield any real answers to guide people through their emotional trauma.

"I basically knew what others were feeling, that feeling of over-whelming numbness and not knowing how to take those initial baby steps," said Martha, whose husband perished on the TWA flight that blew up over Long Island. She believes the message these survivors can convey to others is that "there is still joy and there is still love, and the world is going around and you can learn to reinvent your-self." Elise Richman wishes someone had guided her to charity work earlier. "My sister was with my father when he was murdered and she committed suicide three years later," says Elise. "I never had an outlet for my grief and anger until twenty-four years later when I joined the Million Mom March. It has helped me so dramatically to help this cause."

Dr. Therese Rando, clinical director of the Institute for the Study and Treatment of Loss in Warwick, Rhode Island, says these efforts can be therapeutic. "They allow a person who has been through it to go back and make a difference and help someone else," she says.

There are also many other ways to honor the memory of a loved one and feel good doing it.

- Create art: In Sarajevo, in an effort to turn destruction into beauty, artists polished and carved intricate designs on mortar shells that fell on their city. These bullet shells are now used as small bud vases for flowers, or just as a reminder of the fragile line between war and peace. One of these beautiful bullet shells now sits on my desk.

- Paint a house: Ernie Cote, who runs Compadres, a volunteer big brother program at the Wesley Rankin Community Center in Dallas, helped friends organize a memorial service for fourteen-year-old Sammy Salazar, who had been killed in a drive-by shooting. He also encouraged Sammy's friends as a community service to spend three days making improvements on his mother's home, which helped the kids feel useful.

- Donate a bench where someone dear liked to be: Even a simple gesture of erecting a bench on a school campus can be a comfort to those who miss a friend and schoolmate. Rippowam Cisqua School in Bedford, New York, created a wooden bench on a grassy knoll where kids hang out in tribute to Gillian Roth, a student who died in a car crash. Some teachers encourage kids to write poems or songs about their loved one, to encourage both resolution and an outlet for their emotional pain. I know another family who took the ashes of their son and mixed them with cement to create a bench at his favorite park.

- Invite a deceased friend's child over for the weekend, or send them a memento of their loved one: On many Saturday nights, Annabel has what she describes as "sleepover dates" with seven-year-old Olivia. She fills Olivia's head with stories about her mother, Karen. Stories about how they bumped into each other as overly ambitious typists, stories about the killer miniskirts her mother favored, stories about her mother's heroic battles climbing the corporate ladder.

"I tell her what I remember and what I loved," says Annabel. "But I also try not to mythologize her. Olivia needs to know that her mother wasn't perfect so that she will feel she can make mistakes too. What I often tell her, and what she needs to hear, is how much her mother loved her. I can never tell her that enough."

"At first, I was afraid that my memory of Karen was going to slip away as it had with other people who have been close to me. You so want the glue to hold it together. That's what these Saturday nights are, the glue. It's so fulfilling for me. Talking about Karen makes her presence real to me, makes me feel that my best friend is with me. It's good for her, and it's good for me."

Carol Higgins Clark remembers busily scribbling her signature at a book-signing event in Palm Beach, Florida, when a smartly dressed older woman approached her. "You're Warren Clark's daughter, aren't you?" she asked. Carol's heart skipped a beat. It was rare that someone had referred to her as "Warren Clark's daughter" and this acclaimed mystery writer was intrigued.

"Why, yes, I am," said Carol tentatively.

Pulling a piece of paper from her charcoal leather purse, the woman handed it to the author. "This was written to me by your father long before he married your mother, when I was dating his friend Frank," she said. "I thought you'd like to have it."

The letter was written in 1938 when her father was in college in Alabama, and reads in part, "You ought to have some fun with this letter. Just show Frank the envelope and let him guess what I wrote. I'll write him and tell him that I gave you the 'low-down' on him and that I told you everything about him."

Gingerly touching the letter, Carol quietly admits that this is one of her most treasured possessions.

"I've been told I'm like my father, and that he had a great sense of humor," says Carol. "He was nineteen years old when he wrote this letter. Even though I was only eight when he died, I do remember his sense of humor. When I read the letter, I'm reminded of what he was like and it makes me feel good."

I remember visiting the Vietnam Memorial and seeing a family wistfully touching the engraved name of a fallen son, high on the black granite tribute. Tears were running down the mother's cheek, and a younger son hugged her close to him. I observed other families following the same ritual. At one point the families gingerly looked at each other, their eyes locked together for a split second, magnetically drawn together by their mutual loss, each silently acknowledging how the power and beauty of this memorial was providing a window to their loved ones. Memorials can be created on a small scale. One family erected a beautiful sculpture on their front lawn.

You don't have to be a star to put your hands in cement like they do at Mann's Chinese Theater in Hollywood. One family had an ailing father make a hand impression into a block of cement that was put in front of the walkway to their home.

In Mount Kisco, New York, little kids in Gap jeans play tag on the playground of Jenny's School for Children, a popular spot for toddlers. Though it is named for Jenny, she never lived to see it. Her love of children inspired her parents to create the tiny school after their daughter died in a car crash at eighteen. She is buried in the back of the school next to a bench. Her kind spirit, it is said, fills the school with goodwill and good luck.

Linda Bloodworth-Thomason, the writer of such megahits as *Designing Women*, has started a mentoring program in her hometown of Poplar Bluff, Missouri. Named after her mother, a champion of female education who had died of AIDS from a transfusion of contaminated blood during a routine heart operation, Linda has now helped 102 girls from abusive homes get scholarships. She not only provides the funds, but is a mentor to the girls who often visit her home. "The Claudia Foundation has also started a mentoring program where English teachers work with various people in the community to give them an expertise, and they help teach kids the classics," says Linda. "One woman who works at JCPenney is the town expert on F. Scott Fitzgerald. My mother would be so proud, and these efforts make me feel closer to her."

Create a birthing room in someone's honor. When Parker was born, I was stationed in a special birthing room at Mt. Sinai Hospital named after Jonathan Levin. It was a peach-colored room with a big open window facing Central Park where those in labor can be distracted by a lush landscape of maple trees lining Fifth Avenue.

My husband set up a boom box to play boy-oriented tunes that a friend had compiled to welcome my son into the world, songs like Paul McCartney's "Young Boy," John Lennon's "Beautiful Boy," Bonnie Raitt's "Baby of Mine" and the Four Seasons' "Walk Like a Man." All were playing when a complication developed. I contracted a raging fever during the long labor and a cesarean would have been too life-threatening to perform. Parker's heartbeat had soared to 210 instead of the normal range of 160, and the doctors had to deliver by forceps. "Don't move," Dr. Michael Plotnick ordered.

For some reason, knowing that this room was a tribute to someone special gave me comfort and enabled me to be calm in a crisis situation. Parker Leon was one of the first births in this room.

I'll also never forget the kindness of Lisa White, a girl I didn't know well, but who gave me the most memorable gift following my father's death. Her note read "In memory of your father, a tree has been planted in Israel." Planting a tree that will grow over time is a wonderful gift. I sometimes look outside and see the dense foliage on the trees that surround our house and think how these trees have been here for hundreds of years and that somewhere far away, a tree now grows in my father's name. I wish I could have this tree near my house, but I know it exists elsewhere.

Give a scholarship in honor of someone you love. Steve Sussman, founder of the legendary Texas law firm Sussman & Godfrey, will never forget the kindness of his father's Yale classmates. After his father died when he was eight, his dad's friends combined forces and promised to pay for Steve's and his brother's college tuitions. "This gift inspired me to work hard so I could attend Yale," he says. "Now all my children as well as my brother's kids have also gone to Yale. It will always be a very special place for us." There are many variations on this theme. For example, if your friend liked literature, launch an annual award at a school in his or her name for a student who wins a contest for creative writing. These scholarships do not have to break the bank. They are simply a way to link your loved one to a pursuit they cared about and continue this legacy throughout time.

Sometimes late at night, I'll look heavenward and think about what C. S. Lewis wrote about his wife in *A Grief Observed*. "I look up at the night sky. Is anything more certain than that in all those vast times and spaces? If I were allowed to search them, I should know where to find her face, her voice, her touch."

Today, Lewis could find the star and even name one after his wife.

When Parker was born, my friend Christina purchased the most unusual but memorable gift—a star named after Parker. Based in Switzerland, the International Star Registry assigns a star in honor of the person and gives you a map of where the star is located in the sky. The Registry can be reached at 1-800-282-3333.

This is yet another way to remember, to give your loved one immortality and give yourself comfort in feeling their presence always. In a 1974 study, Dr. Joseph Bess and Gene Bartlett wrote, "In whatever form it may appear, the outlet for our sorrow often may be ministering to the wider needs of the world or in the unending battle against injustices. The question becomes, Where do I use the passion of my grief?"

Memorials and charities are worthwhile endeavors to channel these passions and make the world a better place.

17

Buried Treasure: How to Start a Family Genealogy

As the plane took off, Mary inhaled deeply. Well, this is going to be quite the adventure, she thought. Her sister Maureen squeezed her hand softly, acknowledging the unspoken. With their hectic work schedules and child-care demands, this annual get-together was normally spent hiking in the mountains or basking in the sun at a summer resort.

However, this trip was going to be different. They were heading to a remote place in England outside Darwen, a place so small that it was a mere speck on a map. Only thirty thousand people lived in this working-class district where small two-story houses dotted the hilly landscape.

Ever since their father had suddenly died two years ago, Mary had been filled with remorse. At first she shrugged it off as a normal reaction to loss. Then as time went on, she realized it was something more. It wasn't only loss but regret. "He had been an orphan and never told us much about his life," says Mary. "I felt like I really didn't know him."

The purpose of this trip was to see the old haunts of James

Entswhistle, and to fill in the gaps about their father's life and hope-fully get to know him better.

As soon as they arrived, Mary walked down the narrow cobble-stone streets and felt inexplicably close to her father. She brushed her fingers over the stone buildings, as though her father's finger-prints were indelibly printed on the rough knotted surface. Some older storeowners remembered their father, and the sisters were mesmerized by every mundane detail. Going to the town hall, they also found records of their family—marriages, births, deaths and deeds to houses.

The whole process started to feel like a treasure hunt, and in a way it was, since mapping out the trajectory of their father's life be-came a game, a game where each clue led to a new discovery.

The vacation was the starting point that led them to research their family genealogy by reading books and using the Internet to track down clues to the past. Mary also summoned the courage to start calling the names in her father's worn leather phone book, of people who could tell them stories about their father.

"It's been a wonderful project," says Mary. "It's brought the whole family closer."

This is a sentiment felt by many grievers. Often the pursuit of mapping a family tree is driven by health reasons after a loved one has died. At the local genealogical society, I ran into a stylishly at-tired woman in Burberry tweed who was busy rummaging through the death records of distant relatives. "I am trying to determine fur-ther links between my mother's breast cancer and other family mem-bers down the line," says Ann soberly. "I've discovered that breast cancer has been in my family for many generations. This information can save not only our lives, but our children's, because we'll all be more vigilant in getting checkups."

Michael LeClerc noticed that many males in his family had died young and started investigating his roots to find a pattern. "It con-firmed my worst fears," he says. "The males in my family died at fifty-four, forty-two and sixty-one. But this knowledge has been lib-erating because it forced me to look at each day as a gift." The joy he found in becoming a modern-day Sherlock Holmes while hunting down clues also inspired him to leave his previous sales job and become a professional genealogist. LeClerc is now the reference librarian at the New England Historical Genealogical Society.

Cyndi Howells really appreciated her expertise in genealogy when she was struggling with infertility. "It became like therapy for me," says the force behind Cyndi's list, a must-read Internet stop that includes more than 80,000 genealogical sites worldwide, covering everything from ships' passenger lists to starting tips. "Even though at the time I wasn't able to have a child, I became connected to a larger family. I later learned that infertility ran in my family. When things go bad for me, genealogy puts things in perspective. My grandmother lived in a dirt house on the soddy plains of North Dakota. Another relative was a prisoner in the Confederate Army. Meanwhile, I have a microwave, a home and a husband. Life doesn't seem so bad."

Richard, a seventy-two-year-old widower I met on the Internet, just wanted a hobby to occupy his time after his wife of forty-six years died. "I did it strictly for the therapeutic value of having a distraction," he says. "It's a hobby that required concentration to do the research. I started looking into my wife's family. It did make me get to know her family better even though we had been married forty-six years. Pretty soon I knew more about their family than they did."

An unexpected perk to all this research was a surge in his popularity at family events. For grieving people, genealogy can be helpful in relieving loneliness and providing a lifeline to family members. Thanks to this prized information, younger family members were suddenly interested in what Grandpa Richard had to say, especially now that he could weave tales about colorful characters from the family's past, including those about a legendary crook.

"We used to think of him as the cranky guy who couldn't find the remote control," said one great-niece. "But now when we visit, he tells us these stories and shows us all these old papers and trunks of documents, and it's all so interesting." Mark Myers, a successful computer executive, also found that learning about his past gave him a heightened appreciation for older family members. "My generation thinks they're so smart, making million-dollar deals," he says. "Well, maybe my ancestors weren't as educated, but I feel grateful that they got the hell out of eastern Europe. Someone had to have the balls to take this voyage. I never transferred anyone across an ocean. You now want to thank your ancestors for making the choice that affected you so favorably."

Another reason for the surge in genealogy is that many people feel so disconnected from their immediate family. These days, instead of relatives living in the same city, providing support, babysitting duties and daily gossip, modern-day families are more like Kinko's, with a relative in every city. Compelled by the need for a sense of belonging, genealogy is helping restore to people a sense of their roots.

"A family tree is the most precious of gifts," says interior designer Victoria Hagan, whose grandparents crafted one as a Christmas present. "I am so happy for my sons that they now will have a history of my family's past. But I'm also sad that my husband Michael's family can't have one because so many have passed away without telling anyone their stories."

Yet even with skimpy information, anyone can still retrieve data and construct a family tree. First, do a little homework. You can buy a how-to book such as *Finding Your Roots: How to Trace Your Ancestors at Home and Abroad*, click on a Web site such as the National Genealogical Society at www.ngsgenealogy.org as well as the homespun but helpful www.cyndislist.com, which will also lead you to other sites. Or buy one of the many CD ROMs designed for novices such as the popular Family Tree Maker by Broderbund. Other options include taking a course on family history research, joining a genealogical club, or hiring a professional genealogist to map out your family tree.

Most local historical societies have lists of professional genealogists, as do Internet sites. Get friendly with the librarians at the societies or click on to chat sites, and they'll lead you to the genealogist best suited for your budget and family background. "Some genealogists are specialists in Hispanic families while others have an affinity for *Mayflower* descendants," explains Harry Macy, editor of the New York Genealogical Biographical Record. "For example, it requires different research if a Hispanic family came from Puerto

Rico or had roots in Mexico. A *Mayflower* family may have migrated to the West Coast or stayed in Massachusetts. But most qualified genealogists have the expertise to create histories that date back many generations."

Before starting, agree on a final budget and what you can expect at the end of the project from the genealogist. Prices range from twenty-five to seventy-five dollars an hour, and most require at least a ten-hour minimum. Adds Macy, "It becomes a lot less expensive if the person requesting the information also helps with the fact-finding."

For self-starters, determine where you will put the data. Whether you use the computer or go with the traditional route of note cards and three-ring binders, each fragile new twig on the family tree must be documented with notes on its source. Make sure you are organized in your filing system because paper will pile up as you collect all sorts of data ranging from death notices and house deeds to dusty military records.

The next step is to write down everything you know about your family. Afterward, it's time to "pick the brains of all living relatives, the oldest ones first," advises Hank Jones, a California-based genealogist and author of *Psychic Roots*. "Ask them about what they remember about their childhoods, who their relatives were and where they came from. What did the family cook for dinner? What did they do for fun?" Questions can include what each family member was like, how they made you feel, any interesting physical characteristics or hobbies, what illnesses affected the family and what places relatives moved to. Then visit those musty attics and comb through trunks and drawers for all documents including marriage certificates, death certificates, wills, family Bibles, land deeds, school records, military papers, as well as old pictures and letters. Invitations are also a telling clue because they will provide a mirror to the past, and invitation lists are often saved. Also speak with friends, colleagues, shopkeepers, waitresses or anyone who may have known your loved one.

If it's not sitting in a drawer or trunk, much of this information can be retrieved from a local branch of the National Archives as well as state archives and local historical societies. These are great starting points because they yield a treasure trove of information, including details such as listing everyone in the family by name, age, occupation and place of birth; whether the house was owned or rented; what language was spoken at home; and military records dating back to the Revolution along with individual pension records.

Clicking on to the Internet on any of the genealogical sites will also provide addresses where you can send away for this information, and they can direct you to sites that specialize in various documents from land deeds in Maine or Mozambique to death indexes and immigration records.

To flesh out the stories from these documents, genealogists suggest reading newspapers and periodicals to give a clearer picture of ancestors' lives. "When you see the tax records, compare them to others so that you can determine if the family was wealthy or poor for that era," says Michael LeClerc. "Let's say you find out that your great-great-grandfather came over from Italy in steerage to Ellis Island in 1890. Find out what conditions they lived through."

In searching for his beloved grandmother's roots after she died, Michael LeClerc combed through pension records and discovered that his grandfather had an uncle who had died in World War I. "His pension money was given to my grandfather and enabled him to buy a house," says Michael. "Growing up, there was always a picture of my grandfather next to this other man. Now I know he was the uncle who was responsible for helping my family."

In most cases the Web is a surefire winner when it comes to saving time and connecting with other genealogical sleuths. Years ago one could go blind searching through old phone books looking for people with the same last name. Today a click on the Web will locate all members of the family name. Then the technological filing system can narrow the focus by typing in ethnic indicators such as German, African-American or Brazilian.

Chat rooms are also a welcome source for comparing notes, research techniques, information and dead ends. Often immigrants slipped into countries under assumed identities or changed their names upon arrival. Many ethnic Web sites help maneuver these minefields ranging from www.Jewishgen.org, www.nypl.org/research/sc/sc.html

for African-American seekers to www.columbia.cu/libraries/indiv/ eastasia for those with Asian roots. Again, all major sites have detailed information categorized by ethnic groups, which makes the search far easier.

Be prepared for some stumbling blocks. "Sometimes records aren't as well preserved," warns Harry Macy. "You can go back in Italy to the fifteenth century but in Ireland, the Catholic Church didn't keep as meticulous records and you'd be lucky to get back to 1800." These snafus can be overcome but require more detective work and resourcefulness in finding other institutions that kept more revealing records.

Roger Friedman believed he had a lead in tracking down his grandmother's uncle Morris Marsden, in South Africa. "I e-mailed the Cape Town archives and the local libraries asking them to help in researching any Marsdens and British Jews who had immigrated there at the turn of the century. At first, I was thrilled that I had found the only two Marsdens in the area. Then we started e-mailing each other like old friends," says Friedman. "But later I discovered that we weren't related, though now I have new friends in South Africa."

After losing a loved one, it feels as though the world has shrunk. Yet genealogy expands one's scope. You can meet not only friends, but also relatives in far-flung places. "I've discovered thirty new cousins online," says genealogist Hank Jones. "I have a whole new family with whom I now correspond by e-mail." Dave Distler's genealogical voyage resulted in a trip to Germany. As was reported in a *Time* magazine article by Margot Hornblower, vague records indicated that his great-great-great-grandfather Friedrich Jakob Distler had either been born in 1814 in Germany, Prussia, Rhineland or Northern Bavaria. Surfing the Net, Dave found an organization called Palatines to America, which referred him to a German genealogist who found his grandfather's hometown, Hinterweidenthal. When he entered the village name in a search engine, he found a private e-mail address. Three weeks after e-mailing, he got a response from a local resident with the phone numbers of two Distler families in the town. In May of 1996, three New World and fourteen Old

World Distlers met at a cozy German inn to celebrate. "Old Uncle Fritz had told me about the mysterious Distlers who journeyed to the other side of the Atlantic," says Brigitte Schubert, a newfound German cousin. "I was so glad to sit behind Dave. I didn't want to let go of his hand."

The benefits to searching for one's roots are well documented by the millions of people now surfing the Web and busily researching deeds and documents at local historical societies. "If we do it right, you can bring the dead back to life," says Hank Jones, who became closer to his deceased father as a result of his genealogical search. "My father seemed very reserved and remote to me but through finding letters, tax records and talking to people, I learned that he was much more of a generous, giving man than I remembered. I got to know him in a totally new way."

Aside from discovering sentimental details of his father's life, he also uncovered the possible reason for his great-grandfather's success as a hotelier in San Francisco, with an establishment known as Hillman's Temperance House. "Going through an old trunk, I found a recipe for some hotel medicine. No wonder he was so successful. The main ingredient was ten gallons of pure grain alcohol with opium added to it," chuckles Hank proudly. "Checking it all out is part of the fun," he says. "It lets us all put on a Sherlock Holmes cap, and the case we get to solve is finding out about ourselves."

Over at the New York Genealogical Society, where well-worn couches sit underneath looming portraits of the early pioneers in the field, Harry Macy is busy directing new converts to research sites and wooden cabinets filled with old biographical records.

"This is a way to keep the memories alive," he muses. "So many of our ancestors were ordinary people. By making the effort to collect this information and preserve it, they won't be forgotten. Most are not going to get their name in a history book, but they can certainly attain immortality by someone constructing a family book about their lives along with the rest of the family's."

Buried treasure can be found all around you through the memories of others. I remember as a child being starved for information on my father. What happened over time is that my brother and I made a concerted effort to contact those who knew him. "What do you remember about him?" I would ask. "Please tell me a story."

Reconnecting to our loved one is no easy task. The mere mention of the deceased is often discomforting. Unfortunately, in our culture grief is expected to be unspoken, hidden and publicly ignored. Tears are only permitted to be shared openly at funerals and then only for a short time afterward. Within weeks after my father's death, I remember being expected to shut off my emotions like a faucet as friends quickly tried to change the subject whenever he was mentioned. But that drip, that drip of constant sorrow, continues throughout your life, sometimes loud and incessant, other times barely audible, but it's always, always there. It never goes away. That's why we need to rekindle memories to ease the lasting chill of our loss.

One time I remember cornering a friend of my father's like a trapped animal, grabbing his arm with an urgency that caused him to shudder while I blurted out in a voice laced with desperation, "I'm so sad. Many days I wake up missing him, and I feel as though someone is stabbing me in the heart. Do you feel the same? What do you miss most about him?" Not surprisingly, this approach got me nowhere. Instead, he touched my shoulder and said, "Don't let it upset you so much," and left as quickly as possible.

The trick, I later learned, is making the other person feel comfortable by leading them into a conversation, since people prefer to avoid the subject of death at all costs.

I would say things like, "Daddy always talked about you … What do you remember about him? What was one of your funniest moments together?" This was far more productive than my initial approach and furnished me with wonderful insights into my father's life as a boy and as a man, to supplement my own images of him as a parent.

One story came from an old friend I tracked down in California who told me about a love affair from my father's youth. Another in Maryland shared the story of a bet my father made that he could hold a dinner party for six for under twenty dollars to prove that guests savor conversation and company more than a five-course meal.

I cherish these insights. Because what people rarely realize is how much survivors want to talk, how their souls scream for some dialogue, some discourse, some little conversation about their loved one, some morsel to hold on to.

"You become literally starved for memories," says Rosie O'Donnell, who lost her mother to breast cancer when she was ten. "I have so few of her."

Recently, Rosie was standing on the stage of Radio City Music Hall accepting an Emmy Award as best talk-show host. Looking into the audience, as her fans clapped in delight, she drifted back to a time when she was there with her mother. As she started her speech, her eyes started watering, and she burst into tears, explaining to the audience, "I remember when I was here with my mother. She would take us here to see shows and buy us lemon gumdrops. She would be so happy right now."

It wasn't only the joy of receiving such an honor from the television community, but the memory of her mother that moved Rosie to tears that night. Later, I interviewed her for CNN, and I whispered how I understood, that I too had lost a parent in childhood.

"Your life is never the same, is it?" Rosie said as though we were old pals meeting on the family porch, instantly bound by our deepest secret.

"No, it's not," I replied. "I work very hard to keep his memory alive."

"We talk about my mother all the time," Rosie's sister Maureen chimed in. "Just last weekend, our kids got together, and we told them stories about our mom."

On that weekend, as on many others at the O'Donnell house, the songs of Barbra Streisand play on the stereo along with *The Lion King*, *Sesame Street* and favorite show tunes. The music selection isn't only for the adults, but deliberately designed for the children. Rosie and Maureen's mom would sing Streisand tunes while preparing meat loaf for the kids, and now the girls are passing along the tradition, telling their kids how their grandmother loved the music.

Years from now, when Streisand tunes are on the radio, the kids will think back to their mothers, as well as to the grandmother they never knew but heard so much about.

"It helps. It makes you feel she's still with you," said Rosie, as we all nodded in agreement.

PART FOUR

Family Politics

~

"Do you prefer to be right or to be happy?"
——A Course in Miracles

18

❧

Remarriage and Stepchildren

In the film *Lethal Weapon 4*, Mel Gibson is sitting at his wife's grave-side confused and upset. He has been mourning her for years—and several sequels—and now he has met someone else, whom he also loves. Yet he feels if he marries Rene Russo, it is a betrayal of his beloved wife, who was murdered.

"Please, God, give me a clue about what to do." he asks.

At this point Joe Pesci stumbles to the rescue. He tells Mel that just because you loved someone doesn't mean you're being disloyal if you love someone else. "It's just different," says Pesci, explaining that each person has a different piece of your heart. No two loves are supposed to be the same.

Pesci doesn't conjure up images of Cupid, but there is eternal truth in what he says. People often struggle with the balancing act of honoring the memory of a loved one while embracing a new love. One older widow was so conflicted that in her will she decided to split her ashes—between her old and present husband. Sandy can relate to this dilemma.

"When I met Stephen on a ski trip, I was overjoyed to be excited about being with someone once again," recalls Sandy, a dynamic forty-four-year-old. "You miss the little things like having coffee in the morning and reading the newspaper together. After we got engaged, he demanded that I remove all the pictures of my former husband from the house. He wanted all the memories to be erased. It's not that I don't love Stephen, but I also loved my husband and want him remembered, too."

Naturally distressed, Sandy consulted a therapist. She discovered that Stephen's concern was rooted in his fear that he would never measure up to the "sainted" former husband, nor did he want to be compared.

"We worked on ways to make Sandy help Stephen feel very secure in her love for him," says Dr. Sam Klagsbrun, a noted psychiatrist at the Four Winds facility in Katonah, New York. "She started to put pictures throughout the house of times Stephen and Sandy shared together, which gave a permanence to his place there. Now he doesn't feel as though he is competing with her former husband."

Because the children were very attached to their natural father, pictures of the family pre-Stephen are placed in the kids' rooms.

"One of the hardest challenges was talking about Dave to my kids without upsetting Stephen," says Sandy. "It was very important to me that they have a daily reminder that they were loved by this man and enough stories so that he is not a phantom. In the first year, instead of talking about Dave all the time, I would save it for when we had our own bedtime rituals together. This helped a lot."

After two years of marriage, Stephen's insecurity waned and conversations about Dave seeped into family life more easily.

"I always think of Dave but in a new way," says Sandy. "On our anniversary or his birthday, I will open my jewelry box and put on a bracelet that he bought me and wear it all day. It's my little memento from him, and it gives me great pleasure. I'll look up in the sky and say 'hi,' and hope he's doing well. But then I put it back in my jewelry box. It's the ritual of paying respect to him and acknowledging that he is not forgotten even though I have a new life."

Dr. Ken Doka, a Lutheran minister and senior consultant at the American Hospice Foundation, counsels newly formed families to create some sort of ritual in the home to honor the deceased parent and welcome the new stepparent.

It can be a simple or an elaborate gesture but should signify a transition. Sandy could have invited Stephen for dinner and made a toast welcoming him into the family and, at the same time, stating in front of the children that their father's spirit still resides in the home and within them. Kids will often act out when a new person arrives, because they feel threatened. They wonder, "Will Mommy go with him and leave me?" They also feel loyal to the deceased parent and may not want him or her to be replaced.

"During this type of transition, it is useful for families to do something that marks the fact that somebody new is now in the home," he says. "One father took a group shot together with his new wife and then asked his kids for suggestions where to put the picture, giving them a sense of inclusiveness."

This picture can be a simple one, or you can plan a day at the museum or the beach. Take the new family to a theme park. Go for a fishing weekend in a log cabin. This picture will then represent not only a transition but also the promise of enjoyable times as a new family unit.

Another suggestion for Sandy and Stephen was to ask Stephen to bring some photos of his life before Sandy into the house to symbolize that each of them had a life before they were joined together.

To help with the transition, Doka also suggests moving the furniture around when a new person arrives, to acknowledge that a change has taken place. You might shift around the family couch and chairs. Paint a room a cheery yellow. Or reposition the kitchen table and reupholster the chairs in a new fabric found on a family outing at a flea market. Just do something new and different.

"Too many times, families do not acknowledge that a change has taken place and they try to resume everyday life as though nothing has happened," says Doka. "A monumental change has occurred. These ceremonial gestures help mark that something new is taking place."

Remember that stepfamilies have been brought together by a form of loss, and therefore do not follow the traditional models of an intact family. In this family structure, the surviving parent can't neglect the importance of symbolic links between the biological parent and the child. Even if Tommy and Johnny must share a room, let little

Tommy have a shelf or drawer with space for his deceased parent's mementos. Also give Johnny a space for his parent. "Too often the child gets the message consciously or unconsciously that Daddy doesn't want to upset Stepmommy so the child shouldn't talk about his own mommy," says Jeannette Lofas, president of the New York–based Stepfamily Foundation. To design a peace treaty so that the home doesn't become a war zone, the two adults must address these issues at the onset of cohabitation. For example, would the new wife be upset if, when her husband remembers a story from his past, he mentions it at the dinner table? Or would she be more comfortable if he takes his son aside at bedtime and discusses it then? Just decide what the terms will be. But be sure to create terms where the child can feel safe discussing their deceased parent.

"The shadow of the former husband or wife should and will be always in the house," says Jeannette Lofas. "Parents have to be adults and not act like little children. An adult can have several spouses. A child only has one biological mom and one dad."

Jeannette favors rituals that foster inclusiveness. "Let's say Jack wants a picture of his father in his room. If his new stepfather goes with him to pick out a nice frame for the picture, the stepfather is creating a bonding experience with the boy as well as involving himself in the child's life," she says. "It's a small but meaningful gesture." This also gives the child the unspoken permission to love his father and also like his stepfather, since he may indeed want and need a male figure in his life.

If the finances of the family permit this luxury, another idea would be for the stepparent to help his or her new stepchild redecorate their bedroom. It could be as simple as buying a new lamp or purchasing a new down-filled bedspread. All members of the family could help with painting or perhaps stenciling a favorite cartoon character on the wall.

To forge bonds with teenagers, go out and buy music together and get to know the stepchild's taste. Or try to watch a TV show together. Find common ground. I often score points with Jessica and Vanessa by sharing tidbits about their favorite stars. "Did you hear that the WB network wants all the girls to have long hair because the ratings for *Felicity* plummeted after Keri Russell cut her hair?" This sparked a whole conversation and made it seem that I was an insider in their lives. Furthermore, any adult can plug in by simply reading the TV pages of any newspaper or magazine to learn what shows appeal to your kids' age-groups, which will in turn provide material for dinner conversation.

Be prepared for some initial resistance and silence. However, keep prodding. Ultimately, we all want to be loved, and someone's continuous kind efforts will break down these barriers.

19

~

Dealing with the Possessions of the Loved Ones

Family politics also come into play when the possessions of loved ones are dispersed. Most therapists advocate leaving the room, apartment or house intact for a period of time and then after the acute phase of mourning, steps can be taken to make this transition. "There is no right time to do this," says Dr. Carter Potash, president and executive director of Stony Lodge Hospital in Briarcliff Manor, New York. "Some people are emotionally ready for this after a few months, while others need more time." Often what prods this decision are the particular needs of the family—both emotional and economical. "If someone has twelve rooms in their house, one room can remain a shrine to the memories of the person they loved," says Dr. Potash. "This is perfectly healthy and should not be discouraged, especially if this brings comfort. Others with limited space may want to convert a bedroom into a playroom."

Another issue is how many possessions one should keep. Sometimes in the heat of emotion, people throw out all the possessions except for a few prized objects. Clothes are often boxed and sent away. Yet clothes can carry the perfume of Mom or the salty sweat from a hard day's work from Dad. My brother and I wish my mother had kept some of my father's classic striped ties or soft camel hair coats so that my brother could now enjoy them. Because Peter was so young at the time of my father's death, my mother discarded all his clothing, and therefore the connections that could have been made.

Tennessee Congressman Bart Gordon is grateful that he and his mother resisted advice to throw away all the possessions of his deceased father. "Recently, I went upstairs to the attic with my mother, and lying across the trunk were some of Daddy's khaki pants and a flannel work shirt he wore all the time. It made us feel that he was right there in the room," says Bart. "It was a very nice feeling."

Some err in throwing out too much, but there are also many families who veer to the other extreme and keep too many possessions of their loved ones stored in their house.

When Dan Radice's dad died, Dan wanted to keep so many of his father's possessions that his wife felt as though their house had been invaded by clutter. "It is when your house suddenly has to absorb furniture and objects due to the death of your partner's parent that normal rules of compromise disappear," says Dan's wife, Sophie. "Any sense of propriety over what goes into your home must be forfeited to your partner's feelings of grief, attachment to childhood objects and love for the deceased."

In less stressful times, a wife can ditch the old leather couch or a husband can veto the frilly bedspread. But with death, the politics shift.

"The nonbereaved half of the couple has to shut up, put up and somehow make way for the inheritance of someone else's history," says Sophie. "One room of our house had to become a storeroom for boxes of precious books, strange plants, a collection of trumpets, stuffed animals, a grandfather clock and an extraordinary hand-painted wardrobe. The look of pain on my husband's face when I said that I thought the shell-encrusted umbrella stand was grotesque was enough to make me understand that I would have to keep these judgments to myself."

At least she did for a while. After a year, Sophie had had enough and blurted out that she wasn't feeling comfortable in her own home. Dan then realized how much the situation was upsetting his wife. They then devised a compromise: Sophie and Dan kept the items that worked for their lifestyle and gave the others away.

Many charitable organizations always need household goods, furniture and clothing. Helping others can also take the sting out of relinquishing the possessions. If you don't want to donate to a charity, have a yard sale and use the money for some special family event. Or spend the money in having the remaining possessions stored in a rental unit.

Because discarding the possessions of a loved one will affect family members, here are some tips from therapists on the best ways to handle this task.

- Agree on a time to make this change. At a family dinner ask, "What do you think we should do with Amy's room? She's still with us in spirit but doesn't need to live there anymore." One can easily substitute the name of brother, father or mother.
- Mutually decide what the room will now become. Have a special memento strategically placed in the room to acknowledge that it once belonged to the deceased. It could be a favorite teddy bear, a cherished lamp or a family picture.
- Think about what to do with possessions no longer needed. Offer to donate them to a charity. "Would Amy rather we give these toys and clothes to someone in a hospital or someone from a school?"
- Decide which special mementos and favored clothing will be saved as souvenirs. Allow each family member to be present when this takes place. Max still resents that his parents didn't include him in this process. "They were trying to protect me from this painful necessity," he says. "But instead I lost out on choosing something of my brother's that meant something to me. I would have wanted to keep a sweatshirt that they threw out. I still think of that sweatshirt to this day." Joanna had a different experience. She is very grateful that her parents had the foresight to keep her sister's clothing and let her choose what she wanted. "When I wear one of her favorite pink sweaters," says Joanna, "it's as though her arms are wrapped around me."
- Do not throw away art projects, diaries, doodles, prom invita-

tions, phone books—all of which will later be trigger points to remember the child or adult. Pick and choose the special ones. "Too often therapists tell you to get rid of everything as a form of moving on," says Dr. Richard Tsenudi, a therapist and researcher at North Carolina University. "I disagree. These tangible physical items allow you to continue to have a relationship with your loved one."

Sometimes World War III erupts when siblings start dividing a parent's possessions. Sally wanted Mom's pearl necklace, causing Amanda to scream, "You always got everything." Such emotionally charged times often trigger deep-rooted rivalries that can create lasting scars. Cory still resents his brother Michael for taking their father's cuff links. "He got to the house before I did, and Mom was too wigged out to make any sane decisions," says Cory. "It would have been so much better if it was all spelled out beforehand. What annoyed me is that I have to go to functions where I could wear the cuff links and think of my father. Michael works in jeans and a T-shirt."

Some advance planning would eliminate these types of disappointments. Perhaps Grandma could ask all her beneficiaries to compose a wish list of mementos. This way family members can anticipate conflicts and negotiate issues at a time when there is no sadness or stress.

20

Grandparent Rights

Up until the 1970s, the concept of Grandparents Rights Law wasn't part of the legal lexicon. However, with the rapid rise of messy divorces, splintered families, contentious custody battles and a litigation-happy society, grandparents often get caught in the cross fire and start fighting back. Because of the power of the senior citizen lobby—75 percent of older Americans are grandparents—and strong pressure from national groups such as the American Association of Retired Persons and the Child Welfare League of America, every state had some form of what is known as the Grandparents Rights law that permits grandparents to seek court-ordered visits with a grandchild. Recently the Supreme Court ruled that grandparents can't interfere with the rights of parents to decide what is best for their children. But the ruling left room for issues of safety and protection.

While visitation is an understandable request, the most controversial aspect of the grandparent movement is when Grandpa starts meddling with what school Junior should go to and in what religion he should be raised. This becomes especially prickly when grandparents become estranged over matters of money, religion or child-rearing practices and want to enforce their beliefs on the grandchild.

Take the case of Manny Eliopoulos, reported in *The Baltimore Sun*. Once a month Manny's father must contain his anger as a car pulls up to his home in Greektown. It's time for his son Manny Jr. to go to his grandmother's house in Glen Rock, Pennsylvania. He has no choice. After her daughter died, Charlotte Fowlkes took over custody of Manny for two years over the father's objections. Now the courts have ruled that Manny Sr. has custody of his son but allow the grandmother to have visitation rights to her only grandson.

"It's like she's my wife," fumes Emanuel Eliopoulos, a truck driver who has spent more than $35,000 on lawyers fighting this issue. "It gets in the way." Eliopoulos believes she undermines his relationship with his son, while the grandmother questions his ability as a parent.

"All I want to do is be around my grandson," retorts Fowlkes. As for eight-year-old Manny, he's now caught in an ugly tug-of-war that's more combative than anything played on his Nintendo games.

"When the law views a grandparent as being an equal to a parent, that's wrong," says Charlotte Eliopoulos, sister of the child's dad, Manny Sr.

Ethel Dunn, executive director of Grandparents United for Children's Rights in Madison, Wisconsin, argues the other side, saying that grandparents can be a last line of defense for a child who is neglected, abused or harmed in any way. "We see over and over again children who say they can only talk to their grandma," she says. "For children who are afraid of their parents or can't speak to them, this is a vital connection."

This is especially true when parents remarry. Grandma's house often becomes a safe place to talk about their deceased parent and hear stories about them as kids. "What did Daddy do when he was my age, Grandma? Was he like me?" is a common question that really helps a child build his self-identity.

Not all arguments lead to permanent friction and tension. After Kerry Ladho died from cancer, her husband, Abe, discouraged his son's relationship with his in-laws, John and Lesley Kemp. As the

Sacramento Bee reported, the grandparents were so distraught over losing Kerry and afraid they'd lose Joey that they got a court order granting them visits from Joey for part of each weekend.

In time, both parties worked hard to make compromises for Joey's best interest. After Abe moved to San Francisco with his new wife, Susan, he welcomed the Kemps' visits as long as they called ahead. They're also invited to Joey's school functions, and he is with them for a week every Christmas and at least two weeks in the summer.

Experts believe that harmony is achieved when the grandparents and surviving parent sit down and communicate what some call the "negotiables" and "nonnegotiables." From the start, grandparents should respect the wishes of the parent. This is not an equal relationship—a parent has more power and does not want to feel undermined or have their authority threatened. Yet if the parent sees a willingness by the grandparent to be thoughtful and accommodating, nine out of ten times the in-law will welcome the love and support of a grandparent.

Here are some points for the grandparents to consider and ways to introduce them:

- The grandparent should open the discussion respectfully to set the tone of the conversation. "You know how much we love little Sammy and want to see him, but you also have your own life. Would it be okay if we call him on the weekend?"
- Offer to help out. "We never want to be meddlesome, but we would like to see Sammy. Just know whenever you need free baby-sitting, we're here. But can you also tell us how often you think it would be reasonable to see him? How should we contact you?"
- Determine what would annoy the parent and create tension in the relationship, and avoid doing those things!
- Don't undermine the parent's authority. If a parent tells the grandson he cannot have a Batman superhero action figure because he is punished for bad behavior, it is not okay to under-

mine his or her discipline strategy and buy it for him to win points. There are other ways to spoil a grandchild—either with a special meal or a favorite activity.

You would be surprised how rarely these frank conversations take place. Another good idea for the surviving parent is to offer the grandparents the opportunity to take a possession of their child's. This sends the signal that the son- or daughter-in-law is respectful of the grandparents' grief. By mapping out exactly what each party expects and needs, harmony normally prevails or at least some form of compromise is forged. Remember that in life, when nothing is perfect, the adaptive soul succeeds.

21

⁓

Holiday Survival Kit

"They should celebrate his birthday, not the day he died." These wise words were spoken by Jacqueline Kennedy Onassis who lamented the excessive coverage commemorating the assassination of her husband, President John Kennedy. "It is his life that should be remembered, not only his death." You don't have to be from a world-famous family to see what wonderful advice this is for anyone. Because the day someone you love dies is a day that is marked in your psyche forever.

Katie's dad died on Christmas Day, and as a result, the thirty-year-old sales executive was never able to enjoy all the festivities of the holiday season: traditions that included sledding at her New England home, having hot cocoa in front of a fire or sitting next to the family Christmas tree. "Anything connected with that holiday made me think of my dad and my loss," she recalls.

One night she was walking home and noticed the way a neighbor had strung holiday lights along his house like ropes of sparkling pearls, and it made her think how much her father loved this season. Transfixed, she flashed back to the time her father sat in his favorite armchair talking about the magic of Christmas and how this time of the year everyone from the surly cabdrivers to the stressed-out executives became kinder. "It suddenly dawned on me how sad my father would be that all of us were missing out on this holiday that he had spent so much effort to make special. When we were younger, he'd even dress up as Santa Claus and was the first one up in the morning preparing coffee and pancakes, even though he wasn't such a good cook," she says, laughing softly. "I just wanted to bring him back into the holiday somehow."

Inspiration occurred in the oddest of ways. She started humming the melody of "The Twelve Days of Christmas" and instead of saying, "My True Love Gave to Me," she inserted the line "My Father Gave to Me." Immediately she called her sister and shared her idea. So now when the family sings, "The Twelve Days of Christmas," lyrics include "ears the size of melons," "a love of outdoor camping," "books by Scott Fitzgerald," etcetera. "It makes it fun, and we'll substitute different lyrics each year," says Katie. "We've started a tradition inspired by him, and it makes us all feel he's with us."

Peter, a TV producer, accomplishes the same feeling by cooking his mother's favorite dishes on her birthday. It came as a surprise to him how much his mother had been the glue that kept the family together, and how, in her absence, family traditions had started to evaporate like a morning mist. Holidays were no longer mandatory get-togethers and birthdays were acknowledged, but hardly with the same enthusiasm. "My mother was the rock of the family," says Peter with a wistful smile. "The loss is so hard to describe. I feel like I'll never be loved as intensely by anyone else. It was Mom who pored over our homework assignments and made sure we wore our hats and gloves. She never missed a game of mine, or a birthday, and I can't tell you how much I miss her calling me at work to make sure I am eating right and telling me that no matter what, I am terrific. We all missed her terribly, and I think it became difficult being together on holidays and birthdays because it was such a reminder of what we had lost."

A few months before Christmas, Peter's sister was having similar thoughts as she drove to pick up her two kids from school. Then she had an idea. When she returned home, she collected all the recipes her mother had given her and printed them along with some of her favorite sayings.

"My sister sent us all her favorite recipes," says Peter. Somehow mixing the sugar and flour in a big wooden bowl and stirring the ingredients into a sticky paste triggered pleasant memories for Peter, as though his mother's presence was nearby and he could see himself as a ten-year-old eagerly licking the bowl. Now the recipes evoke memories of his mother and help him include her in holiday functions.

"Whether it's a birthday, a holiday which brings families together, or the anniversary of a death, it is necessary to acknowledge the significance of the loss," says Dr. Carter Potash. "It doesn't have to be a time-consuming project like cooking a favorite dish. It can be as uncomplicated as calling someone in the family and sharing an anecdote about the loved one."

My brother is a master at this. On my father's birthday, I can expect to pick up the phone, say hello and a familiar voice will say, "Hello, Mrs. Tuckerman," and immediately I will laugh, because Mrs. Tuckerman was what my father would call my mother when she pestered him. Mrs. Tuckerman was a Nancy Walker character from an old-time record who harrassed poor Mr. Tuckerman, and my father would invoke her name in such an endearing way when my mother was trying to get him to take his medicine and eat right. Shaking his head in mock disgust, he'd say, "Mrs. Tuckerman, now I understand how Mr. Tuckerman feels," and we'd all giggle. Sharing this anecdote and bringing him into our lives in a simple, memorable way takes away some of the sting that he isn't with us.

As the writer John Volkan once observed, "We can never purge those who have been close to us from our own history except by psychic acts damaging to our identity." Therefore, talk about your loved one on these days.

Sarah feels her sadness over her brother Richard's death from congenital heart failure is compounded by her family's unspoken vow never to discuss him. "My other brother Stephen and I were at my parents' house, and I mentioned how Richard would have loved the fall season, and my parents looked at me as though I was talking about a stranger. I yelled, 'I'm speaking of Richard, you know, your son and my brother. Today is his birthday.' They looked at me as though I had done something awful. In Britain, you're told to keep a stiff upper lip and shut your emotions in the cupboard. But if I can't talk to my family, who else do I have? It's not like America where you go to a therapist. It's just not done here. But I need to speak of him because I miss him so."

This is why maintaining a relationship with your loved one is so essential, because these annual rites are inescapable reminders of the time when the family was whole, and try as we may, these times will inexorably cause us to relive the initial loss all over again.

Poet Henry Wadsworth Longfellow said that the holiest of holidays are the ones we observe in silence and apart. He called these the secret anniversaries of the heart.

Any significant marker at which the deceased was present—birthday, anniversary of death, holidays—causes sorrow. "As these markers approach, the cycle of grief often circles back, and people will become depressed and sad several days leading up to the event and may not even know its origin," Dr. Gerald Koocher says. "This is why we now encourage people to be aware of these markers and talk about the person. It should not be a taboo subject."

But once we share, they are no longer secret and become honored reminiscence. Dr. Koocher admires one family that declares it a holiday on the birthday of their deceased son. "The parents take off from work and the other siblings are excused from school, and they either go to an amusement park, on a picnic or to the movies," he says. "They are really saying that they're going to promote healing together and want to continually connect to this person they love. They have found ritualized meaning from this day."

This doesn't mean that everyone is blissfully happy on this day. On the contrary. However, these markers will trigger memories, and by being together, the family helps share the experience collectively as well as enhancing the healing through storytelling and remembrance. Denial deepens the hurt and creates isolation and despair.

Carol, a Boston-based housewife, appreciates when people call her on the anniversary of her son's death. Although her son has been gone for ten years, she still feels the pain associated with this day. "There are only a few friends who do phone, but it is one of the greatest acts of kindness," says Carol, blinking back tears. "It can be simply someone saying, 'I know this is a hard day.' Some will be so kind and tell me how they were thinking of Brian. Life may go on but you never forget. This type of support makes you feel there is love in your life even if I no longer have my son."

On Thanksgiving, one mother has her oldest son cut the breast of turkey with a special ceremonial knife that his deceased father used for carving. Another family crafts Christmas tree ornaments with a picture of their father on one of the balls as well as family pictures of him with the kids. For Chanukah, one daughter took her mother's old clothes and, late at night with McCall's patterns, sewed stylish new customized suits for herself and two sisters. Another sister used some old clothing to make doll's dresses for her daughter.

Charlotte Nganele, a Cornell University New York Hospital–trained psychiatrist, says these types of rituals help the person express feelings about the deceased while acknowledging the transition that is now death. "These gestures actually reinforce the continuation of the loved one's life and reflect how family members who have died can still be present in the family," she says. "This way, the loss, along with the memory, coexist forever."

PART FIVE

Making Memories Last

❧

"If it's not documented, it didn't happen."
——Virginia Woolf

22

❧

What Memories We Actually Keep

My mother accuses me of having what she calls "selective amnesia." "Why do you remember only the bad things I did, what about all the good things?" It is a fair question. Why do some memories clamp onto our consciousness while others slip away like water down a drain? What exactly do we remember and when? And why are our kids' memories of family events so very different from ours?

Fortunately, researchers are busy examining all the different ways we can unlock our storage closet of memories and providing helpful clues about how to make more memories stick.

"The best strategy is that after you do anything together, whether it's watching a movie together or going to a park, talk about it," says Dr. Ava Siegler, director of the Institute for Child, Adolescent & Family Studies and author of *What Shall I Tell the Kids?* "The experience becomes more memorable when you and your child discuss it afterward. Repetition is the building block of memory in young children."

Even if what they remember is not the way you viewed the same event, reinforce their memory. Talk about it. Sharing how you all viewed the same event will help your child's memory to have a fuller and lasting picture of it. It's like putting layers of clothing on. Sam might remember that the family vacation included a canoe trip where Jimmy almost fell out of the boat. But Jimmy will remember the campfire afterward where he toasted a marshmallow. These two experiences then become what are known as trigger points. Later Mom and Dad can offer their own take on the event, such as how the family all hugged by the campfire and sang songs.

Keep in mind that most children will not absorb the same impressions as an adult. They are not looking for the "moral" of the story. Often it is an annoyance with a sister for snatching a sweater or the memory of a wacky-looking person they met in an elevator. One family took their kids to Williamsburg, Virginia, to give them a sense of history. What did ten-year-old Will retain? "The plastic tree at the hotel's pool was really cool," he reported. However, parents can layer the story with the moral they hope to imprint on their children about family togetherness.

"The secret is listening to your children," says Dr. Patricia Bauer, a professor at the Institute of Child Development at the University of Minnesota. "Children are very egocentric. The world revolves around them. What they remember must be reinforced with them as the star, and then you can flesh it out with other memories." This advice applies to everyone—no matter the age.

Last year I unintentionally embarrassed Jessica. For her middle-school graduation book, parents were asked to write a paragraph as a send-off. I scribbled some lines that ended with, "Enjoy the journey, even the bumps on the roads can teach you lessons. Always know that we are here with acceptance, love, support and if needed, a credit card." The credit card line was meant as a loving reminder that if she had a real problem, we would help her out. Yet she was furious with me. She worried that it would send a false signal that she was spoiled.

So what's a parent to do? I knew to reinforce to her that my intentions were loving and that I had made a mistake. I didn't dismiss my error—because I knew full well she would remember it. But I also tried to layer the incident with more positive memories. I made her a photo album with pictures I took of her graduation. I bought her a special gift with a note telling her how much I loved her and how proud I was of her accomplishment. I also made self-deprecating jokes about it. "Hey, we all make mistakes. I remember what I did. I know you'll remember this over the thousand other nice things I've done," which made her laugh—a little.

This is not mind control or mind manipulation, but rather a layering of memories with lots of love, showing your good intentions. Explaining that you're human, talking about your motivations, revealing that you are trying—all go a long way in helping build positive relationships and memories with your children.

Many people wonder when children begin to retain memories. There are several theories, but most agree that young kids remember more than we think. From a time a baby is three months of age, he or she has taken in many sensory impressions about you including your smell, the outline of your face, the sound of your voice, and remembers it in a general amorphous way.

"It isn't a specific incident that your child will likely remember when he grows up," says Sirgay Sanger, M.D., a psychiatrist who directs the Early Care Center in Manhattan, "but a sense of it—an aura of safety or fear, joy or pain."

My cousin Justin was only twenty months old when his father died, and he has been haunted by the feeling that he didn't know his father. "Sometimes I had these senses of him, but I wrote it off to being from a story I heard or viewing some picture of him and creating an image," says Justin. "But then my friends started to have children, and I realized how intimate the relationship between babies and parents is even in early years. It was then I felt that I really did have a connection to him, that all the playing, holding and cuddling does have a psychic impact, and I was comforted by that thought."

A survey at the preemie unit at Mount Sinai Hospital in New York revealed that babies who spent their early months in a hospital grew up to be frightened of doctors. "It makes sense," observes Dr. Jonathan Scherr, a fertility specialist and *Child Magazine* contributor. "These babies are living in incubators with tubes attached to them, and they are getting injections almost daily. They have a memory of it in their psyches, which explains why a doctor's office triggers memories of their early discomfort."

Clearly, traumatic events have more staying power than happy ones. At the time of trauma, two hormones are released that etch these memories into the brain. That is why my mother has few memories of her childhood but remembers viscerally the day she was five years old and her mother had a fatal heart attack. "There was a lot of commotion, and the ambulance came to our house," recalls my mother. "I remember seeing her with a sheet over her face and watching my father cry. He had never cried before."

The memories of spilling soda on your new dress in first grade will be more vivid than going to a movie with your family, and the sting of someone's unkind words will resonate much longer than a memory of a friend who never hurt your feelings.

Some people will replay a traumatic event in their mind like a recurring nightmare while others block it out, in what psychologists say is our internal defense system at work. Someone can be in an abusive relationship but look back at the "good" and not remember the black eyes and bruises.

"For everyone, there are certain kinds of traumatic events that are remembered, and some that are not," explains Dr. Siegler. "With sexual traumas or violence, sometimes the mind protects itself by forgetting. It depends on what the mind can bear. Usually humiliation, rage or sadness from grief marks the brain. It isn't forgotten."

We do, however, have the power to flood our psyches with positive memories and often do. "It's amazing how time, the greatest healer of all, can brighten the colors of happy memories while fading the tones of sad ones," says therapist Ted Menten. Nostalgia becomes a way of removing all the potholes and bumps from the road. When you look back, you want to see the journey as a meaningful, pleasant one. This does not mean that you aren't aware of the obstacles and disappointments. Instead, you focus on the destination you reach and try to see value in it. That's much easier to do if you are conscious of the power of memory. Happy times can be etched in childhood memories as well as adult ones. They just take some effort.

Often, because of our hectic schedules—returning from work, cooking dinner, overseeing the kids doing homework, watching TV—we don't take the time to talk about the past because we're so preoccupied with the present. "Janie, what time do you have to be picked up from soccer practice? . . . Jimmy, don't forget to practice piano. . . . Chloe, what supplies do you need for your school project? . . ." etcetera.

However, families should try this exercise periodically. Sit down and ask your kids:

What was the funniest moment they shared with their sister or brother . . . or their parents?
What was the most fun day they had and why?
What moment did they feel you really came through for them?
What was a really happy day for them?
What time did they ever feel disappointed?
What is each family member's quirk?

If presented as a game, you'll see how the family narrative is unfolding before the final act. You'll learn what information your children are responding to and what experiences are forming their personalities and values. You'll also be able to be involved in becoming your own historian because you can embroider their stories with details to help them remember, and which later will be passed on to your children's children.

Because we react to different stimuli that interface with our belief systems and experiences, each person has their own set of wiring. Some people remember the smell of a child's freshly washed hair while others recall the feathery softness of a baby's skin. However, by collaborating on memories, friends, as well as family, will get a richer texture to the experience you all shared.

Of all the things I've done for my friend Roger, the one he remembers is how I called up friends to help him get writing work when he needed it, which to me was a no-brainer. And I'll never forget how after I lost the baby, he came over with a pint of Häagen-Dazs, and though he had traveled a long distance, understood I needed to be alone and just cry. He left, depositing the ice cream near my bed. My friend Elena remembers that I helped her shut down her bakery, and I'll always be grateful for her dating advice in focusing on "why it can work, instead of why it can't." I'll always love Liza for her generosity in throwing me a baby shower, one of the happiest days of my life. She, on the other hand, remembers me writing a story for her daughter.

To learn about our early lives, we can interview our siblings. They slept under the same heart for nine months and carry not only our bloodline but our lifeline. Siblings are our true historians, intrinsically intertwined with us from the first breath to the last. Recently my brother told me a story about this hotel in Puerto Rico, which I said I never had visited. "Oh yes, you have," he said. "Don't you remember, we once went there for Christmas, two years before Daddy died." And suddenly, I remembered the incident as though I was experiencing it for the first time again with my father.

Think back to the times we played with kaleidoscopes as kids and how by turning them, a whole new spectrum of colors appeared. In a way, that's like memory. Each of us filters out different information and chooses what to remember and what to forget, thus creating our very own picture of events. Inevitably your brother's or sister's picture of the same event will be altered by his or her perspectives, and they will remember incidents that you may have not filed in the data banks called memory. As a result, your family offers a whole library of tantalizing stories that you may have not stored yourself and can gain great pleasure and insight from hearing.

By talking about our special experiences, they will become cemented into our memories and reminiscences and not be as fleeting as others. Over a lifetime we have millions of experiences, but by making the effort to highlight certain memories and review them as you would a play, we ensure that these memories have a lasting influence over our lives, and our children's. As writer Søren Kierkegaard said, "Life can only be understood backward, but it must be lived forward."

As we've discussed, memories are cemented by repetition. Rituals can help build memories, because they are a repeated activity. Each family has its own idiosyncratic rituals, whether it's singing a special lullaby or cooking fish on Friday nights. I can still smell the candy-decorated gingerbread house my mother would buy that signaled the holiday season. Experts say that these types of rituals are actually the anchors of childhood and help kids feel secure.

While you can pass on the rituals from your own family, be conscious of creating your own rituals. "As early as possible, couples should clarify which rituals they want to bring from their past, which to let go, and which new ones to introduce," says Dr. Imber-Black, coauthor of *Rituals for Our Times: Celebrating, Healing, and Changing Our Lives and Our Relationships.* "Once implemented, these rituals then offer children a special activity they can count on. They connect us to where we came from, help us stay anchored and simultaneously move us into the future." Dr. Imber-Black points out that children are natural ritual makers and activities can be simple as well as elaborate.

For instance, in one family each member traces an outline of their hand from colored cardboard paper and cuts it out. Then the family scribbles a message for the year on the cutout hand, ranging from a hope for peace on earth to Kristen getting a bicycle for Christmas to Jimmy making goalie on the soccer team. Then by punching a hole in the cardboard outline of the hand, an ornament can be made. This is not only an inexpensive ornament but over the years, the handprints become tangible evidence of family growth. One can also laminate them to ensure they last for years and years. For one family, after the father passed away, these ornaments became precious treasures. Some families have a Chanukah menorah passed down from generations for their ritual celebration. Some make special dishes. Vanessa has helped me mash the sweet potatoes for Thanksgiving pie. My friend Jamie bakes holiday cookies with special cookie cutters.

On the winter solstice, one family has each member light a floating candle and then place it in a bowl of water. Then in turn, they all say what they'd like to see happen in the coming year.

Another family decorates an elaborate gingerbread house each

December and then takes it to the woods for the fairies to dance in, which whimsically celebrates young children's imaginations.

Thanks to the advent of Kinko's, T-shirts, calendars or mouse-pads emblazoned with family pictures can be made. I also really like what the McGuirk family does every year. The matriarch of the family gets all the kids to send pictures of their families from the year—Caroline in the class play, Terry scoring a goal or Emily feeding her pet rabbit, as well as family outings and trips. And of course other shots capture silly moments including Claire making funny faces at her sister. Then Mrs. McGuirk goes to Kinko's and makes calendars comprising all the pictures from the family for each child, which are tacked to their refrigerator doors to keep them all connected.

My husband takes my son to the park each Saturday morning and follows their trip with a McDonald's happy meal. When it's the weekend, this is Parker's special time with Dad. Once a year he also takes Vanessa and Jessica on a separate vacation for their own one-on-one time. (Parker's too young yet.)

A ritual can also be a familiar greeting or gesture. My husband gives each child a "good luck kiss" each morning before he leaves, even if they're sleeping. One time he ran out of the house, and the kids later reminded him that he neglected to kiss them good-bye. Nightly prayers are also treasured rituals. When traveling on airplanes, we all hold each other's hands when we land even if it forms a chain from one side to another.

During one summer vacation, a family collected large stones from a nature walk. Each member put their name on the stone in black marker. For special celebratory dinners, the mother would use the stones as place cards. In time, these talismans were marked with historic dates such as Adam, 1/1/92, 2/14/93, 9/5/89, etcetera. Anyone who came to the house would have their own stone, and when he or she returned, it would be part of the table setting. "Oh, I was here last July, that's the date," remarked one guest. But after a death of a family member or friend, these stones can still be part of the table by being positioned somewhere else—near the centerpiece, on an hors d'oeuvre tray, in a vase full of fresh yellow daisies. Seeing something written in someone's handwriting is like having them nearby.

Other families choose one vacation spot and visit it regularly, giving them a sense of continuity.

For Rosh Hashana or New Year's, I have everyone write down on a prettily decorated card, easily purchased at a stationery store, their hopes for the future as well as what they've learned this year from the people they love. We call this our "Time Capsule." Then we seal each response in an envelope, which is then placed in a box. We put the box in an armoire in the den and don't open it until the following year's celebration, where we see if our wishes come true. Others I know literally bury time capsules like these in the backyard in a family ceremony. Essie adopted the same concept and used balloons that were released in the air with her messages to her loved ones for the New Year.

On Valentine's Day, we encourage the girls to write poems. Have each family member write a poem or find a passage that relates to your loved one. Save each one and put it in a box with rose petals to be savored always. Jackie Kennedy would have her children write or find poems, then illustrate them for any holiday, ranging from Mother's Day to birthdays. "She pasted them all in a special scrapbook," recalls Caroline Kennedy Schlossberg. "It wasn't like a school assignment but an infinite wandering that took us out of our own world and into so many others. The scrapbook has remained one of our most precious family possessions, and when I look at it now, I can see as much about each of us by reading the poems we chose as I can by looking at the photographs. Now I am carrying on the tradition with my children."

For birthdays, make a family rule that presents must be hand-made. Ideas can include a homemade picture frame, a special bottle to house perfume, a spice rack, a wooden tie rack, a book with special inscriptions, a beautiful letter revealing what you appreciate about your loved one. On special birthdays, personalize a gift with engraving.

Create memorable celebrations. I have a friend who is known for having a "Leo" lunch for anyone born under that sign. It started with five friends and has ballooned into many more each year. Long after Molly is gone, she will be remembered for this signature meal. Another alternative would be to have an annual spring dinner to celebrate the end of winter, or a special Halloween party. My friends Nicole Miller and Kim Taipale have an annual Christmas party at their New York loft that has become one of the anticipated dinners of the season. "We didn't have it one year and people were really upset," recalls Nicole.

It can also be done in small ways. For Parker's birthday, I make the effort to create a beautiful centerpiece inspired by the theme of the party. I literally stuff a big basket with all his action figures and insert flowers and props in between. I love seeing his eyes become as wide as saucers and look forward to his giggle of delight after each creation. I hope he'll always remember this effort his mother made for him—that extra special dash of love.

As fashion reporter Elsa Klensch once told me, all the greats created a signature style to be remembered. It doesn't have to be simply a great haircut. It can be a special flower arrangement or a homemade birthday cake. The secret is doing it often and making people anticipate it year after year.

You can choose from hundreds of ideas. Be inventive, and don't make excuses. At a party, my father's friend once complained about her hectic life and its annoyances. Taking her hand, he said, "There will always be annoyances and reasons we say we can't do things. But it is our job to tune them out and have fun. Remember, that is our job in life." Just think of building rituals as a joyous activity. Make every day or a holiday special by that little touch. Your family will remember and cherish these efforts and pass them on. After all, no act of love, however small, is ever wasted.

23

~

Love Letters

At the funeral for her husband, Jay Monahan, *Today* show anchor Katie Couric made an impassioned plea to all his friends and colleagues who gathered to mourn the passing of the forty-two-year-old lawyer, the love of her life and the father of her two young daughters.

She said she was worried that her daughters wouldn't know their father and asked those assembled to write a letter about any experience they had with Jay, any good times shared, any funny moment, anything that would give Ellie and Carrie a sense of the man she loved.

Although her daughters will always feel their loss, thanks to the loving concern of their mother, they now have a whole library of letters to read whenever they miss their father: letters about his love of Civil War memorabilia, letters about some of his first cases, letters about how he met their mother and even letters about what he was like as a child.

Most people recognize that good manners dictate that you write a condolence note to someone suffering the death of a loved one. The most appreciated notes are those that share personal anecdotes about the deceased, stories about who they were. These notes often revive our spirits and become lasting treasures. They reassure us that despite how bad we may feel, someone is watching and cares.

"When my husband was killed in a plane crash, I was so numb, I could hardly function," recalls Karen. "Some days I didn't even shower or get dressed. But the letters I received from people really helped me. I started to look forward to them. I would hear from friends I hadn't spoken to in years who didn't even know my husband. Or I would hear from his acquaintances what my husband had meant to them. Some would share their experiences about losing a loved one. It really made me feel loved and not as alone."

These notes can also provide material for what Bristol Community College professor John Tormey calls "Living Memory Books." He suggests that grieving people buy a special book and label it with the name of the loved one. Inside should be memories compiled of this person. "But you should leave plenty of extra space in this book so that whenever a thought or memory of this person enters your mind, you can write it down," he says. "This is what I mean by a living memory book—because often we forget little details and then when we write them down they become an ongoing narrative. If someone tells you something about a loved one you didn't know, you write it down in this book too. New information is like meeting the person again. The book helps make you feel that the person is nearby, and over time you will read the book on various occasions and be comforted by all the memories inside."

Families and old friends are the best resources for retrieving memories, though the people your loved one may have met at work, at the gym or even at the local bar may have fleeting memories that enhance the script of your loved one's life. The only task involved is just asking them for their memories.

Michael is a cameraman who I worked with at CNN. When his wife's mother died, she didn't realize how much she would miss her. The following year, Ann called her brothers and made this request. "The best gift I could get is memories you have of Mom," she said. "Write them down and send them to me." To her surprise and delight, her brothers remembered times that she forgot, filling in the gaps of a life that blurred into fleeting memories.

That is why more families are now starting to create "Memory Boxes" or "Living Memory Books" at funerals. Everyone who has ever known the loved one pays their respects, and it's the easiest time to make this request—and also the hardest. At these times people are sometimes in so much grief that it's hard to write down all their thoughts cogently.

But who says you can't do this at an earlier time? Like right now, since the memories are so fresh. Write down memories of your own life for your children to have later.

First put on some soft, relaxing music and maybe sip a cup of tea. Now, using either your computer or a pad of paper, write each year of your life and leave a half a page between each year. Go back in time, and try to record memorable moments from each year. Trigger points will often be family holidays—Thanksgiving, Passover, Easter, Christmas, Kwaanza, Ramadan, Chanukah. Think about your birthday parties and friends who may have played with you. Where were you on your birthday? Who was there? Was there anything you didn't get but wanted? Why didn't you get it? What was school like? What sports or school activities did you participate in? Imagine a family dinner. What was the conversation? Who made you feel good? Who made you feel bad? Who gave you your first sense of self-worth? Who made you realize you were good at something? To enhance this memory box, enlist friends and family to fill in some of their memories. This will give you far more material and could remind you of good times, and sometimes trying times, you may have forgotten.

Katie Ford, the president of Ford Models, wanted to give her husband, hotelier Andre Balazs, a special gift for his fortieth birthday. So she contacted all his closest friends, as well as his family members, and asked them to write down one of their favorite memories of Andre. After collecting these letters, and adding some scribbles from their two young daughters, she bound them in a beautiful leather book and presented it to her husband. It remains one of the favorite gifts he's ever received and helps him to appreciate the people who are in his life.

Tears come to my eyes whenever I read the letter tennis great

Arthur Ashe wrote to his daughter Camera. Terminally ill, he wanted her to know how much she was loved. Arthur wrote down his thoughts about all sorts of subjects that he would want to discuss with his daughter over the years, his thoughts on dating and marriage, about combating racism and on self-esteem, about his desire for her to learn two languages, about his childhood and family, about how much her parents loved her and each other. Although she was only seven years old at the time, this record is a permanent document that proves forever how truly loved she was by her father. I doubt many people who have spent lifetimes with a parent have had a glimpse into their parent's heart and mind like this. That's the power of a letter. Here is an excerpt:

> *Dear Camera,*
>
> *You would be sad that I am gone and remember me clearly for a while. Then I will exist only as a memory already beginning to fade in your mind. Although it is natural for memories to fade, I am writing this letter in the hope that your recollection of me will never fade completely. I would like to remain a part of your life, Camera, for as long as you live.*
>
> *Don't be angry with me if I am not there in person, alive and well, when you need me. I would like nothing more than to be with you always. Do not feel sorry for me when I am gone. When we were together, I loved you deeply and you gave me so much happiness. I can never repay you. Camera, wherever I am when you feel sick at heart and weary of life, or when you stumble and fall and don't know if you can get up again, think of me. I will be watching and smiling and cheering you on.*

The power of love endures after death, and this letter revives her father's presence. As Morrie Schwartz said in *Tuesdays with Morrie,* "Death ends a life. Not a relationship."

Some express their feelings in smaller ways, using scrapbooks to convey sentiments.

On one page in a journal, a mother pasted a picture of the scenic French landscape the family visited, along with the picture of their child feeding a horse. She bordered each of these shots with colorful construction paper and pasted it onto the page. Then she took another piece of construction paper and wrote the following:

> *Dear Erin,*
>   *At thirteen months, you are all about discovery. You love wide-open spaces and the feel of cool grass against your tiny bare feet. On this particular day, you were quite taken with the horse, and the corn in Grammy's garden created a jungle for you.*
>   *I love you,*
> *Mom*

Another mother took a picture of her son Chase in a bunny suit and pasted it onto construction paper that was glued to a piece of fabric in a handmade journal. She used pastel stickers of eggs to decorate the picture, and in a script that was purposely drawn to look like a child's handwriting, she wrote, "Chase's Easter Bunny suit started with the ears. We found them at a craft store, and he wore them all around as we shopped. His dad says that someday he'll be totally embarrassed—I hope not. I am so grateful for my little bunny."

And here's what an enterprising father did. To document his special relationship with his little guy, he and his wife made a scrapbook of pages with father and son. Headlined, "Yeah! Daddy's Home!" there is a picture of the son waiting at the window with the following caption, "5:45 P.M. Starting at 14 months, you began to run to the window every evening at the same time to wait for Daddy." Then there's a shot of Dad giving Junior a bath with the caption, "Don't forget your pontoon boat! Clean at last!" followed by a picture of Dad reading to his son with the caption reading, "Every night Daddy reads you a bedtime story. And then he gives you a good-night hug."

By just adding a few words to illustrate a picture, these scrapbooks have a life of their own, filled with the qualities that make your loved ones special.

The next time you wonder what to buy a friend for their birthday, try writing a letter about a special moment you shared, or even frame it, perhaps accompanied by a picture of the two of you.

To Barbara,

Ah, our dating years. Remember trying on ten thousand outfits before choosing one and turning our apartment into a cyclone? Found this picture. Thinking of you,
Love Jill

Letters have enduring power. Buried deep in the pores of the paper are the heartfelt emotions of the author communicating his thoughts to you.

Although e-mails have become a popular form of communication, they don't hold the same resonance as someone's handwriting lovingly composed on a sheet of personalized paper. E-mails can be erased with the click of a button, but letters feel like living entities, and in fact they are, holding the essence of someone's individuality in the nuanced way they dot their i's or cross their t's. Whether someone's penmanship is tightly condensed or large and flowing, handwriting reveals volumes about the author. Just like DNA, letters reveal our inner workings, and whenever we visit them, the experience of the moment the letter was written is immediately relived and revived.

In the same way that little children are given piggy banks to learn the importance of saving, we can instill a love of writing by being a role model. If your children see you write, they will follow this tradition. My sister-in-law Marcia taught her boys the importance of thank-you notes as toddlers by having them scribble a line next to their name, therefore instilling the habit of this gracious courtesy early in their lives. Now at eight and six, Jordan and Oliver are conditioned that writing notes is the proper way to express yourself to people who do nice things for you. Plus, reports Jordan, it's also fun to receive letters. "It's better than a phone call because you get to open up the envelope," he reports. And you can keep the letter.

Keeping a record does not have to be a time-consuming task. Before Parker was born and I started a more detailed diary, I would simply save my appointment books from year to year. Leafing through one of them, I can see how back in the week of May 23, 1988, the entries were simply, "Summit Coverage," "Female Comedians," "Robert." Nonetheless, immediately I am lulled back to the experiences those brief words represent and can use them as trigger points.

There was a time I was certain that I would remember every detail of Parker's life, the day he crawled, the first word he spoke, the exact time his baby tooth peeked through his pink virgin gum. The truth is that I do not remember, and many of these little milestones are jumbled together into a fuzzy timeline consisting of years instead of days. But now in Parker's navy suede diary, I have documented these milestones, sometimes weekly, occasionally monthly. I have a permanent record, so that when he inevitably asks "When did I . . . ?" I can provide a ready answer. I do think this manic desire to document my son's life is one of my legacies of loss. Writer Letty Cottin Pogrebin, one of the cofounders of *Ms.* magazine and author of *Getting Over Getting Older*, says that she religiously kept detailed records and scrapbooks of her children. "My mother died when I was a teenager, and I had so little to remember her by," says Letty. "I wanted my kids to have many memories. Now I am older than when my mother had died with grown children. To see my kids take down the books and introduce their lives to boyfriends and friends through these books makes me feel like I did a good job. These memories they will have forever, and I do believe they will pass on this tradition to their own children."

My diary talks about my son's milestones but also reveals our thinking in how we approached everything from weaning him from a bottle to handling everyday crises.

"Today I had a real conversation with you which showed how you are developing logic. It was snowing outside. Through the window, I showed you how the snow falls from the sky and lands on the ground and on the tree. 'Why is bird not in tree, Mommy?' you asked. 'It's too cold for the birds, sweetheart,' I replied. You then turned to me, and with such sweetness and innocence, said, 'Mommy, get bird a baby coat.' What a moment."

Another entry was, "Dad had a bad day at the office, and my job was to divert his attention so he can recharge his emotional batteries. In a way, that's what you do for him, too, help him escape the pressures of daily life and put life in perspective. When you greet him at the door with a bubbly 'Daddy,' I see his anxiety melt away as he becomes a two-year-old with you, playing with your trucks and cars. Family does that, and it's why I hope you too one day will have a wife and family. It's worth waiting for the right one, but when you have it, it is life's greatest pleasure."

My goal is for him to learn about us as well as himself, and to understand that no matter how old one is, there are uncertainties to work through.

Allyson has written letters to each of her three children. "I made sure to tell them the parts of their personality I not only observed but really liked," she said. "I think it would be really great to know how my parents looked at me at a certain age. This is information that rarely is shared, and my kids will now have it."

Each time I have bought a diary, I've made it a family event as though we were purchasing a brand-new bike or CD, sending the message that this is a valued enterprise. Though I did veto the Superman diary Parker pointed to, I have included the kids in helping choose various diaries, and look forward to the time when these books will be lined up like cereal boxes on a shelf all representing the different flavors of each of our lives.

Vanessa already is a talented artist, turning diary covers into elaborate collages made from magazine headlines and colored glitter. Inside are ticket stubs, photos, autographs, poems, letters next to details documenting her life. Hopefully, Parker will continue this tradition. Jessica made Vanessa a photo album with essays about sisters that will be treasured always.

One family I know writes a long letter each year outlining the milestones in their family's lives and sends it out as Christmas cards. "There are so many things I know I should do," sighs Janet. "But I never find the time. Between work and the kids, I hardly have time to shower. Yet this is one ritual I am disciplined about. The Sunday after Thanksgiving, I know to spend the afternoon writing about the kids' lives. I have made that a priority, and the whole family looks forward to seeing it."

Writing in diaries or composing letters and notes can become as much of a habit as getting a haircut, and over time these short little stories bloom into a novella of a life, tangible and permanent, valued and savored for generations.

24

~

Picture This:
How to Take Family Pictures

What child hasn't asked to see his parents' wedding picture or marveled at the sepia-toned photo of grandparents long deceased? It is said that photographs are mirrors with memories, and I believe this is true. Pictures can capture a moment and freeze it forever in time.

At weddings, custom dictates that we hire a professional photographer to document this most special occasion. Yet so few of us think of using a professional at other times. Sometimes through sheer luck, we amateurs capture a great shot that won't be consigned to the garbage heap. However, the odds of taking a great picture on your own are as likely as winning the lottery. The vast majority of these photos are disappointments. The lighting was wrong, the focus blurred, the kids weren't smiling, blue eyes became glowing red circles. Furthermore, a family member—usually me—is taking the picture, so someone is always left out.

You've heard the sad accounts of people who had once-in-a-lifetime reunions with friends or family, and the pictures taken were either flawed or out of focus. "Can you believe it, that idiot cousin of mine didn't have film in the camera," yelled Christopher. "After the reunion Aunt Mildred died, and we never will be able to get that shot." This is why I started hiring a professional photographer to shoot our holiday pictures. I wanted to limit my risks.

"This is one of the best investments a family can make," says Barbara Vaughn, a family photographer who specializes in natural home settings. "Videotapes are certainly memorable, but often they're put in a drawer and not seen on a daily basis. Pictures are openly displayed in a home, and you have a daily relationship with them. When you go into someone's house, and you see pictures from different generations, it shows the continuity of a family and gives you a wonderful sense of history."

Hiring a professional photographer doesn't have to bankrupt you. Department stores like JCPenney and Sears now have professional photographers on staff for reasonable prices. Usually, these studio shots, with many options for backgrounds, can be achieved for less than fifty dollars, though additional prints may cost more.

If you're on a tight budget, call a film school and see if any students would be willing to take a family portrait for whatever budget you can afford. Ask several students to send you samples of their work so that you can choose a style that appeals to your taste. Hiring a talented student can cost as little as a hundred dollars.

Professional photographers are often far more expensive and can start at $250 an hour and zoom to as much as $20,000. Costs may not include the price of proofs, which can be an additional $100 or more. To find someone, comb through children's magazines, photography books or local newspapers. The magazine, newspaper or book publisher will have a contact number.

Often the professional photographers make profits from charging high rates for prints, so work out a price before agreeing to the shoot. If you can't afford their overall fees, many photographers will either negotiate or steer you to someone else.

As with any endeavor, it is always best to be prepared, and here are some things to think about before the photographer arrives or even if you take the shot yourself.

- Contrary to popular belief, bright sunshine and a sunny day don't produce beautiful pictures. There will be too much harsh shadow and squinting. The best results come from an overcast day, which provides soft, flattering light. Other ideal times are very early in the morning or right before sunset. Therefore schedule the shoots around these times.

- Think about what you're wearing. If the photo is in color, it is best to all wear the same color shirt to create a unified picture. Solid colors like white, black, navy and red are ideal candidates and will blend nicely with most backgrounds. (If the photo is in black and white, avoid anything white because it will make you look larger.) Also, don't make the mistake of putting a child in a striped shirt on a chintz couch. It will ruin the picture no matter how adorable he may be.

- Grooming is essential. Remember this picture is going to be taped to refrigerators or put in a frame to be viewed by family members for many years. Do you really want to be seen with greasy hair or mascara smudged under your eye? Take the time to put every hair in place and use hair spray as insurance. Put on makeup as though you're going to a prom or a special Valentine's dinner. The better you look, the better you feel, and the photograph will reflect this extra effort.

- No photographer is a mind reader, and they will not know what kind of photo you're after. Considering the amount of money and time that is spent on magazine shoots, tear out some pictures you like from magazines and pay attention to composition. What's in the background? What were they wearing? How are the people sitting or standing?

My husband's ex-wife, Alicia, saw a photo of Meg Ryan, Jodie Foster and Michelle Pfeiffer in *Premiere* magazine. Each was barefoot in jeans and a black shirt, curled up next to each other with Jodie in the middle. Alicia liked the image so much that she brought it to her photographer and duplicated it with her daughters resting their heads on her shoulders in the same exact angle. You can also send some of the tear sheets you like to the photographer before the shoot to discuss how you can duplicate them for your own family. This will also give the photographer an idea of your preference, and you can work together to create the perfect, memorable image.

This same advice applies if you're taking the shots at home.

Timothy Greenfield-Sanders, whose celebrity work appears in galleries and magazines, says one of the biggest mistakes an amateur photographer makes is complicating the background. "You'll see a family together, and then the Christmas tree is sticking out of someone's head or there's a bad piece of furniture obstructing the view," he says, smiling ruefully. "Unless you really know what you're doing, stick to clean and simple lines."

Another trick, says Greenfield-Sanders, is to resist centering the faces in the middle of the frame. "You'll see a tourist taking a shot with the family next to the Statue of Liberty. When the film gets developed, it's rarely a good shot because there will be too much space between their heads and the horizon," says Timothy. "By tilting the camera down, you'll get a much better angle where the people will fill up the space and create an image worth saving."

Because people are so weight-conscious, they'll do silly things that are often counterproductive for a pretty shot. To look slimmer, tilt your body slightly sideways versus head-on.

Timothy Greenfield-Sanders urges people who are conscious of weight not to jut their chin straight out. "It happens all the time, and it creates the opposite effect," he says. "Or they tilt their head up and what you see is a bird's neck. The best trick is to tilt your chin down and stretch it out and it tightens everything around the neck. It's the cheapest face-lift around."

One female politician who used to visit CNN would put Vaseline on her front teeth to make them more sparkling, though most of us thought this was an unnecessary exercise. For women, putting on lip gloss does create a nice shimmer, which the light bounces off of and which complements the smile. Also, consciously think happy thoughts because pictures capture this.

The type of camera you use doesn't matter, because there are many "idiot proof" designs on the market that let you simply point and shoot. But read the instructions and invest the time to learn how to use it. Ask the store owner to show you tricks of the trade. Why have red eye when there's a button to minimize it? So often people don't make the simple adjustment from landscapes to portraits and miss out on a good shot.

Here is one other pitfall. Make sure the equipment is ready before you assemble the family. Load the film. Check the lighting. Plan the background composition of the shot before anyone sits down. When all systems are go, then assemble your family.

"Too often, the photographer will take two or three shots and think that's enough," says Jeffrey Saks, the art director for *Parents* magazine. "Set up the same shot and take at least one full roll of the image you want. This way you have a far better chance of having everyone look good."

For photographing children, let the child play with a favored toy until the moment you want to shoot the picture.

"Then call his name, and he'll look up and you'll get a spontaneous picture," adds Jeffrey. "Children have short attention spans. This concept can also be applied to photographing elderly people. Have them read a book and then at the moment that everything looks perfect, call their name and they'll look up."

Jeffrey, like many experts, also suggests photographing people doing the daily rituals of life. "It's a mistake to think that all shots must be portraits," he says. "Let your child see himself playing with his cars or reading with Mom. Pictures are supposed to be reflections of life."

I agree wholeheartedly with this advice. In Parker's album, there are pictures of him pounding the piano like a pint-sized Beethoven and of him dancing with his sisters. These shots say more about our family life than a mere "stand up and say cheese" portrait. Annette Bening once commented on how her husband Warren Beatty takes pictures of their kids sleeping. You too can be inventive.

So try taking pictures of:

Your kids waking up
Your kids dressing
Your wife on the phone
Dad watching a football game
Your two daughters watching TV on the bed
(A picture to document how messy their rooms really were)

Your family blow-drying their hair or putting on makeup
Mom reading a recipe book while cooking vegetable stew
The inside of your car

Barbara Vaughn spent almost twenty-four hours photographing a family for a *Day in the Life* documentation. Her client was so happy with the results that she plans on doing it annually. Incorporate this idea into your own life.

For developing prints, you can go to the one-hour photo shops. However, not every store has the same quality. Some use different chemicals or have machines that aren't as current. Shop around. For special prints, ones that are keepers, it's always a good bet to go to a custom printer. Most local phone books will have listings for professional labs.

If you're willing to spend the extra money, many labs can also touch up these photos in the same way that magazines erase blemishes from bodies and faces. Technology does exist so that you and your family can look like movie stars, but every added layer increases the overall price.

With the advent of digital cameras and high resolution printers, images can be taken that can be immediately plugged into a computer or television set. You can even print out the pictures on the computer or send them on the Internet.

AOL has a service where simultaneously you can order traditional prints from the camera store and for an additional fee, have the images digitalized and sent to you through e-mail. Over 40,000 camera stores participate in this program.

After capturing a memorable shot, there is one last task that cannot be overlooked. On the back of each photo, write down the date as well as the people who are in the photograph. Over time, years merge into seconds, and the concept of time becomes blurred. No matter how clear your recall, the day-to-day details of dates, places, names and times inevitably begins to fade. By simply writing down the date of the photo and the people who are in it, you can immediately revive your memories and help future generations learn vital clues from their past.

It's also appreciated when you share pictures with others by making copies. "The Japanese will send off a copy of a picture even to someone they hardly know," says my friend Lisa. "I think that is a marvelous tradition."

Where you house these pictures is also important. Too many of us toss pictures into boxes and neglect to make albums. Go out and buy some albums and spend a few hours sorting through pictures. They're easier to enjoy and far more accessible when compiled in albums. According to the Hobby Industrial Association, consumers spent $300 million in 1999 to safeguard memories—in 1997 the number was $200 million and in 1995 it was virtually nothing.

Julie Roe-Smith, a consultant for Creative Memories, a firm that specializes in scrapbook products, has a theory on scrapbooks' sudden popularity.

"In this crumbling society, people are looking for something family oriented," she said. "It's the whole family thing. I have heirloom furniture. I want my son to know about the people who gave it to me. It's keeping in touch with the past."

If you're displaying a picture of someone you loved, put the shot in a special frame that shouts, "This person is special." Or to personalize it even more, make a homemade frame. Make copies of pretty shots to dispatch to relatives for their enjoyment and safekeeping in case of loss or damage.

Also make sure your photos are preserved in acid-free albums or frames so that vivid colors in pictures won't fade over the years. I have a friend whose lemon-colored prom dress is now the color of mustard in the photo. Let the color and personality of your life live on by putting these treasured mementos in a protected place. In the same way many put valuable jewelry and documents in a safe-deposit box, put these precious jewels in a safe place too.

25

The Movie of Your Life: How to Make Family Videotapes

It happened so suddenly. One day Bobbi Galex was playing tennis, and the next day she was in the hospital's intensive care unit. She had had a bad reaction to osteoporosis medication and was gravely ill. But while her family kept vigil near her bedside, they had a lot of memorabilia to help comfort her.

Her daughter Audrey owns an Atlanta-based company called Roots & Wings—Life Stories, which makes videotapes for families, creating what she calls family histories. The year before, she had videotaped Bobbi.

"We learned that she loved to paint as a child, so we brought in paintbrushes for her to feel with her hands, and we pasted up Monet prints on the walls of the hospital," recalls Audrey. "I fortunately had asked her about her favorite music, so we brought in Sinatra and Streisand songs."

The family also brought pictures of a healthy Bobbi Galex so that the nurses could relate to her as a strong, vital person.

The combination of luck, an expert medical team and loving care helped their mother survive her ordeal. However, the experience taught Audrey many things.

"I didn't even know what her favorite passage of the Bible was until I asked," she says. "These are questions you never talk about, yet they become so important. These videos are not only living histories of the person you love, but they can give you information about what to do when a loved one is dying so the transition can be as pleasant as possible."

Audrey learned another lesson. Compile video histories early in life before memory fades and intricate details unravel in the mind. These videos became dear companions after a loved one dies. "At eighty, you don't remember as much," observes Audrey. "I'll ask clients to tell me something about their kids, and they forget the small things. They end up talking in generalities instead of remembering specific details that add the color to our lives."

So now Audrey advises people to compile videos early in life. Information to help novices can be provided by logging on to www.personalhistorians.org, which lists many companies that provide the video services. Genealogy sites also offer suggestions.

It isn't difficult to incorporate videotaping into family rituals on a regular basis. Every year before Christmas, the McDonald kids are given the assignment to be Hollywood directors in the making. Armed with a video camera—which many families now own but can be rented if needed—they are asked to compile an annual movie about their family complete with interviews and embarrassing moments. Once Tommy did his whole sketch on the family's bathroom schedules, including how Emily exasperates her brothers by taking too long getting dressed. "It becomes a game to them, a competition," says John McDonald, the family patriarch. "But often they capture very funny moments, and we have it all on tape for our family and ancestors to appreciate for many years to come."

British actress Kate Beckinsale (*Pearl Harbor*) gets constant comfort from videos of her father, a TV star who died of a heart attack when she was 5. "I learned very early that hot is hot, cold is cold, and very healthy people can drop dead in a second," she says. "Suddenly, everything was over, but then again, it wasn't. My father has been dead for 22 years, and he's still on TV all the time. I'm so used to seeing him. Whenever there's a really significant moment in my life, he's on the TV. When my daughter, Lily, was born two years ago, I said, 'Let's turn on the TV,' and there he was. At first, it was hard to watch him, but now I see it differently. Now it almost feels like he's watching me. My father's death has given me a strong sense of the power of film."

A life is not only defined by major milestones. In the movie *My Life*, Michael Keaton has been diagnosed with terminal cancer and wants to leave his unborn son memories of him. In addition to videotaping conversations of his thoughts about important issues, he brought his video camera to his favorite restaurant, showed his son how to shoot a jump shot and shared what he loved about the boy's mother. One touching scene has him reading a Barney book to his son because he won't be there to do it himself. His presence is so real, so lifelike, no longer an abstraction but someone with a beating heart with flesh and bones, which is exactly the point.

With the aging of the world population, more and more families are recognizing the value and need for documenting the histories of their loved ones. They know that the experiences that shaped their parents and grandparents have an ongoing impact on their own lives. They know that their parents' stories will shed light on parts of their own personalities and how their parents' fears and triumphs helped form the people they've become. And they also know that if their grandparents and parents die, their stories die with them, and so does a piece of their own history.

Yet where do you start? And what do you say?

I remember interviewing Steven Spielberg for his *Shoah* project, where he compiled the stories of Holocaust survivors to ensure that history never forgets the horrors that took place. I asked him what was the hardest part of the project. "It is not easy unlocking the secrets," he said. "Many are buried so deep. Until we started this project, many of these survivors didn't even tell their families what they had gone through."

Whether you're Steven Spielberg or Steven Smith, getting people to talk about themselves is no easy task. Ask someone to start talking, and they often close up like a clam. Their mind goes blank.

Thirty-two-year-old Heidi tells a typical story. "I tried to videotape my grandmother, but when I asked her to tell me her life story, she couldn't think of what to say. Then she became frustrated and said, 'I'm no one special or famous, so why would you want to bother with this?' And that was the end of that."

If only Heidi could have met Dr. Robert Akeret, her job would have been so much easier. For thirty years as a practicing psychologist, he has helped people build self-esteem through self-knowledge. He is also the author of four books, including *Tales from a Traveling Couch* and *Family Tales, Family Wisdom: How to Gather the Stories of a Lifetime and Share Them with Your Family*.

As a result of speaking to so many patients, he developed a program called "Elder Tales" to help families "tap into the wisdom of elders through their stories." Unlike others, he combines the technical skill of a top-notch interviewer with the probing acuity of an Ivy League psychotherapist. "As Flaubert once said, every life has a novel in it," says Dr. Akeret, a knowing smile spreading across his lips.

The best way to start his Elder Tale program is to look at it as a project that needs preparation—not as a spur-of-the-moment task. Think of it as a labor of love. Do it in leisurely sessions over the course of several afternoons.

He suggests organizing the videotaping sessions into groups. "Snapshots from Youth," "Snapshots from the Adult Years," "A Day in Your Life," "Turning Points," "High Points and Low Points," "Epiphanies and Lessons." Dr. Akeret says you should collect photos and souvenirs from each period. "Look for those pictures that seem to have stories leaping right out of them or pictures that have some significance to you." You may want to accompany these photos with memory joggers.

Memory joggers are diaries, ticket stubs, invitations to special events, graduation books, arts-and-crafts projects, notes you wrote in the margins of books, old schoolbooks, appointment books, your mother's Lenox china and white linen tablecloths. Memory joggers can also be a well-worn baseball mitt stuffed deep inside a trunk, records from musicians no longer heard, as well as clothes from earlier eras now long out of style.

A school yearbook can trigger all sorts of memories. Stacey's grandfather Dan became a giddy teenager as he leafed through the yellowed pages. "See that boy? Johnny was his name, and he was the biggest bully. My father said I should leave him alone. But I got sick and tired of him beating me up, and one day I just smacked him back and he never messed with me again."

Then Grandpa Dan pointed to another picture of a fifteen-year-old with a gingham skirt and golden hair. "Darcy Enghart, boy did I love her. She was my first love outside your grandmother. Didn't like me, though, but it turned out all right. She drank too much and made her husband miserable. Your grandmother, though, she was as sweet as blueberry pie. But she also knew how to get her way too, that one. In her sweet little way, you know the way she had that soft voice and all, she got us to move to South Dakota after the war because she had relatives there and her uncle had offered me a job. I think she didn't care so much about the job but wanted to get me away from Darcy."

Thinking back to Darcy reminded him of what it felt like to have a crush at the dawn of World War II, and soon other memories were summoned up, memories of his family listening to the radio and of his mother's needlepoint.

"It was in the air, and folks talked about war, but we were busy living our lives, doing our chores and trying to have some fun," says Dan. "I do remember my mother feverishly sewing when the news came on and the reports kept on getting grimmer and grimmer. I guess she realized her sons would have to go to war." And from that, Dan gave a detailed narrative of fighting in the war as a pilot, all because of one look at a photograph of Darcy.

Each memory jogger provides clues and stories from the past and creates a sweeping narrative that becomes interconnecting stories of a life. Sometimes these memories can be enhanced by what experts call "hypnotic" motivators. For example, if someone is reflecting on a picture from 1950, find props that relate to that period. Props such as old newspapers, records, aluminum tins that stored flour, bottles for milk help revive the ambiance of the period. They can be found in flea markets and antique stores as well as on the Internet. Many newspapers have services that enable customers to buy old copies from times long ago.

These props can make a difference. One friend told me how her father was answering questions in monotonous one-syllable answers until she put some Glenn Miller tapes on. "Suddenly, he was transformed. He was a young vital man again twirling his wife while dancing the Lindy. You could see it happen right before you. His memory became fresher, and he could provide many more details of his life."

Smell is often the most potent of memory joggers. If you have a teapot from another era, make a simmering cup of tea and let the aroma evoke a whiff of the past. When would your parents use this tea set? What else was served with it? What other smells permeated the house? Hold an antique watch in your hand and remember the time your father wore it going to church. Was he very strict about reading the Bible? Did he like to be nicely dressed? What was his favorite part about Sundays? Feel the pages of an old newspaper. Take your old passport, open to an entry and remember what it felt like to be holding it tight in your hand as you embarked on your journey. Dr. Akeret told me a story about how the smell of turpentine helped an elder remember his father, who was a painter.

All these tools activate what Dr. Akeret calls the kinesthetic memory, the memory that resides in muscle movement as well as the memory that lives in your other senses—hearing, sight, smell and taste.

It all helps set the mood.

After selecting twelve or so pictures and corresponding souvenirs for each session, Dr. Akeret suggests the person being videotaped arrange them in whatever order they'd like. On a file card they should write down:

- The names of the people in the photo
- Where and about when they were taken
- Any special circumstances they can remember—was it a trip or a special occasion
- A single line to sum up the feeling of the event—Bobby's graduation. School play. Got my first car.

Dr. Akeret says these file cards are "crib notes" to help organize thoughts and remember details in case you forget during the taping.

Now it's time to videotape. Make sure you use fresh, never-been-used videocassettes. Since this tape is going to pass on from generation to generation, it is vital that the master be a clean copy. Clarity and precision diminishes each time a tape is recorded over, and sound quality can suffer as well. If you are shooting outdoors and using a battery-powered video camera, make sure the batteries are fully charged. Also test that the equipment is working properly.

As discussed in the previous chapter, think about the setting. Harsh lighting will bleach the image. If there's not enough light, your subject matter will look like a shadow, and the wry, crooked smile of Grandfather that amused you so much will be lost. Your goal is to have even light that blends in to the surroundings. Do not film in front of a window because it creates a backlight that obscures the subject. Another helpful hint is to film your subject at a 45-degree angle, or slightly sideways, for the best image.

A tripod is a worthwhile and inexpensive investment. The apparatus allows the camera to rest in the same position without moving. A tripod enables you to sit with your subject without the distraction of holding a camera and speaking at the same time.

Keep the tripod three feet away from the subject. Look inside the lens to ensure that you have the right proportions of the person you're shooting in relation to the background. You don't want to see the tape later and realize you only captured the top of your grandfather's head because of faulty framing.

To start the videotaping, open with the date and the purpose of the shoot. "Today, Grandfather is telling us stories about his childhood for the session on Snapshots from Youth . . ."

Have Grandfather pick a photograph and start telling its story. What does it mean to him? Who were the people in it? What was life like for him during this time? "Let each story run as long as feels natural," says Dr. Akeret. "Often the listener wants to ask questions, but try to wait until the person being videotaped completes his or her thoughts on the photograph. This helps with the narrative flow."

Amusing tales and mishaps will follow as well as a surprising bonus. Your loved one will find it cathartic to share this information, tapping into what psychoanalyst Erik Erikson identified as "the desire to integrate the various parts of life as fundamental to life's final stage." Elder tales fill a primal need to be worthy of respect from the society at large, and traditionally it was always the older people who were the repository of wisdom from the past. Many don't have fancy possessions to leave to their children, and their stories become the children's inheritance.

After the childhood session, proceed to the next section of "Snapshots from Adult Life" the following week. "Usually the session takes an hour, and the inevitable questions and answers that follow extend another half hour or so," says Dr. Akeret. The person whose life story is being documented should also show a variety of stages from courtship, to marriage, to children, to pictures from your professional life. It doesn't have to be the obvious photograph of an event. It can be of someone you met who inspired you to think in a new way. It can be of a child interacting with the world, and having this moment captured made you think about the wonders of the childhood and your child. Or it can be a picture that shows how life can change and teach many lessons.

Dr. Akeret shares an anecdote from a great-grandfather:

This is my favorite photo. The photo says it all—financial success beyond my wildest imagination. I'm sitting in the garden waiting for the furniture to arrive. I had just purchased the estate with the profits from my new import/export company. I was pleased with myself that I could afford such a fine house and proper garden. At the time, my sole companion was Jack, a great horned owl. Just about fifteen years later, when Hitler started the Second World War, I lost everything. I carry this photo to remind me that no matter what misfortune comes my way, I can always succeed again and always have.

For the "Day in Your Life" section, one can focus on one day or several days. Dr. Akeret suggests asking what someone remembers about: an ordinary routine day—a typical school day from when you were nine; a holiday—say Christmas, Passover or Fourth of July; a unique day in history where you remember where you were—the day Princess Diana died, the day President Kennedy was assassinated, the day a parent died.

Aside from telling the stories, try to focus on aspects of the day that stirred the senses such as the smell of coffee brewing in the kitchen, the cool air from a fall breeze or the style of clothing. Help your subject remember the rustle of your mother's apron, the smell of wood chips in your father's rec room, the hustle-bustle of commerce in the community, etcetera. The tiny details will flesh out the narrative.

"Turning Points" are usually preceded by some form of a crisis that alters the course of a life. Decisions have to be made—or in retrospect are made for you—which lead you on a new course. And as Dr. Akeret says, "either by action or default, you can see that the way you responded to that crisis defined who you are."

For example, I love the story that singer Julio Iglesias told me years ago about how a personal crisis became a turning point in his life.

"I was a soccer player earlier in my life. That's all I did was play soccer, day and night. I even slept with a soccer ball in my bed. I was already starting to play in the pros and getting good notices too when I was in a terrible automobile accident. The doctors told me I was never going to walk again. You can imagine how upset I was. All my hopes and dreams were smashed like my legs. I had no idea what else to do. But then a medical assistant brought me a guitar to give me something to do. And I started playing. And playing. And that's how my music career started."

Meeting someone who makes you look at the world differently can be a turning point. One woman remembers the compassion of a neighbor helping a sick friend. She so admired the woman that she later decided to become a nurse.

And sometimes turning points can reveal lifetime regrets, as one elder told his grandson in this cautionary tale.

"I wanted to marry a girl named Sarah," recalled one elder. "I had met her at school, and we just enjoyed each other's company immensely. But my family forbade the marriage because she wasn't from a prominent New England family and mine was. Even my brothers discouraged me, and I buckled under the pressure. I always regret that decision. I never was as happy with anyone as with Sarah. Your grandmother was a nice woman, and I cared for her immensely. Not like Sarah. If you love someone deeply, you know it and you should go for it. Otherwise you'll have regrets."

For the Epiphanies and Lessons session, the focus is on closing the narrative of a life by addressing various themes that make up your life. The response should sum up your life in a sentence or two. Who are you? An epiphany, says Dr. Akeret, is a sudden realization of a significant truth, usually arising out of a commonplace event.

One of my epiphanies is based on something that happened years ago. I was told a story in confidence about an ailing political figure. If I had given the story to my producer, it would have made national news (and eventually did) as well as boosted my career, which at the time sorely needed some help. Yet I couldn't betray a confidence, even though many of my other colleagues would have pounced at the opportunity for a career-making scoop. I think when I reflect on my life, I've cared more about being an honorable person than being someone who will stop at nothing to get ahead. This philosophy has also hurt me sometimes, but now after all these years, it's a price I've not only accepted paying, but learned to appreciate. It is who I am. As Eleanor Roosevelt once said, "Somehow we learn who we really are and then live with that decision." These video sessions reflect that wisdom.

Not every video session has such a regimented approach. Some prefer starting from early childhood and moving on biographically. Since asking about parents can be an emotionally charged question, family historian Vera Rosenbluth starts off her sessions by inquiring about grandparents. "Most people had at least one grandparent, so I often start my sessions by asking, 'Who was your favorite grandparent and why?' This is a safe way for the person to open up about their family."

Many questions can lead to meaningful discussions.

The following list is culled from many experts and hopefully will be a doorway to open a wide range of conversations with your loved ones. Do not be overwhelmed by the number of questions. Use two or twenty. They're here for you to pick and choose from.

When did you feel you had any special talent? Who made you feel that way?

Who was the person who gave you your first sense of self-esteem?

When did you realize you were good at something?

When did you realize you couldn't do everything you wanted to do?

How much do you think luck plays a part in life?

Were you lucky?

If you could do anything over again, what would you do?

What are you most proud of?

What was your biggest disappointment?

Who made you feel loved?

Who have you loved?

Since each person is unique, what gave you the most pleasure with each child?

What values do you think you leave your children?

What quirks do you think you have?

What gave you the most pleasure with your spouse? What did you enjoy doing together?

Who has affected you the most?

What compromise did you have to make for your close relationships?

Who was your best friend and why?

If you had a second chance to change the outcome of an experience with someone, either with something you said or did, what would it be?

What person have you most admired?

What virtue is overrated?

Was it because of someone you met, parental pressure or a genuine interest that you got involved in your profession?

Did you like work? What didn't you like about it? If you could do it all over again, what would you be doing?

What did you do for fun?

How has God helped you in your life?

Questions can also be designed to trigger memories from various key periods of life. The secret, of course, is to revive the senses that bring people back into the past.

What were you like at ten, fifteen, twenty-five?

Did you have a pet? Can you remember what its fur or feathers felt like?

Do you remember your first-grade teacher? What's your first memory of school?

What did your mother often cook for dinner? What did she put in your lunchbox?

What did the dishes look like? The tablecloth? What did it feel like?

What was the conversation at the table? Was it quiet or lively?

What did the neighborhood kids do for fun?

Do you remember a birthday party?

Would you skin your knees? Did you ever have a bad fall?

Were your parents strict? How would they punish you?

What made them laugh?

What did your bedroom look like at ten, fifteen, twenty-five, forty-five?

What music did you play in your teens?

What did it sound like when you awoke? Were there birds? City traffic?

What was your most expensive splurge?

What was one of your favorite vacations?

Who would you have liked to have been friends with?

Who was the first person you kissed?

Who was the first person you made love to?

Who was your first crush? Do you remember her voice? How her hair felt against your skin?

How do you fight fear?

What did you learn most from love?

Although these questions can help, make sure you also think about listening. Too often the interviewer rattles off questions like a machine gun without allowing enough time for the person to reflect on the question. As *60 Minutes* producer Don Hewitt once told me, the best information comes from the pauses. Vera Rosenbluth, an author and personal historian based in Canada, says that listening is as important as the questions. "Allow the silence. Allow the space," she advises. "The more deeply you listen, the more eloquent people will be. They'll feel it's safe to talk, and many of these people need to be heard. When people are focusing on them and listening to them, they'll say a lot."

This process is also therapeutic for the families who watch these tapes. Think about seeing a movie for the first time. Then years later, you see it again but notice different angles. I remember renting *The Sixth Sense* after seeing it in the movie theater. When I first saw it, I was so focused on the plot that I didn't realize all the little clues that were dropped cleverly in the dialogue. But after reviewing it, I saw a whole new movie. I noticed the scenery more vividly. I focused more on the behind-the-scenes characters and the acting performances of the stars. It was a new experience.

The same is true when we go back and look at the lives of our loved ones. As an adult, we will view the same event we saw as a child differently.

"The life story of a loved one possesses a wealth of complexity, depth and meaning that furnishes us with valuable opportunities for learning and growth even after the person has died," says Dr. Craig Vickio. "Reinterpretation is always possible and can yield new insights into the lives of our loved ones. Such new insights are likely to occur as we age and encounter changing life circumstances— circumstances that enable us to consider the deceased from a different vantage point."

Which simply proves that there is no one script for any story. So the movie of your life can be an ongoing miniseries.

PART SIX

Leaving a Legacy

"A rock pile ceases to be a rock pile the moment a single man contemplates it, bearing within him the image of a cathedral." ——Antoine de Saint-Exupery

"Praising what is lost makes the remembrance dear . . ." ——William Shakespeare

26

A Will to Live

In the movie *Stepmom*, Susan Sarandon has done an admirable job of letting her kids know she is dying. In her last few weeks, she makes every moment count, whether it's taking her kids ice-skating or putting extra care into making a Halloween costume. However, as her condition deteriorates, she leaves each of her two children with a special gift.

She presents her daughter with a quilt. Along with the black-and-white fabric squares are pictures of moments the two had shared: the ice-skating rink, the school plays, the plays. You just know that whenever she needs her mother's arms wrapped around her, this quilt will serve as a standby.

For her son, the aspiring magician, she made a cape. Like the quilt, the cape had stenciled pictures of their good times together. When she presented the gift, she said that, like magic, she would appear, not in person, but in spirit. He too would have something to remember.

I wish I had tangible memories like that. I cling to a silver charm bracelet that my parents bought me when they traveled through Europe. Each charm was purchased in a different country and though most are broken or chipped, I still hold on to this talisman of a time when a gift card said, "Love, Mom and Dad." I realize in retrospect that my parents didn't consider gift-giving as symbolic acts that later hold meaning. "We gave you what you needed at the time," my mother explains, rattling off the sneakers, sweatshirts and bicycles that were presented to us at the appropriate times. Just recently my mother gave me one of her old designer dresses that was in mint condition. I already treasure it, the feeling of the clingy material against my skin and the way the black ruffle circles around the hem so delicately. It is the first item she ever gave me which has the magic of history woven into it, because I remember vividly that my father proudly escorted my mother wearing this dress while Peter and I peered through the staircase.

This is why I am making the effort to buy gifts that will help Jessica, Vanessa and Parker remember me. Along with the requests list from the kids, the Abercrombie & Fitch pants, the Hard Candy makeup, the Batman action figures, I also include an item that is unique—a poem I've read that makes me think of them, a special book with an inscription, a photo album handcrafted from silk, a pair of classic earrings that can be worn at thirteen as well as thirty. I want to ensure that they have tangible memories of me always.

I also intend to leave other gifts for their future use. Since we never know when our time may come, plan for certain items to be bought or saved in your will.

Wouldn't it be so wonderful if, in their will, a parent had left a whole box of gifts that would be dispersed at various points in time? Like these for example:

"Son, these were my cuff links I wore when I went on my first job interview. I got them from my father, your grandfather. For your high-school graduation, I want you to have them. I'm sorry I can't be there for you, but you are always with me and I am with you."

"My Beautiful Daughter. I am so sorry that I am not here to be at your wedding. To help you pick out your dress. To register for your gifts. To help plan the seating arrangements. But here is something for you to let you know I'm thinking of you. Here is a blue garter, something new."

Since this is a traditional gift, it wouldn't matter if the blue garter was purchased twenty years before the actual event. The thought was there and would be so very meaningful. The mother's presence would be felt at a time when her daughter would have conflicted feelings, happiness over a marriage but sadness that her mother couldn't share in it.

Moreover, when parents die, families customarily disperse the possessions at a time when they're also coping with the death. You're on emotional overload and can't really appreciate the significance of seeing your father's ties hanging like toothpicks in a cedar closet.

Yet if, in the will, some of these possessions were taken immediately to be dispersed later, rationed for key times, these mementos would provide so much more meaning as well as comfort.

You can also be inventive. Tom Fontana, the legendary TV writer of such hits as *St. Elsewhere* and *Homicide*, has left a $25,000 provision in his will for his friends to have a big blowout bash on him. I intend to use this same concept in my will, but instead I will earmark funds for a lavish lunch in an expensive restaurant to be enjoyed by my best friends annually. Even the most expensive restaurants are less than fifty dollars per lunch. It would cost only a few thousand dollars for ten years' worth of lunches with each of my six best friends choosing a different locale each year. Of course, to reduce the cost of such an extravagance, it could take place at a modestly priced restaurant with the same results.

Most of us don't want to think of writing a will for obvious reasons. It forces us to face our mortality. "More than 70 percent of the population die without wills," says Artie Langhaus, an estate planner with KLS Planners. "Without a will, the family's problems are multiplied because it puts everything into complete chaos. This is not only a problem with property dispersion and taxes, but also with the distribution of personal assets."

Instead of thinking about a will as an unpleasant task, try to think of it as insurance. I remember driving one day and hearing Martha Stewart on the radio talking about the importance of documenting all your possessions. "Go into each room and write down everything that is in the room," she instructed. "Do not miss a detail. In the kitchen, document all the silverware, the plates, the dessert dishes, the special glasses, the pots, the pans. You should also take a picture of all the important possessions as proof of exactly which pieces are in your home. Also write down the approximate value of each piece." She then encouraged that each room have its separate list and that listeners should take the list, along with the pictures, or videotape if that's your preference, and seal it in a plastic bag. "This bag should be kept outside the home so that in the case of a robbery or fire, you won't forget all the possessions you actually own," she concluded.

Well, this same exercise can also be part of your will. For many reasons this is a smart move. First, it gives you a record of all that you have. Second, by documenting all your possessions, it prevents anyone from staking claim to your possessions. The courts are filled with cases where distant relatives suddenly appear out of nowhere wanting Aunt Wanda's Tiffany watch. Third, it also prevents wounded feelings among your surviving heirs.

Writing a will is a task that everybody, regardless of age or financial status should do. With a properly planned will, you can ensure that your property will be distributed exactly as you would have wished and not on an arbitrary basis, you can name your own executor to administer your estate, your children's guardians will be named as you wish and individual causes or charities will receive the support you want. The following paragraphs are guidelines for you to consider, but make sure you also consult an expert.

Although in twenty-five U.S. states you can make out your own handwritten will, mail it to yourself and then file it unopened with your personal papers to make it legally binding, it is still best to contact a lawyer or trust company in order to avoid possible confusion later. Having a will drawn up is one of the cheapest things you can have a lawyer do, and many lawyers charge hourly.

You can, however, lower the costs of drawing up a will by some early planning. Both books and software on wills can help you organize your records and ask the right questions when you meet a lawyer. This way you won't be using as many hours of the lawyer's time. Here are some books and software I've found to be helpful:

- *The ABA Guide to Wills and Estates* (Time Books $12). Covers estate planning.
- *Simple Will Book* (Nolo $17.95). Includes a pullout will form that you can fill out and step-by-step instructions stated in easy to understand language.
- *The Complete Will Kit* (John Wiley & Sons $19.95). Goes over all the issues involved in drafting wills.
- Willmaker 5 (Nolo, Windows or Mac $70. 800-992-6656). A friendly fill-in-the-blank method of creating a will that you can print out and sign. Nolo is the expert at turning this complicated maze of information into concepts that anyone can understand and follow.
- Quicken Family Lawyer (Parsons Technology, Windows or Mac $49) More detailed and more time-consuming but provides thorough information on over sixty types of documents you may need over a lifetime ranging from a will to a residential real estate lease.
- Internet Sites: www.nolo.com: Click to "Wills & Estate Planning," www.savewealth.com/planning/estate/charitabletrusts.html, www.ljextra.com/practice/trusts/index.html, www.netplanning.com/estate/index.html.

You should educate yourself on wills and use a lawyer, because as one expert said, it's foolish to jeopardize your family's future by doing it yourself.

A simple goof can have disastrous results. In one case, the courts threw out a will because its author hadn't realized he had to have his signature witnessed. The man had wanted all his assets to go to the stepchildren he raised as his own after his wife's death, and not to his estranged son. However, the court declared the will invalid, and all the assets went to the son, in accordance with state law. The stepchildren were left with nothing.

To ensure you have an ironclad will for your relatives, follow these guidelines provided by Nolo.

Go through all your possessions and decide to whom you want to give Aunt Rosie's chintz couch or the stained-glass lamp. Write out your final designations along with whatever comments you'd like to have read at the unveiling of the will.

Assemble all legal documents, leases on houses, marriage certificate, birth announcements, stocks and bonds, life insurance policies—any asset that has value and has proof of purchase. Copies of these should be kept in a special binder, with the originals kept in a safe-deposit box.

Also keep in mind:

- You must date and sign the will.
- The will must be signed by at least two witnesses. Your witnesses must be people who don't inherit anything under the will.
- You don't have to have the will notarized, but if you and your witnesses sign an affidavit before a notary public, you can help simplify the court procedures required to prove the validity of the will after you die.
- A will does not need to be filed with a government agency. Keep it in a safe place and be sure the person who is taking care of your estate knows where it is. Store it in an envelope marked "Will" and place it in a fireproof metal box, file cabinet or home safe.
- There is also an Internet site, www.FinalThoughts.com, that allows you to share your wishes. If you join, you can file information about where documents are stored as well as your desires for funeral arrangements.

Your will should also:

- Include information on who you intend to leave your property to, whether it's an individual or an organization
- name someone to take care of your minor children
- name someone to manage property you leave to minor children

if the person taking care of your child isn't capable of managing the property

- name your executor, the person with authority to make sure the terms of the will are carried out

Now it's time to plan ways your heirs can avoid paying excessive estate taxes, primarily through circumventing what is known as probate. Probate is a legal process that takes place after someone dies. The executor of the will proves the validity of your will and presents the local probate court with lists of property, your debts and who is to inherit what you've left. Then relatives and creditors are officially notified of death. If you don't have creditors, it is worthwhile to avoid probate because it can take up to a year and often cost as much as 5 percent of the overall estate in legal fees.

Here are ways to avoid probate:

- Get a Payable-On-Death Bank Account: By filling out a simple form provided by the bank, you can name the person you want to inherit the money in your account at your death. The beneficiary then goes to the bank, shows proof of the death and his or her identity and collects whatever funds are in the account without the probate court ever being involved.
- Funds in retirement accounts such as IRAs, insurance policies and 401Ks do not have to go through probate after death. The beneficiary you've named can claim the money directly from the account custodian.
- Stocks and Bonds: Almost every state now has adopted a law called the Uniform Transfer-On-Death Securities Registration Act that lets you name someone to inherit your stocks, bonds or brokerage accounts without probate. When you buy a stock, ask for a beneficiary form.
- Joint ownership of deeds on homes or businesses avoids probate with assets being automatically transferred to the surviving owner. Usually couples use this measure to protect themselves. This is not considered a good option unless it is with a spouse

because the co-owner can make claims on property at any time or sell or mortgage his share—or lose it to creditors. An added headache is that if it's not a spouse, you may be liable to taxes if value of interest share will automatically belong to the surviving joint tenant.

- The law enables you to give $10,000 a year to one recipient. If you have two children and give each $10,000 a year, in ten years, there is $200,000 that would not be taxed. You are also not taxed for donations of any amount to tax-exempt charities, gifts of any amount to your spouse or for someone's tuition or medical bills.

- Living Trusts: Property you transfer into a living trust avoids probate. In the trust document, you name the people or institutions you want to inherit trust property. When you die, the person you named as the successor trustee transfers the assets to the people you want to get it.

None of the beneficiaries has any claim to the assets until the will is read. Most experts say you should review your will every few years or at a time of a life change like a birth for whatever changes you want to insert. If you decide you want to disinherit one of your relatives, do not assume that if they are not in the will, they won't receive some of your estate. A child is often entitled to some of your assets even if he or she wasn't included in the will. So if Bobby is a lazy good-for-nothing louse and not worthy of your assets, make sure you state in the will that he is not to get anything, to ensure he has no claim to your Chevrolet.

For most people, their children's welfare and security are the primary reasons to write a will. One of the first considerations, especially for parents of younger children, is who will be little Katie and Kevin's guardian. Often people choose a family member with children so their kids are linked with familiar surroundings.

A guardian is the person who raises and cares for minor children in your absence. Choose the person whom you feel will raise your children as you would have and with whom you believe your children may feel most comfortable. Decide whether you want your children to be raised in your home or the guardian's, whether you want to name an individual or a couple as the guardian and whether you want to leave the guardian a cash bequest in recognition of the service.

A trustee is the person who administers the terms of the trust, arranging for investment of the assets for the beneficiaries and making distribution of trust assets in accordance with the trust terms. Think about appointing those who are intimately familiar with your wishes regarding the beneficiaries, and with whom the beneficiaries feel comfortable dealing.

Some parents may name one person to be the children's personal guardian and a different person to look after financial matters. Often this is because the person who would be the best surrogate parent would not be the best person to handle monetary concerns. Sister Molly may be a loving parent, but Uncle Charlie may be a whiz with finances.

The executor will be the person who administers your estate, offering your will for probate in court, inventorying your assets, having them appraised, arranging for the preparation of the estate tax return and paying all relevant taxes, arranging for the investment of estate assets during the administration process, and ultimately distributing the assets in accordance with the terms of the will. Think about appointing family members or trusted friends or advisers.

This is by all accounts the hardest part of the process. Rarely is a person suited for all these roles, but you must work with what you've got. Interview prospective guardians, trustees and executors of the will. Your sister Sally may love little Samantha and delight in playing with her Barbie dolls, but she may not want the responsibility. Your brother Paul may be the quieter personality, but might gladly agree to this request and consider it an honor to be asked. Do not assume you can predict people's responses. Even though the death of both parents is highly unlikely, it is still best to be prepared for the sake of your children's happiness and welfare.

Often people earmark fees for the guardian and trustee for the effort in managing your children's lives and security. This is a wise decision, especially if the estate has many assets.

"One of the biggest reasons people don't write wills is that they can't decide on who will be the executor, trustee and guardian," says

Alan Lustrin, a senior partner at KLS Estate Planning in New York. "Then they unwisely think, 'Okay, we'll wait until later to do this' and it's too late. In each of these categories, you should choose alternates to serve if the person you have originally chosen cannot."

Lustrin says the best litmus test in deciding who will be a good candidate is to think of the people you would say yes to if they would make a similar request.

Last but not least, one must also consider a living will. Because doctors are required to preserve a patient's life through whatever means is medically possible, you could be hooked up to a machine for months, causing both a financial and emotional drain on your family. A living will ensures that the doctors will withhold life-prolonging treatments. Your health care directive doesn't become effective unless you are diagnosed to be close to death from a terminal condition, permanently comatose, or if you cannot communicate your own wishes for your medical care.

I highly recommend the CD-ROM called Completing a Life and the Web site www.completingalife.msu.edu, which were created by Michigan State University. This way you can examine your options in the privacy of your home, fill out the easy-to-understand forms and file them with your family and doctor.

"We were hoping that by providing information in a non-threatening way, we can empower people to look at it long before they need it," says Dr. Leslie Bricker, who helped develop the CD-ROM and is an oncologist and palliative medicine specialist at the Henry Ford Health System in Detroit. "Because we're a sensationalistic society, people only hear the horror stories. But if you plan ahead, you don't have to be in pain."

Dr. Kathy Foley from New York University Medical Center and the president of the Project on Dying in America believes these documents help diminish the fear associated with death. "One of the reasons people are scared of death is that they've seen someone in pain and are afraid of the process," she says. "Today, technology exists so that the patient need not suffer. But the doctors and the family must be told in advance the extent of medication that can be administered. Sometimes for the pain medication to be effective, the patient becomes sleepy and groggy. One patient may want to be more alert while others want the pain medication at whatever cost, even if at the final moments they are not as communicative. It is important to discuss these issues with your family and in the living will."

Other medical issues include whether or not the doctors should continue with diagnostic tests, blood work, dialysis, respirators, surgery as well as cardiopulmonary resuscitation, following a terminal diagnosis.

Living wills should also include your feelings about being moved into a hospice center. "Everyone is entitled to die with dignity," says Dame Cicely Saunders, the founder of the modern-day hospice movement. "We're here to prevent pain rather than have people feel they have to earn pain medication." Now in her eighties with a halo of thick white hair, Dame Cicely oversees St. Joseph's Hospice in England and believes that it's easier to make people trust in death if they are treated with care and compassion. "In hospices," she says, "we help people die peacefully and help them live life to the fullest until that time."

At the hospice, volunteers and nurses talk to the patients, hold their hands and comfort them. Days are filled with reading, writing and arts-and-crafts projects ranging from stenciling scarves for final gifts to making ceramic pots molded from red clay. In the days leading to death, many choose home care where nurses administer pain relief.

Hospice care became a covered benefit under the Medicare program in 1983 and is covered by Medicaid in forty-three states in the U.S. According to a 1999 study conducted by the National Hospice Foundation, only 24 percent of Americans put into writing how they want to be cared for at the end of life. Yet 83 percent knew what they wanted from end-of-life care—they wanted their wishes to be honored.

We all want to feel that life is a continuous journey and that when one door closes, another one opens. But it is so much easier to travel from one place to the other if you feel you are prepared. Being prepared is more than a comfort. It lets the people who you've left behind know that they were loved.

27

The Grande Finale

Over lunch one day, I was telling my brother about a short story I had read by poet Maya Angelou. She writes about how certain places resonate deep within while others don't move the senses in the same way. It sparked a conversation about the places we have loved.

"Do you have a favorite place anywhere?" I asked.

"That's a no-brainer," he replied. "It's the Half Moon Hotel in Jamaica. I've had my best times there. A matter of fact, I want to be buried there."

"You want to be buried there and not somewhere close to home?" I asked, my eyes wide with surprise. "Why?"

"I want my ashes spread near the beach, since this is the place I felt most at peace," he explained.

If it hadn't been for this conversation, I would never have known my brother's wishes. The truth is, most families do not have a clue about the final resting place for their loved ones. We often say good-bye in the course of a day, but the good-bye that really matters, we never discuss.

By telling our loved ones about our wishes, about songs that we like or poems we hate, we can ensure that our grande finale will be a memorable one, and that our loved ones need never wonder what our wishes would have been.

"Good funerals are marked by a high degree of pomp, drama, creativity and a liberal dose of family involvement," says John De-Pretis. As manager of the world-famed Frank E. Campbell Funeral Chapel in Manhattan, he knows a thing or two about the subject. Their clients have included the families of Judy Garland, Yul Brynner, Jackie Kennedy Onassis, Joan Crawford, Rex Harrison, John Lennon, Mae West, Billy Martin, Tommy Dorsey and Fred Trump, to name a few.

"It's said that Queen Victoria loved planning funerals," he adds. "That's my type of gal! And why not? The funeral is every bit as valid as a wedding, sweet sixteen or a bar mitzvah. A life, whether of one week or 106 years demands recognition."

The send-off for Jim Henson, the brilliant creator of such beloved *Sesame Street* characters as Kermit the Frog and Big Bird, was anything but somber and sad. "We wanted to make it a celebration of his life," says his daughter Sheryl. Although he was only fifty-four years old when he died of a viral infection from pneumonia, Henson had made his wishes for his service known. The bearded puppeteer with a Pied Piper personality had written down in a letter five years previously that no one should appear in black at his funeral. So walking through the corridors of St. John the Divine Cathedral were hundreds of friends, family and well-wishers, all dressed in the brightest of colors and costumes. The church was decorated with thousands of butterflies made from the puppeteer's workshop. The childish joy he brought to his work and life was reflected in every detail of the ceremony, from the poems, to the music—a New Orleans jazz band greeted guests with a roaring rendition of "When the Saints Come Marching In"—to the eulogies.

England's Lord Mountbatten had a similar idea. The last viceroy of India said that he couldn't "think of a more wonderful thanksgiving for the life I've had than that everyone should be jolly at my funeral."

"A greatly staged funeral helps in the healing process," explains John DePretis. "A funeral is a place for people to come together to grieve, laugh, honor religious traditions and accomplishments for a departed member of the group. There isn't a society on earth that doesn't mark, honor and celebrate this transition."

Stylish flourishes and little telling details are important to illustrate the person's individuality and tastes. The riderless horse at President John Kennedy's funeral, so steeped in symbolism, was inspired from accounts of Abraham Lincoln's funeral. Coretta Scott King, the wife of civil rights leader Martin Luther King, arranged for her husband's mahogany coffin to be drawn through Atlanta on a crude farm wagon pulled by two mules, symbolizing King's identification with the poor. Legendary entertainer Frank Sinatra, an insomniac and world-class partier, was buried with a roll of dimes, because when he was out on the town he always worried about having enough change to make phone calls—back in the days when a phone call only cost a dime.

Mystery writer Agatha Christie requested that she be buried with her wedding ring, although she was divorced, and that Bach's Air in D from his third suite be played at the funeral. Mark Goodson, the producer of such game shows as *Password*, *Family Feud* and *The Price Is Right*, made the unusual request that following his death he be paged once a week at the Beverly Hills Hotel pool, a famous hangout for Hollywood types.

Gene Schwartz, the president of Frank E. Campbell Funeral Chapel, says families use these same ideas in many ways. "Someone who loved golf is buried with his golf club," he says. "Billy Martin of the Yankees was buried with baseball caps. Another person filled the room with aromatic candles."

Of course, the ideal situation is to also have a "living funeral." Morrie Schwartz, the irrepressible professor of philosophy immortalized in Mitch Albom's book, *Tuesdays with Morrie*, knew he was dying and gathered all his friends and family together while he was still able to enjoy a loving review of his life. However, not everyone has the gift of knowing death is near. So it is wise to be prepared by writing down your wishes.

Because we avoid the discussion, funeral plans are usually made at the last minute when the stress level is highest. People are in such vulnerable positions that they can be easily exploited. This is totally understandable. Thinking about your own funeral, or planning a will, stirs the superstitions within us. I got an ache in the pit of my stomach just thinking about it, as though, if I focused on the plans, it would turn into a self-fulfilling prophecy. This is when you have to fight the feeling of believing that tragedy is imminent and instead focus on the advantages of being prepared.

From a practical standpoint, a funeral is often one of the biggest expenses one has, besides purchasing a home and a car. The average price is around $8,000, but it can cost more. Planning ahead saves money. Nolo offers this advice.

Most people start by deciding where they want to be buried and finding a local mortuary. Many want to be where their mother or father are buried, next to a hill or near a bed of flowers. The mortuary can handle such tasks as collecting the body from the place of death, making burial arrangements with the cemetery, preparing the body for burial, arranging to have the body transported for burial. They can also suggest ideas for conducting the ceremonies. Most families then arrange for their personal pastor or rabbi to come to the service, though the mortuary will often have a list of suggestions if you don't belong to a church, temple or mosque.

To ensure that your local mortuary is the best option and meets your needs in terms of style and cost, funeral societies are great resources for comparison shopping. Names of various societies are listed in the telephone book under Funeral Information and Advisory Services. Another option is contacting the Funeral Memorial Societies of America at 800-458-5563. If you join the society, you will receive a form that allows you to plan for the goods and services you want—and to get them for a predetermined cost. Many of these societies also are watchdogs, making sure that you get and pay for only the services you choose.

After you have decided where you want to be buried, here are some thoughts that should be included in a note to your family:

- The name of the mortuary or other institution that will handle the burial or cremation.
- Whether or not you want to be embalmed.
- The type of casket you would like.
- Your pallbearers.
- Where you want to be buried or whether you want your ashes scattered and where.
- Whether you would like your organs donated.
- Details you want in the service, ranging from a selection of music, poems you may have loved, people you care about to make a eulogy and whether you want something special written for your epitaph.

Your wishes should not be included in a will, since these documents are read days or weeks after the death. Instead, write a note and put it in a drawer, safe-deposit box or jewelry box, and don't forget to tell your loved ones where it is. Sometimes even these notes are memorable. After Gracie Allen died, her husband, comedian George Burns, went through her drawer and found this note to help him prepare for her funeral:

> George,
>   Don't put a period where God intended a comma.
> Love,
> Gracie

Music often sets the mood for the event. In black churches all over the world, gospel music is as much a part of the service as the sermon. Hearing powerful voices belting out such goosebump-making songs as "Amazing Grace" is an uplifting experience. Some choose classical selections. Others have hired guitar players to strum soft melodies. Sarah McLachlan's angelic voice is now a popular choice. The more iconoclastic are opting for bagpipes. The crucial decision is figuring out what type of sounds the person listened to and bringing their musical pleasures into the service.

Don't think you have to be consistent. I know that for me, I would like a choir singing uplifting happy songs, a little Elton John,

Sting and Santana's version of "You are the Love of My Life" in gratitude to my husband and children and then to have the service conclude with a guitarist singing the Beatles lyrics "And in the end, the love you take, is equal to the love you make."

There are no rules here. Finding the right music to reflect the person you love is one of the most important elements in a memorable service. For as Aldous Huxley wrote long ago, "After silence, that which comes nearest to expressing the inexpressible is music."

Not everyone chooses to read poetry in the service, choosing instead to focus primarily on eulogies and music. Yet, as F. F. Leavis said in 1932, "Poetry can communicate the actual quality of experience with a subtlety and precision unapproachable by any other means." To many, poetry has its own lyricism that lulls the listener into deep reflection. T. S. Eliot had this explanation for its power. "Genuine poetry can communicate before it is understood." Yet the reason some don't utilize poetry in the service is not a dislike for the literary art but an absence of readily available choices. Jill Werman Harris, whose book *Remembrances and Celebrations* offers many selections, has a list of favorites that she generously shared with me.

"My favorites are Longfellow's 'Footsteps of Angels' as well as his triumphant 'Psalm of Life.' Inge Auerbacher's 'Something to Remember Me By,' Langston Hughes' 'The Bitter River,' Auden's 'Blues for Hedli Anderson,' Thomas Hardy's 'The Going' and the Twenty-Third Psalm."

My own personal favorite is a poem written by an anonymous writer called "Do Not Stand at My Grave and Weep."

> Do not stand at my grave and weep
> I am not there, I do not sleep
> I am a thousand winds that blow
> I am the diamond glint on snow
> I am the sunlight on ripened grain,
> I am the gentle autumn rain
> When you wake in the morning hush
> I am the swift, uplifting rush,
> Of quiet birds in circling flight,

> I am the soft starlight at night,
> Do not stand at my grave and weep
> I am not there, I do not sleep.

Remember that there is no obligation that a poem be about death. It can be a few simple lines about the pond by the hill that brought joy to the person who is now deceased.

A eulogy has no special format. It is an essay from the heart. As Garry Schaeffer, the author of *A Labor of Love: How to Write a Eulogy*, pointed out, a eulogy isn't a person's life story but instead, your story about the person.

However, some helpful tips can enhance these farewells.

A eulogy does not have to be long. Just remember that at Gettysburg, there were two speakers. One was Edward Everett, who spoke for two hours. One was Abraham Lincoln, who spoke for two minutes. You know whose speech is still remembered. So try to keep your eulogy from three to five pages at the most.

The opening phrases set the tone. Some open with an anecdote about the person, "I remember when Sam . . ." or "I once asked Sam what he felt . . ."

In describing her lover Dashiell Hammett, Lillian Hellman opened his eulogy by saying, "A few weeks ago, on a night when he was having a tough time, I said, 'You're a brave man.' I had never said such a thing before, and as he came out of that half doze the very sick have from minute to minute, he smiled and said, 'Better keep words like that for the end.' "

I tend to agree with comedian Alan King, who says that using humor "is a relief from the pain." So in writing the eulogy for comedian Henny Youngman, whose famous joke was, "Take my wife," King opened the eulogy by saying, "If Henny was alive right now, he'd be very sick. But to paraphrase him, I think he'd say, 'Please, take my life.' And instead of giving his body to science, he'd want to give it to Madonna."

"In writing the eulogies, I just think of ten memorable jokes or experiences with the person," says King, who has also eulogized

Frank Sinatra and Myrna Loy. "The bottom line is that it has to be well-intentioned."

In composing your thoughts, find stories that reveal the quirks or humanity of the person. Although you should and can list someone's accomplishments, such as "he was a great business leader, a fine musician and terrific tennis partner, but mostly, he was a great friend and father," it is the essence of the person that people want to remember.

Some opt to start their eulogies with famous quotes about loss found in books and then attribute it to someone's life, such as using Thoreau's quote, "In the end, may it never be said that we never lived," to be followed by a variation on, "We can say without a doubt, that Samantha truly lived . . ."

When a death was sudden and unexpected, often people start the eulogy by acknowledging why the mourners are gathered, such as the opening remarks from Charles, the ninth Earl of Spencer, at the funeral of Diana, the Princess of Wales:

> I stand before you today the representative of a family in grief, in a country of mourning, before a world in shock. We are all united not only in our desire to pay our respects to Diana, but rather in our need to do so. For such was her extraordinary appeal that the tens of millions of people taking part in this service all over the world via television and radio never actually met her, yet feel that they, too, lost someone close to them in the early hours of Sunday morning.

The middle of the eulogy should be a list of what made the person special. "She was a loving mother, a gourmet cook, a kind person who was the first to bring a casserole to any neighbor . . ." And perhaps it should include a brief summary of a life's accomplishments.

Not every paragraph needs to be glowing. Again, this is where humor helps. A friend of someone who was always late said, "I guess you can say this is the first time that Jane was ever on time. And it is the one time we wish she wasn't." My friend Mark read a eulogy for someone who was very loved but who also was very cheap. So

he brought smiles to the audience when he said, "David was wonderful in many ways. The most generous person you ever met.
He would come over to your house in the dead of winter to help you
shovel snow. He would pick up your kids if they needed a ride and
even take them out bowling. But let's face it. He was a little cheap.
Can you imagine what he'd say to Janet if he knew how much this
casket cost! He'd get up and walk out."

The end of the eulogy should sum up the impact the person had
in life and how he will be missed but never forgotten. Former New
York mayor David Dinkins has a wonderful line he often uses at eulogies that is worth repeating because it could apply to so many of
our loved ones. It reads, "Helping others is the rent you pay for the
space you take up on earth. And with (fill in with name), his rent has
been paid in full. We'll miss him."

Most epitaphs can be as dull as spending New Year's Eve watching C-Span. They simply state name, status, and dates of birth and
death. Yet tombstones can and should be a form of modern-day
haiku with well-chosen words to describe the deceased. "Given our
culture's deep fear of death and hence denial of its absolute reality,
it's not hard to imagine many people simply not wanting to think
about their epitaph," says Jill Werman Harris. "I think that the
thought of the tombstone for many of us is a somber experience. But
it doesn't have to be."

Some that have stood out from the pack include one which says,
"Cheerio, see you soon." Comedy writer Art Buchwald told me he
wants to write, "He Rented" on his pal Mike Wallace's tombstone
because the journalist never bought a house in Martha's Vineyard.

Some oldies but goodies include:

Too bad for Heaven
Too good for Hell
So where he's gone
I cannot tell

In this place lies William Yeast
Pardon Him for Not Rising

> *Shoot 'em up Jake*
> *Run for Sheriff in 1872*
> *Run from Sheriff 1876*
> *Buried 1876*

> *Stranger, tread*
> *This ground with gravity*
> *Dentist Brown is filling*
> *His last cavity*

Excuse My Dust (Dorothy Parker)

Fred Schneider of the band B-52's wins the prize in creativity. He has ordered a solar-powered microchip for his tombstone to play the sound of mourners weeping and project a picture of Fred laughing, along with a message saying, "I hope I haven't gone to hell" while listing the titles and prices of all B-52's albums. Though the cost of the albums could seem cheap a hundred years from now, the lasting entertainment value is priceless.

Because so many baby boomers are heading toward what the *New York Times* called "the period of perishing," increased attention will be put on making memorable funerals. After all, the baby boomers are still the largest and noisiest bunch in the population and have a knack for pushing pop culture in directions that affect them.

Which explains the advent of another trend, burials for beloved pets. In 1972, there were 96 pet cemeteries; today there are more than 700. "Your pet is a family member who you love and miss," explains Andrea Eastman, a Hollywood agent who had a funeral for her dog where Richard Gere gave the eulogy. "You want to honor his life and how he contributed to yours. I cried more at my dog Oliver's funeral than my own mother's. He had always given me joy."

Already, companies are offering future customers the ability to compile video biographies that can be viewed on touchscreen kiosks at the cemetery as well as on a Web site called forevernetwork.com. Forever Enterprises, a company based in Missouri, told *Time* magazine that it hopes to change the cemetery by making the biography rather than the remains the focus of a visit. Eventually, they hope to insert touchscreens right into the tombstones.

"At traditional cemeteries, all you have is something carved in cold stone," says owner Tyler Cassity. "There's nothing alive. This way you can see them as they were in life."

With these flourishes, one can be laid to rest with a dusting of revisionist history that diminishes the harsh features and enhances the more flattering ones. The best part is that you can present your life in any way you like and create a glossy Hollywood production that would make Cecil B. DeMille proud. It also has the added bonus of comforting family and friends, and insuring your immortality.

28

⁓

Good-bye Is Not Forever

At a sold-out performance in New York City, the mustached medium and best-selling author James Van Praagh asked the audience this question:

"How many of you have had your loved ones contact you? Did you ever find pennies? Hear their voices? Have unexplained feelings that they were near?"

Sheepishly, a few raised their hands, followed by more and more. Soon more than half the audience waved their hands high in the air to share in the affirmation of what they long believed but were scared to admit.

"You have to be open to these signals," said Van Praagh encouragingly. "Don't be scared. Your loved ones want to contact you. But they do it in their own way."

Too often we dismiss the unexplainable, yet the unexplainable is all around us.

At the moment my father died, my brother bolted up in his bed with the sense that someone was saying farewell, minutes before the priest at his boarding school came to tell him the life-altering news.

How can one explain why, the night before my father died, instead of giving him a hug good night, I hesitated because a bright light seemed to envelop him like a force field? It kept me away, and I simply said "Sweet dreams, Daddy." And how else can you explain what happened to Mary Morris?

Five years ago, Mary's twin brother, Frankie, was diagnosed with an inoperable brain tumor. After the diagnosis, Frankie went to Mary's house for the afternoon.

"You know, I'm not sure if I believe in God," Frankie said to his sister.

"Yeah, I know, Frankie. Does it worry you?" she replied.

"No, not really. Ever since Vietnam, I'm not sure I know what I believe in. I do think there is some higher source out there. At least, I hope so. I'd hate to think that there is nothing and that's it, I'm gone."

"It's just so unfair," Mary sighed, holding back tears. "What am I going to do without you?"

"Maybe if there is something more, I can give you a sign."

"What do you mean?"

"You know, a sign. Maybe I'll will it so flowers appear someplace. Like in your bedroom."

"Flowers. Nah, think of something else," laughed Mary, playing along.

"Okay, how about pennies. When I'm gone, if pennies appear out of nowhere, you'll know that I'm okay and I'm watching over you."

"All right, Frankie, if I see pennies, I'll think of you."

The hours sped by that long afternoon until it was late in the evening. By the time Mary crawled into bed, she was too emotionally drained to say even two words to her husband Donald.

That night after Frankie went home, he died of an aneurysm in his sleep. He was forty-six years old.

The following morning, Frankie's daughter-in-law, Janis Palmero, took care of the body while Mary's husband Donald went to his brother-in-law's apartment to pick out a suit for the funeral.

Donald climbed the stairs to the bedroom en route to the closet, when he was distracted by something lying on the bed. It was a penny, so bright it looked as though beams of light were reflecting from it.

"I picked up the penny and put it in Frankie's suit pocket because he was always broke in this life, and I figured, well maybe this would be good luck in heaven," recalls Donald. "I didn't know about Frankie's promise to Mary."

That day others had similar experiences.

Frankie's wife found a penny underneath her husband's body in the EMS van. His best friend found one by his gold Buick.

"Over forty people found pennies," recalls Mary, shaking her head in disbelief. "It was amazing. People started to find pennies in pantyhose, a plastic box, on the floor. One of his friends who was in a rehab center found one in a drawer. And when I went to pick up my son Geoffrey at school to tell him about his uncle Frankie, I saw a penny right next to the ledge of the high-school sign. I couldn't believe it. I felt Frankie was talking to me. He was there."

Sitting in her homey peach-colored living room, Mary walks over to her Memory Shelf and softly touches the penny. "That's the penny from Geoffrey's school. The one I found."

A sweet smile spreads across her face. "You know what they say about pennies from heaven. Pennies are from heaven. I know that my brother is with me. Even if I can't see him, Frankie is here."

Linda Elders is certain her mother writes to her from heaven. A few years ago, Linda was sitting at her desk at her California home, feeling the heartache of missing her mother, Ruthie. Suddenly she got this urge to start writing her feelings down on paper, and her words mysteriously took on the tone of her mother's. "My mom was from Kentucky, and her whole way of communication was Southern," says Linda. "These letters were in a Southern dialect, which is not how I talk. I'm a Yankee. There was not a doubt in my mind that my mom was communicating to me from my own handwriting."

"What did she say?" I asked.

"She thanked me for being generous with my sister and told me to lose weight." Linda laughed. "She also commented on how beautiful our children were and wished she could be there with them."

After she wrote the first letter, Linda was emotionally drained and teary-eyed. She didn't dare write again for several months. Sometimes her mother's voice would visit her, and other times it didn't. Each time Ruthie did come, Linda was so very happy to hear from her.

"You have to have an open heart for this to happen," says Linda. "If you do, it will."

Others find messages in all sorts of places. Bridget had a ritual with her husband that on special occasions he would bring a big bunch of flowers. After he died, she was sitting by the kitchen table glum as can be. From the corner of her eye, she saw some flowers. "Couldn't be," she said to herself. Walking to the counter to investigate, she saw a bunch of daisies on a chair. "I knew they were from Brian; there couldn't be any other explanation," she told me. "It made me feel he was with me on this day." Elisabeth Kübler-Ross says her husband, Manny, promised to leave flowers in the snow after he died and she found a bunch outside her home, as did their daughter.

It is the business of mediums to listen to these messages. Years ago, my husband brought a friend of his whose brother had committed suicide to Lillydale, a summer facility in upstate New York, which is like a psychic camp. Lucy was haunted by his death and wondered if she could have done something to prevent it.

Walking into a room, the psychic told Lucy that she saw someone with a bullet in his hand. "He's telling you that you had no control over it," the psychic said. "He just couldn't live up to your father's expectations of him. It was too much. He's happy and doesn't want you to be upset. He wants you to know that."

Having your deepest secret exposed by a stranger in such a fashion is an emotionally charged experience. "How could she have known?" wondered Lucy. "But I strangely feel as though a huge burden has been lifted. I've often wondered why he did it and now I feel I know."

These are not isolated examples. Most people after a few beers will confess that they have had strange sensations about their loved ones as though information is being transmitted through another frequency. The frequency is usually our senses.

Before dozing to sleep, Jane could swear she heard her mother's voice telling her to be wary of a law partner. Phyllis was thinking about her sister and walked into a room and inexplicably smelled her perfume. The television in Parker's room will suddenly go on without anyone touching a button, and I'll wonder if any of his grandfathers are checking in. Michael suddenly craved his mother's veal piccata at the moment he was proposing and felt this was her way of showing approval for his fiancée Stacey. And then there are the secrets widows have shared with me how late at night, when they've been crying, they can feel a soft caress on their shoulder, even though no one is in the room.

In all these cases, their "intuition" told them their loved ones were communicating with them. While most of us believe in intuition, it still cannot be explained logically. "A gut feeling," "goose bumps," "a feeling in your bones" all describe a sensation that occurs deep within. Intuition is knowledge that comes to you through a seemingly unknown source. Yet no one denies its wisdom. An intuition may give you a nudge to do something, an inspiration to try something. The great psychic Edward Cayce described it as a natural channel for guidance.

"The key is always to pay attention to what you're getting," says Char Margolis, a celebrated psychic and author of *Questions from Earth, Answers from Heaven.*

Char believes that intuition is a mystery sense we all possess. She says we should look at our brains as being like radios receiving several stations simultaneously. "One station is louder than the other, therefore we pay more attention to it," she says. "That station is what we define as our physical reality, which is made of the information we take in through our five senses and process in our brains. Intuition is simply information coming in on a different, quieter channel, so that it's often overshadowed by our other five senses."

The best way to become more intuitive is to trust your heart. Intuition exists through our essential oneness with creation. It is listening to the force that pours from all aspects of life: the trees, the streams, the flowers, the light from your desk lamp. If you want to summon someone you love, think about them. Focus your attention on an object they may have given you. Listen to music they may have played. Take a walk outside and breathe in the fresh air. Cast your eyes heavenward and have a conversation. Dream about them and see what they say.

As with any pursuit, this should be done using good sense. This is not an invitation to live in the past. Some people become prisoners of the past. You want to be a person who not only finds meaning from the loss but can draw sustenance from your loved one in the ways you pursue your goals, the ways you love, the ways you shape your thoughts and in the ways you build memories of your own.

I do believe that there are many ways to connect to our loved ones. Some are simple rituals, such as making a toast at a family dinner or baking a Viennese torte on holidays. Some are more complicated and require us to listen quietly to the voice inside when we seek to draw on their wisdom. Others require a heightened sensitivity to all the signals that flicker along the fringes of our everyday lives and give us important messages.

Collectively, all these efforts will help you live more fully, more happily, more at peace.

It is interesting that more and more scientists are exploring the spiritual nature of the universe, thanks to the advent of quantum physics, which reveals that we are more than our physical beings. "Einstein in his theory proved that $E = mc^2$, which essentially means that matter is condensed energy," explains Dr. Gerald Schroeder, a nuclear physicist and author of *The Hidden Face of God*. "If you take the leading edge of what's going on in quantum physics, which moves this theory a step further, we see a world where nothing is solid, but instead wavelengths of energy create the impression or sensation of solid mass. Our senses on earth only filter in the material aspects of the world because we can't see the movement and dimensions of the atoms at the subatomic level holding everything up, including the chair on which you're sitting. Therefore, it looks like the world and everything in it may be associations of waves of energy. Which means that all the world is integrated. This has been the eternal message of biblical religion, that a unity pervades the world, and that there is a universal consciousness."

Without the physical presence of our loved ones, we can still connect to their wisdom, which is now part of the universe. Oprah Winfrey has been particularly successful in condensing this into everyday terms when she says that the universe is an expression of information and wisdom that you tap into.

This is not to say that given the choice between our newfound wisdom or having our loved one in our arms, we would choose the wisdom. But that is not our choice. As Rabbi Harold Kushner wrote in *When Bad Things Happen to Good People*, "No one promised us a life free of pain and disappointment. The most anyone promised us was that we would not be alone in our pain and that we would be able to draw upon a source outside ourselves for the strength and courage we would need to survive life's tragedies and life's unfairness. We can, by our responses, give suffering either a positive or negative meaning."

It does take time, this process. The heart is not as elastic as one would hope. But we don't have to accept a life where we allow the emotional scars to disfigure. Instead, we have the choice to embrace strategies that will diminish the pain and enhance our appreciation of what we have left and what is still possible for us.

With every ending, there is a beginning. May your memories soothe you, sustain you and inspire you.

APPENDIX

~

Achievers Who Lost a Parent Early in Life

Provided by Dr. Marvin Eisenstadt

Person	Age When Parent Died
Political Figures	
Alexander the Great	19 (Father)
Mark Antony	10 (Father)
Tony Blair	22 (Mother)
Simón Bolívar	2 (Father) 8 (Mother)
Guy Burgess	9 (Father)
Aaron Burr	1 (Father) 2 (Mother)
Julius Caesar	15 (Father)
Caligula	7 (Father) 21 (Mother)
Catherine I (Russia)	2 (Father) 3 (Mother)
Neville Chamberlain	6 (Mother)
Salmon Chase	9 (Father)
Chiang Kai-shek	8 (Father)
Winston Churchill	20 (Father)

Claudius I	1 (Father)
Henry Clay	4 (Father)
Cleopatra	18 (Father)
Grover Cleveland	16 (Father)
William Jefferson Clinton	0 (Father)
Oliver Cromwell	18 (Father)
Jefferson Davis	16 (Father)
Abba Eban	1 (Father)
Elizabeth I (England)	13 (Father) 2 (Mother)
Alexander Hamilton	13 (Mother)
John Hancock	7 (Father)
Hannibal	18 (Father)
Benjamin Harrison	17 (Mother)
Rutherford Hayes	0 (Father)
Henry VIII	17 (Father) 11 (Mother)
Adolf Hitler	13 (Father) 18 (Mother)
Ho Chi Minh	9 (Mother)
Richard Holbrooke	10 (Father)
Herbert Hoover	6 (Father) 8 (Mother)
Sam Houston	14 (Father)
Harold Ickes	16 (Mother)
Ivan IV the Terrible	3 (Father) 7 (Mother)
Andrew Jackson	0 (Father) 13 (Mother)
Thomas Jefferson	14 (Father)
Benito Juárez	3 (Father) 3 (Mother)
Kagawa Toyohiko	4 (Father) 4 (Mother)
Jomo Kenyatta	5 (Father)
Genghis Khan	8 (Father)
Nikita Khrushchev	16 (Father)
Kenneth Kuanda	8 (Father)
Robert E. Lee	11 (Father) 22 (Mother)
Vladimir Ilych Lenin	15 (Father)
Abraham Lincoln	9 (Mother)
Slobodan Milosevic	21 (Father)
James Monroe	16 (Father)
Napoléon Bonaparte	15 (Father)
Gamal Nasser	8 (Mother)

Horatio Nelson	9 (Mother)
Nero	2 (Father) 21 (Mother)
Eva "Evita" Peron	7 (Father)
Peter the Great	3 (Father) 21 (Mother)
Maximilien de Robespierre	19 (Father) 6 (Mother)
Eleanor Roosevelt	9 (Father) 8 (Mother)
Franklin Roosevelt	18 (Father)
Teddy Roosevelt	19 (Father) 25 (Mother)
Alfred Smith	12 (Father)
John Smith	16 (Father)
Sen. Olympia Snowe	8 (Mother) 9 (Father)
Joseph Stalin	11 (Father)
Queen Victoria	0 (Father)
George Washington	11 (Father)
Roger Williams	17 (Father)

Religious Leaders & Philosophers

Saint Augustine	17 (Father)
Buddha	0 (Mother)
Albert Camus	0 (Father)
Confucius	1 (Father) 24 (Mother)
Charles Darwin	8 (Mother)
Mohandas Gandhi	15 (Father)
Pope John Paul II	8 (Mother)
Mohammed	0 (Father) 6 (Mother)
Friedrich Nietzsche	4 (Father)
Plato	3 (Mother)
Jean-Paul Sartre	2 (Father)

Artists, Writers, Musicians

James Agee	6 (Father)
Steve Allen	1 (Father)
Hans Christian Andersen	11 (Father)
Johann Sebastian Bach	9 (Father) 9 (Mother)
Francis Bacon	18 (Father)
Baudelaire	6 (Father)

Ludwig van Beethoven   22 (Father) 16 (Mother)
Cate Blanchett   10 (Father)
Charlotte Brontë   5 (Mother)
Emily Brontë   3 (Mother)
Mel Brooks   2 (Father)
Dame Barbara Cartland   5 (Mother)
Ray Charles   10 (Father) 15 (Mother)
Mary Higgins Clark   10 (Father)
Sean Puffy Combs   2 (Father)
Joseph Conrad   11 (Father) 7 (Mother)
Dante Alighieri   17 (Father) 6 (Mother)
James Dean   9 (Mother)
Daniel Defoe   8 (Mother)
Edgar Degas   13 (Mother)
Eugene Delacroix   7 (Father) 16 (Mother)
Benicio Del Toro   9 (Mother)
Fyodor Dostoyevsky   17 (Father) 15 (Mother)
George Eliot   29 (Father) 16 (Mother)
Ralph Waldo Emerson   8 (Father)
Desiderius Erasmus   18 (Father) 17 (Mother)
Eric Fischl   22 (Mother)
Helen Frankenthaler   11 (Father)
E. M. Forster   1 (Father)
Robert Frost   11 (Father)
Thomas Gainsborough   21 (Father)
George Gordon, Lord Byron 3 (Father) 23 (Mother)
Kelsey Grammer   13 (Father)
Joseph Heller   5 (Father)
Alfred Hitchcock   15 (Father)
Victor Hugo   25 (Father) 19 (Mother)
Aldous Huxley   14 (Mother)
Samuel Johnson   22 (Father)
Immanuel Kant   21 (Father) 13 (Mother)
John Keats   8 (Father) 14 (Mother)
Larry King   9 (Father)
Nathan Lane   10 (Father)
John Lennon   19 (Mother)

Jerry Lieber	6 (Father)
Madonna Ciccone	5 (Mother)
Thomas Mann	16 (Father)
Somerset Maugham	10 (Father) 8 (Mother)
Paul McCartney	14 (Mother)
Herman Melville	12 (Father)
H. L. Mencken	19 (Father)
Michelangelo	6 (Mother)
Charles Mingus	0 (Mother)
Molière	10 (Mother)
Marilyn Monroe	9 (Father abandoned her and mother institutionalized; put in orphanage)
Thomas More	6 (Mother)
Rosie O'Donnell	10 (Mother)
Dorothy Parker	5 (Mother)
Edgar Allan Poe	1 (Father) 2 (Mother)
Anthony Quinn	10 (Father)
Jean Racine	3 (Father) 1 (Mother)
Raphael	11 (Father) 8 (Mother)
Paul Revere	17 (Father) 3 (Mother)
Julia Roberts	10 (Father)
Jean-Jacques Rousseau	0 (Mother)
Bertrand Russell	3 (Father) 2 (Mother)
George Sand	4 (Father)
William Saroyan	3 (Father)
Franz Schubert	15 (Mother)
Martin Short	20 (Father) 18 (Mother)
Gertrude Stein	14 (Mother)
Stendhal	7 (Mother)
Tom Stoppard	4 (Father)
Harriet Beecher Stowe	5 (Mother)
Barbra Streisand	2 (Father)
Pyotr Tchaikovsky	14 (Mother)
Alfred, Lord Tennyson	21 (Father)
William Thackeray	5 (Father)
Leo Tolstoy	8 (Father) 1 (Mother)

Mark Twain	11 (Father)
Voltaire	6 (Mother)
Richard Wagner	0 (Father)
Virginia Woolf	13 (Mother)
Orson Welles	13 (Father) 8 (Mother)
Edith Wharton	19 (Father)
James Whistler	14 (Father)
Theodore White	16 (Father)
Elie Wiesel	16 (Father) 14 (Mother)
Oscar Wilde	21 (Father)
William Wordsworth	13 (Father) 7 (Mother)
Emile Zola	6 (Father)

Scientists

Sir Joseph Banks	18 (Father)
Robert Boyle	3 (Mother)
Sir William Bragg	7 (Mother)
Sir Thomas Browne	8 (Father)
Henry Cavendish	2 (Mother)
Nicolaus Copernicus	10 (Father)
Marie Curie	11 (Mother)
René Descartes	10 (Mother)
Sir Arthur Stanley Eddington	1 (Father)
Sir Francis Galton	22 (Father)
Sir Andrew Huxley	16 (Father)
Antoine Lavoisier	5 (Mother)
Gottfried Leibnitz	6 (Father) 17 (Mother)
Sir Isaac Newton	0 (Father)
Blaise Pascal	3 (Mother)
Hermann Rorschach	18 (Father) 12 (Mother)

BIBLIOGRAPHY

Albom, M. *Tuesdays with Morrie,* New York, Doubleday, 1997

Altschul, S. *Childhood Bereavement and Its Aftermath,* Madison, CT, International Universities Press, 1988

Akeret, R. *Family Tales, Family Wisdom: How to Gather the Stories of a Lifetime and Share Them with Your Family,* New York, William Morrow, 1991

Ashe, A. *Days of Grace,* New York, Alfred A. Knopf, Inc., 1993

Baumgardner, B. *A Passage Through Grief,* Broadman & Holman Publishers, 1997

Bentley, R. "Heaven Can Wait," *The Fresno Bee,* April 20, 1999

Besdine, M. "The Jocasta Complex, Mothering and Genius: Part 1," *Psychoanalitic Review,* Vol. No. 55, 259–277, 1968

Bowlby, J. *Attachment and Loss: Vol. 1, Attachment,* Harmondsworth, England, Pelican Books, 1971

Braverman, N. *The Bible for the Clueless but Curious,* Baltimore, MD, Leviathan Press, 1999

Calhoun, L., Tedeschi, R. "Beyond Recovery From Trauma: Implications for Clinical Practice and Research," The Society for the Psychological Study of Social Issues *Journal of Social Issues*, Vol. 54, No. 2, 357–371, 1998

Campbell, J., Moyers, B. *The Power of Myth,* New York, Doubleday, 1988

Chadwick, D. "BBC Program Teaches Listening, Understanding," *The Providence Journal Bulletin,* September 19, 1999

Chang, D. "Day of the Dead: A Latin American Way of Remembering," *The Orange County Register,* October 29, 1999

Chopra, D. *How to Know God,* New York, Harmony Books, 2000

Chopra, D. *The Seven Spiritual Laws of Success,* San Rafael, CA, Amber-Allen Publishing, 1993

Coleman, R. *Lennon: The Definitive Biography,* New York, Harper Perennial, 1985

Corcoran, M. "An Actress Takes on an Activist Role," *In Style,* 2000

Curnutte, M. "Buried with Their Treasures," *The Cincinnati Enquirer,* December 9, 1998

Denes-Raj, Erlichman, H. "Effects of Premature Parental Death on Subjective Life Expectancy, Death Anxiety and Health Behavior," *Omega,* Vol. No. 23, 1991

Denniss, H. "Scrapbook Keepers Cut Up and Paste Up a Storm," *Orange County Register,* July 1, 1999

Dickey, M. "Starting Up Without Stalling," *Chronicle of Higher Education,* February 23, 1999

Dominguez, R. "The Star of *She's All That* Emerges from Dad's Shadow," *Daily News,* January 27, 1999

Doueck, J. *The Hessed Boomerang,* Deal, NJ, Yagdiyl Torah Publishing, 1998

Edelman, H. *Motherless Daughters,* New York, Bantam Books, 1994

Eisdenstadt, M., Haynal, A., Rentchnick, P., Senarclens, P. (Eds). *Parental Loss and Achievement,* Madison, CT, International Universities Press, 1989

Emerson, B. "Living with Death," *The Atlanta Journal and Constitution,* July 22, 1998

Ephron, N. "The Real Rosie," *Redbook,* February 2000

Ferry, M. "Preparing a Will is Easy to Do," *St. Louis Post Dispatch,* 1998

Forero, J. "From Shared Experience, an Offer of Comfort: A Support Group Helps to Repair Lives Shattered by Plane Crashes," *The New York Times,* 1999

Freud, S. "Mourning and Melancholia." In *G.H. Pollack*, Madison, CT, International Universities Press, 1993

Furman, E. "Children's Grief Patterns," 1989

Goertzel, V., Goertzel, M. G. *Cradles of Eminence,* New York, Little, Brown, 1962

Goode, S. "Angels Look Homeward," *News World Communications,* June 7, 1999

Grandinetti, D. *Leave Nothing to Chance in Your Will,* Medical Economics Publishing, 1998

Haas, J. G. "The Sexes Take Different Approaches to Coping with Death of a Spouse," *Calgary Herald,* August 9, 1999

Harris, J. W. *Remembrances and Celebrations,* New York, Random House, 2000

Harvey, K. "Embracing Sorrow," Knight Ridder News Service, September 10, 1998

Heath, C. "Portrait of a Trash-Talking Lady," *Rolling Stone,* March 2000

Hornblower, M. "How to Find Your Roots," *Time,* April 19, 1999

Hudson, G. "Favorite Family Rituals," *Child,* January 2000

"An Interview with Natalie Cole," *Jet Magazine,* February 24, 1999

Jensen, P. "Relative Losses," *The Baltimore Sun,* November 7, 1999

Johnson, J. "Talking to Children About Grief and Death," *Mothering,* January 1, 1998

Jones, L. "How the Young Grieve," *The Dallas Morning News,* May 25, 1999

Jozefowski, J. *The Phoenix Phenomenon, Rising from the Ashes of Grief,* Jason Aronson, Inc., 1999

Kalb, C. "Stars, Money and Medical Crusades," *Newsweek,* May 22, 2000

Kase, L. M. "Babies Do Remember," *Child,* February 2000

Klass, D., Silverman, P. R., Nickman, S. L. *Continuing Bonds: New Understanding of Grief,* Washington, D.C., Taylor & Francis, 1996

Kübler-Ross, E. *On Death and Dying,* New York, Collier Books, 1969

Kushner, H. *When Bad Things Happen to Good People,* New York, Avon Books, 1981

Laumann, S. "Grief," Knight Ridder News Services, 1998

Lee, W. "A Father's Tragic Loss," *Entertainment Weekly,* March 19, 1999

Levy, N. *To Begin Again: The Journey Toward Comfort, Strength and Faith in Difficult Times,* New York, Ballantine Books, 1998

Lightner, C. "A Grieving Mother Helped America Get MADD," *People,* June 17, 1999

Margolis, C. *Questions from Earth, Answers from Heaven,* New York, St. Martin's Press, 1999

Marks, D. F. "On the Relationship Between Imagery, Body and Mind." In P. J. Hampson, D. F. Marks, J. T. E. Richardson, *Imagery: Current Developments,* New York, Routledge, 1990

Marwit, S. J., Klass, D. "Grief and the Role of the Inner Representation of the Deceased," *Omega,* Vol. 30, No. 4, 283–298, 1996

Menten, T. *Gentle Closings,* London, Running Press, 1991

Menten, T. *Going Solo,* London, Running Press, 1995

McDonald, J. "Web Sites Keep Loved One's Memories Alive," *The San Diego Union Tribune,* April 12, 1999

Mims, B. "Modern Fascination with Hereafter Is Really as Old as Mankind," *The Salt Lake Tribune,* 1998

Mitchell, M. "Grandparents Have Rights Along with Responsibilities," *Chicago Sun Times,* October 3, 1999

Moody, R. A. *Life after Life,* New York, Bantam Books, 1975

Moody, R. A. *Reunions: Visionary Encounters with Departed Loved Ones,* New York, Ivy Books, 1993

Okasky, M. "Death: Not Very Sexy, But Let's Talk About It," *The Dallas Morning News,* May 29, 1999

Parkers, C. M. *Bereavement: Studies of Grief in Adult Life,* London, Penguin, 1986

Pelletier, C. "The Last Money You'll Ever Spend: Planning for a Funeral," *Chatelaine,* July 1998

Pelletier, C. "Planning A Funeral," Maclean Hunter Ltd., 1998

Pittman, F. "A Buyer's Guide to Psychotherapy," *Psychology Today,* February 1994

Pliskin, Z. *Happiness: Formulas, Stories & Insights,* Baltimore, MD, Leviathan Press, 1993

Pollack, W. *Real Boys: Rescuing Our Sons from the Myths of Boyhood,* New York, Henry Holt & Co., 1998

Poole, M., Germino, B. "A Practical Guide to Funeral Planning," American Nephrology Nurses *Association Journal,* December 1998

Powell, J. "The TV Show that Works Miracles," *Good House-keeping,* 1997

Radice, S. "Disposing of Loved One's Possessions," *The London Guardian,* May 29, 1999

Rando, T. A. *How to Go On Living When Someone You Love Dies,* New York, Bantam Books, 1988

Rando, T. A. *Treatment of Complicated Mourning,* Champaign, IL, Research Press, 1993

Reed, H. *Edgar Cayce on Channeling Your Higher Self,* New York, Time Warner, 1989

Reep, T. "Many Religions Link Death and an Afterlife," *The Orlando Sentinel,* January 9, 1998

Rowling, J. K. *Harry Potter and the Prisoner of Azkaban,* New York, Arthur Levine Books, Scholastic, 1999

Rowling, J. K. *Harry Potter and the Sorcerer's Stone,* New York, Arthur Levine Books, Scholastic, 1997

Schaeffer, G. *A Labor of Love: How to Write a Eulogy,* San Diego, CA, GMS Publishing, 1998

Schucter, S. R., Zisook, S. "Widowhood: The Continuing Relationship with the Dead Spouse," *Bulletin of the Menniger Clinic,* Vol. No. 52, 269–279, 1988

Seale, C. *Constructing Death: The Sociology of Dying and Bereavement,* Cambridge University Press, 1998

Sheehy, G. "The Clintons," *Vanity Fair,* February 1999

Silverman, P., Worden, J. W. "Children's Reactions in the Early Months After the Death of a Parent," *American Journal of Orthopsychiatry,* Vol. 62, No. 1, 93–104, 1992

Silverman, P., Worden, J. W. "Children's Reactions to the Death of a Parent." In *Bereavement, A Sourcebook of Research Intervention,* Cambridge University Press, 1993

Silverman, S. "Parental Loss and Scientists," 1973

Simpson, E. *Orphans: Real and Imaginary,* New York, Weidenfeld & Nicholson, 1987

Squires, S. "Scientists Learn More About how Brain Creates Memories," *The Washington Post,* December 14, 1999

Stroebe, M. S. "Myths and Misconceptions about Bereavement: The Opening of a Debate," *Omega 94,* Vol. 29, No. 3, 187–203, 1992

Stroebe, M. S., Stroebe, W., Hansson, R. *Handbook of Bereavement: Theory, Research and Intervention,* Cambridge University Press, 1993

Tedeschi, R. "Violence Transformed: Posttraumatic Growth in Survivors and Their Societies," *Aggression and Violent Behavior,* Vol. 4, No. 3, 319–341, 1994

Tedeschi, R., Park, C., Calhoun, L. *Posttraumatic Growth: Positive Changes in the Aftermath of Crisis,* London, Lawrence Erlbaum Associates Publishers, 1998

Travis, N. Fred Schneider item, *New York Post,* 2000

Tucker, K. "The Celestial Triumph of Touched by an Angel," *Entertainment Weekly,* June 13, 1997

Van Praagh, J. *Talking to Heaven,* New York, Dutton, 1997

Vickio, C. "Lost and Found: Finding Value in Life through Imagining Loss," *Death Studies,* Vol. 18, 609–621, 1994

Vickio, C. "Together in Spirit, Keeping our Relationships Alive when Loved Ones Die," *Death Studies 99,* Vol. 23, No. 2, 161–175, 1998

Weiser, C. "Actress Lobbies Congress," Gannett News Services, 2000

"Why Laughter Is the Best Medicine," *Jet Magazine,* July 27, 1998

Winslow, L. "Death Denial: Baby Boomers Must Discuss Parents' End of Life Wishes," *Tulsa World,* September 12, 1999

Wolfelt, A. "Companioning Versus Treating: Beyond the Medical Model of Bereavement Caregiving," *ADEC Forum,* September 1998

Wolfenstein, M. "Loss, Rage and Repetition," *The Psychoanalytic Study of the Child,* New York, International University Press, 1969